THE FABRICATED LUTHER

The
Fabricated
LUTHER

Refuting Nazi Connections
and Other Modern Myths

Second Edition

Uwe Siemon-Netto

CONCORDIA PUBLISHING HOUSE · SAINT LOUIS

Published 2007 by Concordia Publishing House
3558 S. Jefferson Ave., St. Louis, MO 63118-3968
1-800-325-3040 • www.cph.org

Luther als Wegbereiter Hitlers? copyright © 1993 Gütersloher Verlagshaus Gerd Mohn, Gütersloh, Germany

English translation and revision, *The Fabricated Luther* © 1995, 2007 Uwe Siemon-Netto

Unless otherwise noted, translations from foreign-language sources are the author's own.

Manufactured in the United States of America

Library of Congress Cataloging-in-Publication Data

Siemon-Netto, Uwe.
    The Fabricated Luther : refuting Nazi connections and other modern myths / Uwe Siemon-Netto. — 2d ed.
        p. cm.
    includes bibliographical references.
    ISBN 978-0-7586-0855-0
    1. Luther, Martin, 1483–1546. 2. Two kingdoms (Lutheran theology)—History of doctrines. 3. Germany—Politics and government—1933–1945. 4. Germany (East)—Politics and government—1989–1990. 5. National characteristics, German. 6. Lutheran Church—Doctrines—History. 7. Goerdeler, Carl, 1884–1945. *. Shirer, William L. (William Lawrence), 1904– Rise and fall of the Third Reich. I. Title.
    BR333.5.P6S54 2006
    284.1092—dc22

                                                                                2007000993

1 2 3 4 5 6 7 8 9 10   16 15 14 13 12 11 10 09 08 07

Contents

FOREWORD

Uwe Siemon-Netto's book combines a number of themes in an original and ingenious way—the place of clichés in modern culture generally, the particular cliché according to which Luther is to be seen as the spiritual ancestor of Hitler, the manner in which this cliché violates the historical facts about Luther's understanding of the relation of Christianity and the world, the practical consequences of this cliché during World War II and after, and, finally and in the most ringing manner, the continuing relevance of Luther, correctly understood, for our own time. This is quite a table of contents, and it is a measure of Siemon-Netto's abilities that he carries off this project with both scholarly competence and verve. Obviously, different parts of this argument will be more interesting for different groups of readers. I can only make some general observations here.

It is debatable whether, as Siemon-Netto believes, clichés are more pervasive in modern times than in earlier periods of history. They can certainly be diffused more rapidly and effectively as a result of modern media. Once a cliché is firmly established in the minds of a particular group of people, it attains the quality of taken-for-granted truth and is very difficult to dislodge even by clear empirical counterevidence. Human beings do not like to be confronted with what the psychologists call cognitive dissonance ("I have made up my mind; don't confuse me with the facts"). What is more, thinking in general and rethinking in particular are fairly painful processes, and most people prefer to avoid this pain. The plausibility of a cliché does not depend on the amount or the quality of the evidence for it, but on the way it meets the social and psychic needs of a particular situation. This is not necessarily a bad thing. All of us believe in propositions for which the evidence is dubious or, in any case, not available to us, and some of us hold beliefs that are contradicted by all sorts of "confusing facts." We cannot be careful scientists in our everyday lives. What is more, a good many beliefs based on factual error can have quite benign effects. A child in Lower Poldovia, a country recently blessed with a democratic government, may learn in school that King Bogumil, founder of the nation, was a fervent humanitarian who practiced respect of human rights, justice for minorities, and sensitivity to the environment. The empirical evidence, as known to the historians, may be that Bogumil was a homicidal maniac, terror of peasants, and polluter of rivers. Yet the cliché that transformed Bogumil the Terrible into Bogumil the Good may, on balance, be considered a morally tolerable error.

The "Luther Cliché," as analyzed by Siemon-Netto, was clearly not benign. If Siemon-Netto's argument holds up (and I think that it does), this cliché had very deleterious consequences during World War II, preventing important decision-makers among the Allies from taking seriously those elements in the German resistance that were inspired by Lutheran ideas: If all Lutherans were really Nazis underneath, then these people could not be trusted. I have no expert knowledge of this episode in the history of World War II and thus cannot make any useful observations on it. But I do know something about the ideological uses of the same cliché in the postwar era, and some observations on that may be appropriate.

The cliché, as Siemon-Netto shows, is not just an assertion of a direct lineage between Luther and Hitler as two "bad Germans." The cliché also contains the proposition that the reason for this lineage is Luther's doctrine of the two realms. This doctrine supposedly relegates the world of social and political realities to some sort of amoral cynicism. This supposition, of course, completely distorts the Lutheran doctrine both as promulgated by Luther and as developed in later Lutheran thought. This is not my concern here. Rather, I want to ask: Who benefits ideologically from this distortion? I think I know the answer: It benefits those who understand Christianity in terms of an agenda of political utopianism. In recent times this has been an agenda of the Left.

According to the cliché, Lutheranism separates politics from the constraints of Christian morality and, therefore, opens the way for every sort of evil, culminating in the evil of the Third Reich. The doctrine of the two realms must be repudiated. God's grace is active in this world, and especially in the political world, and Christians must be active in, as it were, helping God's grace along. Put differently, the Christian task in the world is to work toward a Christian society—that is, a society that will embody the imperatives of Christian morality. In its Left version, this society will be a socialist one, and we all have heard the proposition that the task of Christians of our time is "to build socialism." But there is no compelling reason why the utopian agenda must be on the Left. It could also be proposed as the task of "building true Poldovianism" (and in the course of this "ethnic cleansing" the nation of all non- or not-quite-true Poldovians) or as "building white America" (with whatever homicidal implications that agenda might involve). Needless to say, utopianism of any political coloration has never been averse to homicide—the more grandiose the utopian vision, usually the more grandiose the scope of the homicide.

The ideological function of the "Luther cliché," as defined by Siemon-Netto, could be nicely observed in the former German Democratic Republic. An embarrassingly large number of Protestant clergy and laypeople were prepared to collaborate with the Communist regime out of a sense of guilt over the role of the churches in the Third Reich (just *how* embarrassingly large the number of collaborators was is only now becoming evident as the files of the security organizations are made public). Now, let it be stipulated that this role was not one of unblemished heroism (though, of course, there were genuine heroes). But the notion that the passive response of many in the churches was the result of Lutheran doctrine has little going for it. For one, the role of Roman Catholic clergy and laypeople during the same period was not at all more heroic or resistance-prone, despite the obvious absence there of the doctrine of the two realms. In the retrospective of DDR Protestants, though, the alleged Lutheran cynicism in the face of the Nazi evils was now to be repudiated in the name of a new (if you will, post-Lutheran) dedication to social justice—which in turn was understood to be participation in the task of "socialist construction." In other words, the repudiation of Lutheranism served to legitimate the participation of Christians in the utopian project of Marxism in general and of the Marxist regime in Germany in particular. The phrase *Kirche im Sozial-*

ismus ("church in socialist society"), which some simply understood as a realistic assessment of the churches' situation in Soviet-dominated Europe, was understood by many others as a political agenda with high moral legitimacy: Not that the church had to find ways of surviving under socialism, rather that the church should make itself part of the socialist project. It was precisely in this positive, utopian sense that this phrase found wide resonance in wide ecumenical circles outside the DDR and is the reason why for many years Protestant churchmen from the DDR were the darlings on the World Council of Churches circuit. This understanding of the Christian mission in our time was also, of course, linked to the triumphant ascendancy of various "liberation theologies" in both Protestant and Roman Catholic communities.

It is precisely this sort of utopianism that the Lutheran doctrine of the two realms was intended to forestall. And, as Siemon-Netto shows, it is not Martin Luther but Thomas Münzer who is the ancestor of twentieth-century utopianisms, the Nazi one included. And it is precisely for this reason that the sober realism of Lutheranism continues to be highly needed today. It remains to be seen whether the dismal collapse of socialism in most of the countries where it held sway only a few years ago will put an end to the Left version of modern secularized Anabaptism. As suggested above, beliefs are not usually either adopted or abandoned on the basis of empirical evidence, and the myth of socialism meets very powerful individual as well as collective needs. But even if that myth should have really died in the cataclysmic three years following the east-European revolutions of 1989, other utopian myths are already standing in line. Some are on the Right, such as various nationalisms and religious fundamentalisms (including the Christian right in the United States). Most continue to be on the Left, if not in the old socialist sense, in the sense of being hostile to democratic capitalism and to the bourgeois culture to which it is linked. Thus we have feminist utopias, environmentalist utopias (closely allied with what some have called "health fascism"), multiculturalist utopias. And every one of them has attached to it regiments of Christian theologians, clergy, and lay activists who proclaim the urgent Christian imperative of enlisting under this particular banner. To slightly paraphrase Malcolm Muggeridge, there is no cause mad enough not to enlist the services of demented clergymen strumming their guitars. To legitimate such activities, needless to say, the doctrine of the two realms must be emphatically rejected.

Can a Lutheran morality, even if unintentionally, lead to an amoral cynicism? Perhaps. But, I think, an objective reading of history suggests that much greater harm has been done by utopians than by cynics, certainly in this century. It further seems to me, as it does to Siemon-Netto, that a Lutheran mission in our time would be to preach the doctrine of the two realms at every street corner where utopians gather and thereby to diminish the chances of the homicidal horrors that these types produce with great regularity. It would be nice to be able to record that this is indeed what the Lutheran churches have been doing. Alas, they have not. Not in Germany, not in the United States, not ecumenically. Even in the churches in the territory of the old German Democratic Republic, where one would think that some basic lessons should have been learned, there are powerful residues of the utopian delusions that made the *Kirche im Sozialismus* mischief. Lutherans by and large seem as vulnerable as other Christians to the great utopian temptation. One might perhaps consider this as empirical support for yet another Lutheran doctrine—that of original sin.

Peter L. Berger

PREFACE

Three personal reasons have led to this study on cliché thinking, on Martin Luther, and on Carl Goerdeler, a study in need of an update twelve years after its first publication. My reasons are:

1. I Am a Journalist

I have been a journalist for fifty years at the time of this revision of *The Fabricated Luther*. In this business, clichés are our stock-in-trade. A journalist cannot avoid stereotypes. He receives them, originates them, and, alas, also spreads them. And if he is conscientious, he will constantly strive to find out what is behind a cliché; in other words, he will try to *relativize* and thus undo the cliché.

2. I Am a Lutheran

I was brought up on the works of Johann Sebastian Bach—Lutheran theology put to music. I was introduced to these riches early in life by my mother, Ruth Siemon-Netto, an oratorio singer, who began taking me regularly to the weekly motet and cantata services in Leipzig's *Thomaskirche*—Bach's church—when I was 4 years old. This provided an invaluable education from which I have benefited all my life, especially in times of extreme hardship. (Bearing this in mind, I feel deep pity for today's youth, including Lutheran divinity students, whose upbringing at home and at school has deprived them of any sense of this treasure. This flippant abandonment of a magnificent legacy is all the more incomprehensible as it occurs at a time of great prosperity when it would behoove us to nurture this inheritance; but that is a story for another day.)

The most important person in my childhood, though, was my staunchly Lutheran grandmother, Clara Netto, to whom I owe my values. She taught me Christianity; she taught me to stand up for my beliefs and to be wary of false prophets. In World War II, she simply boycotted her neighborhood church, which was afflicted by the *Zeitgeist* and consequently did not cooperate with the Holy Spirit in the creation of faith. Appalled by the pro-Nazi "German Christian" heresy preached there, she conducted her religious life in a way that will sound familiar to contemporary Christians who are offended by the way their denominations are selling out to the current *Zeitgeist*: She withdrew into her bedroom, lit a candle, read her Bible, and said her prayers. She prayed for an end to the spiritual darkness that had befallen our country.

It was during those frightful years that Clara Netto taught me by her own example what it meant to be a brave Christian—particularly one of Lutheran persuasion. After my parents and I had lost our home in an air raid on Leipzig in 1943, we lived in her apartment. Late every evening, when the sirens sounded the first alarm, she donned her best dress because, as she said, she could well meet her Lord in a matter of hours and wished to be properly attired for that occasion. We lived at a major streetcar crossing, which meant that as the Allied bombings began, passengers, conductors, and drivers of four tramlines would pour into the basements of nearby buildings, including ours, where we stored potatoes and coal and where bunk beds were set up for tenants and visitors.

Among the strangers there were often members of one particular species ordinary Germans heartily disliked. They were Nazi Party functionaries in brown uniforms bedecked with gold tinsel, which is why we called them *Goldfasane*, or gold pheasants. They had two characteristics: They tended to be fat and pudgy, an unusual sight in wartime Germany, and given the macho pretensions of their ideology, they were amazingly pusillanimous. Blockbuster bombs would detonate around us, flattening neighboring apartment blocks so thoroughly that it was often impossible to identify the tenants' bodies. (My grandmother's sister died that way; we buried her right hand bearing her wedding ring.) While this was happening up and down our street, and fire, smoke, and clouds of dust entered our basement through cracks in the walls, we prayed quietly. Only the *Goldfasane* would howl, sigh, and, shiver, and they perspired most unattractively.

This irritated Grandmother Netto, who held me tightly in her left arm, softly singing Lutheran hymns into my ear, hymns that would remain in my head for the rest of my life, even as I covered battles as a foreign correspondent in Vietnam decades later. She lowered her lorgnettes and stared sternly at the gutless Nazi officials. "*Aber, aber, meine Herren* [But, gentlemen]," she said, then immediately correcting herself, "*Ach nein*, gentlemen you are not. Whatever you are, pull yourselves together. You are setting a bad example for my grandson and the other children here. You wanted this war, we didn't. Now face its consequences bravely."

The following morning, Gestapo officers in long leather coats showed up at our front door, accusing my grandmother of sedition. "Come, pray with me," she would say. Of course they did not pray, being atheists or pagans. "Well, then, go ahead, arrest me. Arrest a German officer's widow for admonishing German men in uniform to show valor." At that, the Gestapo men left.

I am not claiming here that my grandmother was a paragon of republican principles. She was not. Born in 1888—the year Germany had three emperors (William I, Frederick, and William II)—Clara Netto was a monarchist to the core, though a monarchist fashioned by the gentle 800-year rule of Saxony's cultured, enlightened, and lighthearted royal family. Being a monarchist of that kind included a mind-set that abhorred the depravity of the Nazi rabble and its inhumanity. And it included a virtue Dietrich Bonhoeffer called *Zivilcourage*, or civil courage, whose dearth in Nazi-ruled Germany he lamented.[1] Bonhoeffer would have been elated observing my feisty grandmother during those bombings in Leipzig and the days that followed. She showed *Zivilcourage*. To her, this was the Lutheran way.

I will not deny that in my childhood I also observed so-called Lutherans act in the opposite manner. I was briefly evacuated to the countryside where I lived in the parsonage of a "German Christian" pastor. He put out the swastika on April 20 to celebrate Hitler's birthday, which scandalized my grandmother and my parents. But I realized that this pastor was not representative of the Lutherans in his village; in fact,

---

1 Dietrich Bonhoeffer, *Letters and Papers from Prison*, ed. Eberhard Bethge (New York: Macmillan, 1972), 5.

his parishioners loathed him, especially his organist, who was also the principal of the local school. I was with this man in the organ loft every Sunday, turning pages. During the sermons, he never failed to whisper into my ear what a specious character he thought the minister was, a traitor to his Lord, an idolater worshiping a false god. This was dangerous stuff to teach a child. Had I denounced the organist, he could have been guillotined. Yet his faith commanded him to take this risk for my benefit; he considered it his Christian duty to teach children to distinguish between the righteous and the unrighteous. On Sundays this minister's church was empty, unless a pulpit exchange brought his colleague from a neighboring parish. According to the organist, this neighboring pastor was a "proper, old-fashioned Lutheran," one who proclaimed the Gospel of Christ, not the false gospel according to Adolf Hitler. Thus everybody came to hear him.

I understand that these anecdotal reminiscences might not carry the weight of empirical evidence, scholarly speaking. But with childhood memories such as these, I was all the more astounded to find out later in life that Martin Luther was being accused of being Hitler's spiritual ancestor. The "Here I Stand" Luther, whom my upright grandmother loved to quote, was supposed to have taught us Germans quietism? This just did not square with my own experiences. And when I studied Lutheran theology late in life, I was cheered that my research proved my grandmother right and William L. Shirer wrong. (Shirer popularized the Luther cliché in *The Rise and Fall of the Third Reich.*)

3. I AM A LEIPZIGER

A few days after I was born, our most popular mayor in recent history, Carl Goerdeler, resigned after the Nazis had blown up the Mendelssohn monument outside the *Gewandhaus*, our concert hall. I remember Goerdeler was mentioned in hushed voices around the dinner table. And I remember the immense sadness in our family when, after the July 20, 1944, coup attempt against Hitler, Goerdeler was arrested and sentenced to death. Everyone agreed that, had the coup succeeded, Goerdeler would have made a wonderful chancellor of a post-Nazi government.

In early 1988, as I was finishing my master's thesis applying Bonhoeffer's theology of the cross to the plight of Vietnam veterans, Dr.

Marianne Meyer-Krahmer visited me in my campus apartment at the Lutheran School of Theology at Chicago (LSTC). Meyer-Krahmer, the retired head mistress of a large high school for girls in Heidelberg, was Goerdeler's daughter. She told me of her futile efforts to have German and other historians evaluate fairly her father's sacrifice. The fact that he was a conservative simply did not tally with the *Zeitgeist*, which happened to be left-wing at the time.

As Goerdeler's daughter and I spoke, I began to realize that it was Goerdeler's internalized Lutheranism that had motivated him to fight Hitler the way he did—for example, rejecting assassination as an option in favor of attempting to have Hitler arrested and tried before a court of law. In all of Goerdeler's thoughts and actions, he displayed typically Lutheran attitudes—from the dauntless way in which he warned the world of the evil of National Socialism, to his willingness to combat that evil at great risk to his life, to his insistence on an orderly form of resistance.

Thus the subject for a doctoral dissertation was born. I thank Dr. Meyer-Krahmer for many enriching hours of interviews and for giving me access to her family files. I am most grateful to my *Doktorvater*, Professor Peter L. Berger, for patiently guiding my research of cliché thinking as a sociological phenomenon. I am equally grateful to Professor Carter Lindberg for his invaluable advice as I was trying to counter the Luther cliché from a theological perspective. And I am indebted to Professor Uri Ra'anan for his inestimable counsel on the historical aspects of my writing. However, none of these gentlemen is responsible for the views I have expressed in this study.

I also owe thanks to Professor Paul Rorem who, as my instructor in church history at LSTC, first triggered my interest in Lutheran resistance theories; to Professor Oliver K. Olson, formerly of Marquette University, who directed my attention to the *gnesio*-Lutheran contributions to these theories; and to Professors Klemens von Klemperer of Smith College and Peter Hofmann of McGill University for their counsel on the history of the German resistance in World War II.

I am indebted to Professor H. Joachim Maître of the College of Communications, Boston University, for making me aware of Thomas Mann's part in the genesis of the Luther cliché.

I am most grateful to the Earhart Foundation for awarding me a grant to fund my doctoral studies.

I thank the scores of pastors and members of the Lutheran laity whom I interviewed during my research into the Lutheran roots of the East German revolution centered in Leipzig, my hometown. That revolution provided me with potent material to argue against the Luther cliché.

I thank my friend Sidney Bertner, whose generosity facilitated my research. I also owe a debt of gratitude to my friends Dudley and Eliane Freeman for giving me access to their extensive library. It proved invaluable for my research on the German resistance.

Most of all, I thank my wife, Gillian, for her patience with her middle-aged husband, who interrupted his career as a journalist and disrupted her life to study theology and sociology of religion. She was the first to read every new chapter, and she proved to be a superb critic.

New York, October 1994 / Gurat, France, July 2006

ABBREVIATIONS

AE   Luther, Martin. *Luther's Works*. American Edition. General editors Jaroslav Pelikan and Helmut T. Lehmann. 55 volumes. St. Louis: Concordia and Philadelphia: Muhlenberg and Fortress, 1955–1986.

AC   Augsburg Confession

DDR/GDR   German Democratic Republic

EKD   Evangelical Church in Germany

LSTC   Lutheran School of Theology, Chicago

OSS   Office of Strategic Services (United States)

SA   *Sturmabteilung* (Nazi storm troopers)

SS   *Schutzstaffel* (Nazi elite guard)

WA   Luther, Martin. *D. Martin Luthers Werke. Kritische Gesamtausgabe. Schriften.* 68 volumes. Weimar: Hermann Böhlau, 1883–1999.

WABr   Luther, Martin. *D. Martin Luthers Werke. Kritische Gesamtausgabe. Briefwechsel.* 18 vols. Weimar: Hermann Böhlau, 1930–1985.

WATr   Luther, Martin. *D. Martin Luthers Werke. Kritische Gesamtausgabe. Tischreden.* 6 vols. Weimar: Hermann Böhlau, 1912–1921.

Chapter One

A Cliché Twice Defeated

More than six decades ago, scores of Germans were rounded up and tortured to death, hanged, guillotined, or executed by firing squads for their attempt to overthrow the National Socialist tyranny. Almost all of them were Christians; some were Roman Catholic, and some were Lutheran. The most famous among the latter group were Dietrich Bonhoeffer, the theologian, and Carl Friedrich Goerdeler, the former mayor of Leipzig. Goerdeler would have become Germany's chancellor had the July 20, 1944, coup attempt against Adolf Hitler succeeded.

This study will show that they acted in accordance with Martin Luther's teachings on how and when to resist secular authority. Yet since the end of World War II, eminent scholars and scribes have promoted the cliché that Luther was somehow to blame for Hitler's rise to power and for the Germans' subservience to this evil ruler.

Let us jump ahead in history for one moment: "Germany will never be reunified—at least not in our lifetime." For decades this is what Communist leaders stated as a fact and Western politicians whispered so they would not offend their West German allies. Most "independent experts" were less bashful. To the well-informed, the impossibility of Germany's reunification was a "given." But in the autumn of 1989, the Berlin Wall came down. And a year later, Germany was one country again, joined together peacefully and democratically. In hindsight, what seemed a verity turned out to be yet another cliché.

Both stereotypes—Luther's alleged authorship of National Social-ism and the presumed impossibility of Germany's reunification—are related, as we shall see. This gives us cause for reflection on the role of clichés in modern times. The word *cliché* is the French vocable for a stereotype printing plate. Its function is to reproduce the likeness of a given object over and over again. A cliché does not give an altogether truthful picture of that object. For one thing, a cliché is never more than two-dimensional; for another, it is not alive—once cast, it will never change. And even the best cliché is never more than a rough approxi-mation of the real thing.

Used as a metaphor for a particular way of thinking, clichés dis tinguish themselves by "their capacity to bypass reflection and thus unconsciously to work on the mind, while excluding potential rela-tivizations," according to Anton Zijderveld.[1] Zijderveld sees a strong affinity between clichés and modernity. I shall take this notion a step further. I will show that cliché thinking is a sibling of the *Zeitgeist*, which also excludes potential relativizations.

The cliché about the alleged impossibility of a German reunifica-tion conspired with the *Zeitgeist* and excluded potential relativizations such as

1. that the Communist system would ultimately collapse;

2. that this collapse could conceivably occur in a largely nonviolent manner;

3. that reasonable leaders such as Gorbachev and Yeltsin could appear on the Soviet scene;

4. that a peaceful and powerful opposition would emerge inside East Germany.

Finally, being twinned to the *Zeitgeist*, which by its very definition is finite and therefore anthropocentric, our cliché excludes the theological option that God might interfere directly with history.

In fairness to our cliché, it must be said that all these potential relativizations had seemed rather remote for the last forty years. But what of more pedestrian stereotypes, clichés about other nations, for example? "Having been fully socialized in a particular society," Zijderveld writes, "the clichés of this society will lie in store in man's

---

1 Anton C. Zijderveld, *On Clichés* (London: Routledge & Kegan Paul, 1979), 5–6.

consciousness, ever ready to be triggered and used."² This surely applies to clichés such as the following: The English are eccentric and scurrilous; the French arrogant or full of *joie de vivre*; the Germans efficient, *gemütlich*, or cruel, and at any rate obedient to authority. Those endowed with a somewhat larger stock of clichés might elaborate that the Germans' submissiveness to any type of ruler, tyrants included, is all Luther's fault; he was Hitler's spiritual ancestor.

Men of renown have enunciated this astonishing lineage running from the sixteenth-century Saxon founder of Protestantism via King Frederick II of Prussia—a former Calvinist turned Deist—to a twentieth-century Roman Catholic Austrian who became the internationally acknowledged symbol of evil. U.S. historian Robert Michael argued that there was a "strong parallel" between Luther's ideas and the anti-Semitism of most German Lutherans throughout the Holocaust. According to Michael, Luther mythologized the Jews as evil, just as the Nazis did.³ Another U.S. historian, Lucy Dawidowicz, suggested that the "line of anti-Semitic descent" from Luther to Hitler was "easy to draw." Dawidowicz asserted that, like Hitler four centuries later, Luther was obsessed by the "demonologized universe" inhabited by Jews.⁴ However, Dawidowicz at least qualified this by saying that *to Hitler*, this was the "real Luther," as opposed to an entirely different Luther we will discuss later. Alan Dershowitz, not a historian but a renowned legal scholar, pulled no such punches:

> Toward the end of his life—and at the height of his influence—Luther articulated a specific program against the Jews, which served as bible of anti-Jewish actions over the next four centuries, culminating in the Holocaust. In many ways, Luther can be viewed as the spiritual predecessor of Adolf Hitler. Indeed, virtually all the themes that eventually found their way into Hitler's genocidal writings, rantings, and actions are adumbrated in Martin Luther's infamous essay "Concerning the Jews and Their Lies . . ." It is shocking that Luther's ignoble name is

---

2 Zijderveld, *On Clichés*, 36.

3 Robert Michael, "Luther, Luther Scholars, and the Jews," *Encounter* 46:4 (Autumn 1985): 339–56.

4 Lucy Dawidowicz, *The War against the Jews, 1933–1945* (New York: Bantam, 1986), 23.

still honored rather than forever cursed by mainstream Protestant churches.[5]

Dershowitz stands in a long tradition. Thomas Mann linked Luther to Hitler, as did Lord Vansittart, who was once the highest civil servant in the British Foreign Office. Archbishop Temple and the Very Reverend R. W. Inge of the Church of England shared this opinion, as did William L. Shirer, the author of *The Rise and Fall of the Third Reich*, a best-seller. And all owe their insights, directly or indirectly, to Ernst Troeltsch, a liberal German theologian considered a tragic figure by many of his colleagues—a man who could not square the church's doctrine with science and consequently lost his Christian faith, though not his belief in God.

One of Shirer's observations has since gained almost worldwide acceptance: He explained the timidity of most German Protestants in the early Nazi years with the assertion that they were imbued with Luther's "ferocious [belief] in absolute political authority."[6] This is, of course, a crass cliché that entirely ignores Luther's advocacy of, in Franz Lau's words, "an almost foolhardy opposition against all governmental injustice."[7] It ignores that Luther provided his followers with precise definitions of the circumstances under which tyrants may be removed by force of arms.

At the time of the National Socialists' rise to power, Shirer was an American radio correspondent in Germany. As I prepared the first edition of this volume, Shirer (d. 1993) was living in retirement in New England. For the purpose of this study, I asked him how he had arrived at this conclusion. He replied, "It came from general reading."[8] This book will demonstrate that if one does one's homework—that is, if one reads those books which Luther himself authored and is not content with doing "general reading"—one will see that Shirer's conclusions are a construct that has no foundation in historic reality. To say it differ-

---

5 Alan Dershowitz, *Chutzpah* (Boston: Little, Brown, 1991), 106–7.

6 William L. Shirer, *The Rise and Fall of the Third Reich* (New York: Simon & Schuster, 1960), 236.

7 Franz Lau, *Luthers Lehre von den beiden Reichen* (Berlin: Evangelische Verlagsanstalt, 1952), 88–89.

8 William L. Shirer in a letter to Uwe Siemon-Netto, dated February 21, 1989.

ently, I hope to demonstrate that Shirer's conclusions are the result of cliché thinking, not the result of work with primary sources.

But this leads us to questions that must be pondered in a study of the phenomenon of cliché thinking: Does modernity allow for differentiated views? Can a media society function without clichés? Would Shirer's work have been a global success had he written, "Well, yes, there were Germans who misunderstood Luther and therefore did not resist the Nazis and who became Nazis themselves; and there were other Germans whose internalized Lutheranism guided them in the opposite direction and made them choose the path of resistance and martyrdom"?

Shirer knew many of the latter variety of Germans. He knew Carl Goerdeler, who will be the focus of a long chapter in this volume. Did Shirer not see that it was Goerdeler, rather than Hitler's fellow travelers, who acted in a truly Lutheran fashion? Or was Shirer insufficiently informed about Luther *and* about Hitler? Or did he not want to know? Like Shirer, I am a veteran foreign correspondent familiar with the pressures and constraints of our trade, and that makes it impossible for me to slam him. Too great is the temptation to reach into your stock of clichés if your job compels you to explain strange societies to readers and listeners who are unfamiliar with such subjects.

The same types of questions apply to our second stereotype: "Germany will never be reunified—at least not in our lifetime." Was it at all possible for journalists to relativize something that *seemed* obvious to everyone? Was there any precedent on which one could base the assumption that things may change literally overnight? Yet on October 9, 1989, this cliché was soundly defeated—along with the other stereotype, which held that Luther had so effectively warped the minds of his followers in Germany (though not the minds of the people in more uniformly Lutheran countries such as Norway or Denmark!) that they would forever be incapable of resisting governmental evil. It was in Leipzig, Goerdeler's city, almost two generations after his death on the gallows, that one of Luther's most famous dicta was proven right: "At no place has Christ's Gospel ever been stronger than where it is the least liked. For when their hour came the tyrants went under, and the Word remains on the agenda."[9]

---

9 WA 19:401.6–9.

On that October day of what went down in history as the year of Germany's peaceful revolution, after the traditional "prayers for peace" in Leipzig's churches, 70,000 demonstrators marched around the medieval city center. Later, Pastor Friedrich Schorlemmer, a leading dissident and seminary professor in Wittenberg, was to write: "Those who marched in Leipzig had a good notion of what might happen. So they took each other by their hands and got started, the fear of a Chinese solution in their bellies and the security apparatus before their eyes. Only later did it became clear to us what was at stake on that day."[10]

Today we know that the Stasi, East Germany's state security agency, had prepared for a massacre. In Leipzig's hospitals, entire wards were cleared of patients. According to Bishop Werner Leich, who was the president of the federation of evangelical churches in the German Democratic Republic (GDR) at that time, hospital staff had their leaves canceled, and ample amounts of coffins and body bags were brought into town. Leich was also the head of the Lutheran church in neighboring Thuringia. And there, in the quaint town of Arnstadt, the Stasi had rehearsed the crackdown it planned for Leipzig two days later.

Arnstadt was where Johann Sebastian Bach had his first job in a pretty church that now bears his name. Demonstrators fled into that church on October 7, 1989, after the Stasi and the "people's police" (*Vopo*) had closed in on them from all sides. Deacon Klaus Gerth and Vicar Anne-Katrin Schiek rushed into the *Bachkirche* to comfort the frightened crowd. When they emerged again, they were immediately handcuffed and led away—an unusual action, even by East German standards. They were released a few hours later. This was, after all, only a rehearsal.

The ninth of October was a Monday. For quite some time, "prayers for peace" were conducted every Monday evening in Leipzig's downtown churches, Protestant as well as Roman Catholic. The worshipers had no idea of what the Stasi had in mind for them. An agricultural fairground on the outskirts of Leipzig was to be transformed into a con-

---

10 Friedrich Schorlemmer, "Die Menschheit reicht weiter," in *Räumt die Steine hinweg*, ed. Andreas Ebert, Johanna Haberer, Friedrich Kraft (Munich: Claudius, 1990), 108.

centration camp for opposition leaders. Lists of prospective inmates were drawn up, which included the names of all prominent clergymen.[11]

One of those listed was Provost Günter Hanisch, the highest-ranking prelate of the Roman Catholic minority in Leipzig. From the very beginning of the protest movement, he had stood faithfully with his Evangelical brother-ministers and preached from their pulpits. The two Lutheran superintendents (regional bishops), Friedrich Magirius and Johannes Richter, were also marked for internment. Also at risk was Pastor Christian, *Führer* of the *Nikolaikirche*, whom anonymous callers had threatened, "One more prayer service, and your church will be in flames!"

There are many explanations as to why Leipzig was spared a bloodbath and mass arrests. One reason is definitely true. The nonviolence of the demonstrators was a crucial factor. Not that all 70,000 demonstrators were Christians. In fact, of Leipzig's total population of 530,000, only 12 percent of the city belonged to the Protestant Church and not even 4 percent were Roman Catholics. "What happened in Leipzig was a good example for Jesus' definition of the people of God as the salt of the earth: 15,000 worshipers determined the behavior of 70,000 protesters," said Superintendent Richter. On the Monday the wall fell, Richter had ended his sermon in the *Thomaskirche* with these prayerful words: "May you be given the courage to be patient. May you and I be given the strength for good language. May you and I be valiant enough to resist anger."

As the demonstrators marched around Leipzig's medieval center, they arrived at the most dreaded place in their city—the local Stasi headquarters, called *Runde Ecke*, or "round corner." Suddenly, *agents provocateurs* in their midst tried to storm this massive building to give the huge army of secret police, militiamen, and regular soldiers waiting in the side streets an excuse for a "Chinese solution" to put down the unrest. But well-organized Christian groups within the crowd separated the agitators from the other demonstrators. They formed a *cordon sanitaire* around the Stasi building. And that was the beginning of the end of Communist East Germany.

---

11 Werner Leich, in an interview with the author, July 1990.

The security forces withdrew. At whose orders? That is still unclear. But this much is certain—they would not have done so had violence broken out. Without the courageous action of the Christians, civil war would have been the most likely result. As it was, tyranny retreated in the face of a few people armed only with candles and singing hymns. Their gentleness turned out to be the first hammer-blow against the Berlin Wall.

That event was a major victory of Luther over Lenin, who had thought the Germans incapable of making revolution, for before storming a railroad station, the Germans would buy platform tickets. To be fair to Lenin, the Leipzig demonstrators proved him right in one respect. In a sense, they did buy their platform tickets. They were orderly. They came after work. They paid their tram, train, or bus fares. They shed no blood and destroyed no property.

But Lenin erred, for this *was* a revolution. But it was a very German, a quintessentially Lutheran, revolution. It was a revolution without insurrection and bloodshed. It was an "orderly" revolution. Some readers might object, "How could this have been a Lutheran revolution if most of the demonstrators were doubtless atheists or agnostics?" Here I have to appeal to Max Weber, who has shown that *internalized* Calvinistic attitudes are still shaping the social behavior even of secularized Americans. If this is so, then it is fair to say that an *internalized* Lutheranism must have had a major influence on the behavior of secularized East Germans.

In my last chapter, I shall return to the events in East Germany. But first I must explain the phenomenon that these events, as well as the resistance against Hitler almost two generations earlier, have reduced to absurdity—the cliché.

THINKING IN CLICHÉS: A PERVERTED TYPIFICATION

Thinking in clichés resembles a process that Alfred Schutz considers an inevitable prerequisite of social life.[12] It is called *typification*.

We typify continuously. For example, being lost in a strange town we spot a blue uniform and a badge and think: *police officer*. We do not think, "Here is an Irish-American who loves to eat oysters and collects

---

12 Alfred Schutz, *Collected Papers* (The Hague: M. Nijhoff, 1962), 1:6.

butterflies." We know none of that; if we did, we might invite the officer to an oyster dinner to discuss butterflies. But having typified this individual as a police officer, we deal with him or her in that capacity. In this case, we ask for directions.

A second time, while speeding, we see a blue uniform and a badge. Again we think: *police officer*. But now we slow down because we do not want to get a ticket.

A third time we may observe someone in a blue uniform with a badge running across the street in the pursuit of another person. Once more we think: *police officer*. But this time we neither ask for directions nor slow down for fear of getting a ticket. Instead, we respond to the officer in his or her present function. We might help to nab the villain, or we might stand and gawk at the unfolding drama of a police chase.

But if we narrowed our typification of the officer to only one aspect of the profession, we might always ask the officer for directions, regardless of whether the officer was chasing a criminal or trying to catch us speeding. Thus we would not only typify the officer but also register his or her presence in a stereotypical manner. And that would be typification of a perverted kind. This typification would resist modification. It would not allow for the possibility that at this very moment the police officer has a different task. Therefore, typification has degenerated into a cliché—the rather idiosyncratic cliché that a cop's only job is that of a guide.

"Clichés manage to avoid . . . relativization brought about by reflections," Anton Zijderveld observes. "They . . . influence people on the attitudinal level."[13] In our example, a multitude of potential relativizations is bypassed in our behavior if we asked every man in a blue uniform with a badge for directions, relativizations such as: (1) at this point it is not his job to show us the way; (2) we may not slow down when we see him and consequently be fined for speeding; (3) we may prevent him from arresting a criminal; (4) we may not need any directions right now.

Clichés come in a host of varieties. Our lives are so filled with stereotypical expressions, acts, and gestures that they have lost their

---

13 Zijderveld, *On Clichés*, 6.

original meaning. When we say that something will happen "at the end of the day," everybody realizes that we are not thinking of the end of any specific day; in fact, whatever will occur may well take place early in the morning or at noon or at teatime.

When we claim "blondes have more fun," we tend to say it in jest, knowing that our statement would only be true from the perspective of an envious brunette vying for the attention of a gentleman who prefers to romance blonde ladies. And even in that case, we know that it takes more than the color of her hair to let a woman have more fun. Moreover, anybody who has ever been in Rio de Janeiro, as well as in Iceland, will find the assertion that blondes have more fun blatantly absurd—an absurd cliché.

Similarly, when we engage in stereotypical gestures such as the French habit of kissing one another on the cheeks, we are aware that in most cases this act signifies neither love nor concupiscence, as it might have centuries ago. Clichés, including stereotypical gestures, are simply "containers of old experiences" that have "grown stale and common through repetitive overuse," writes Zijderveld,[14] who also points out that clichés are exchanged "like the many coins of our inflated economic system."[15] According to Zijderveld, a cliché should be seen "as a specimen of human expression which has lost much of its original ingenuity and semantic power, but gained in social functionality."[16] The kissing ritual serves as a form of greeting. It has no real meaning. The gesture is the mark of a cliché whose meaning is superseded by function, says Zijderveld.

Nowhere is this more evident than in television commercials. We are frequently shown couples clinking champagne glasses to welcome the new carpet in their house, to accompany a microwave meal served by candlelight, or to relax on a cruise ship. These scenes are not followed by information about the different *crus* of champagne or why some glasses produce a wondrous chime when clinked. Neither the champagne nor the glasses really matter in these commercials. Rather, they are components of a cliché whose function it is to impart to the viewers

---

14 Zijderveld, *On Clichés*, 11.

15 Zijderveld, *On Clichés*, 6.

16 Zijderveld, *On Clichés*, 24.

a sense of celebration. The champagne and glasses are another way of communicating that it feels good to have that particular carpet in the house, eat that microwave meal, or travel on that cruise ship. If the same could be accomplished by pouring a cup of coffee over the new carpet, into the microwave oven, or into the ship's funnel, we would probably get more amusing commercials. But for the time being, dealing with coffee in this way would be considered too original to function as a cliché that bestows on television viewers a sense of celebration.

This supersedure of meaning by function affects all aspects of human existence: consumption, work, spirituality, eroticism, politics, and recreation. "Clichés . . . function as beacons in [the] vagueness, instability and uncertainty"[17] of modern society, Zijderveld contends, naming the loss of tradition as this uncertainty's principal cause. Society no longer experiences the past as a meaningful component of the present.[18]

Modern society is characterized by industrialization, secularization, urbanization, galloping progress in science, bureaucratization, and the capitalist mode of production. These features of modernity have destabilized traditional institutions such as the family, the church, and the community. The lack of stable institutions, Arnold Gehlen observes, "makes heavy demands upon man's ability and willingness to deliberate; and, by demolishing the bulwark of habit, exposes him defenseless to the casual flow of stimuli."[19] Thus, Zijderveld explains, clichés function as substitutes for institutions whose stability has been undermined by modernity.

Having coined the neologism "clichégenic society," Zijderveld goes on to say, "Modernity generates and fosters clichés."[20] Cut off from tradition as a potential provider of guidelines for the interpretation of the world around him, a world of rapidly and continuously shifting values and meanings, man has become dependent on society's principal generator of clichés—the mass media.

---

17 Zijderveld, *On Clichés*, 46.

18 Zijderveld, *On Clichés*, 39.

19 Arnold Gehlen, *Man in the Age of Technology*, trans. Patricia Lipscomb (New York: Columbia University Press, 1980), 77.

20 Zijderveld, *On Clichés*, 26–27.

Even the best television and radio reports or newspaper stories are, by their very nature, compelled to avoid most potential relativizations. For one thing, space and time constraints render a truly comprehensive coverage of any event impossible; for another, journalists are themselves children of Zijderveld's "clichégenic society"—therefore they are subject to its shortcomings. Never before has the proverbial "man in the street" been expected to wrestle with such a bewildering array of facts: Fanatical Muslims, most of whom are citizens of Saudi Arabia, an ally of the United States, hijack passenger planes and fly them into the World Trade Center in New York City. They kill some 3,000 innocent people "in the name of Allah," who will reward each of the culprits with 72 virgins in paradise. The United States and its allies invade Iraq, where Muslim terrorists respond by beheading kidnapped Westerners in front of running video cameras. British, U.S., Canadian, Danish, French, German, and other forces patrol the most arid parts of Afghanistan to protect that country's sometimes friendly, sometimes distinctly unfriendly, population against the Taliban or the highly organized terrorists under the command of Saudi billionaire Osama bin Laden. Despite the above, the majority of Western Europeans tell pollsters that they consider the United States to be the greatest menace to world peace—not rogue nations such as North Korea or Iran or rogue organizations such as al-Qaeda, all of whom desire weapons of mass destruction.

During the writing of the first edition of this volume, Serbs were busy killing Bosnian Muslims and Croats; Croats were killing Serbs and Bosnian Muslims; Bosnian Muslims were killing Bosnian Muslims; U.S. and other forces were bringing food to Somalia only to be killed by Somalis; an epidemic was—and still is—ravaging primarily homosexuals in the United States and Europe and heterosexuals in Africa in breathtaking numbers.

Never before have even university-educated Americans, for example, been as inadequately equipped to make sense of the vast amount of information they are exposed to day after day. Never before have history and geography—two key disciplines for the understanding of world events—been held in such low regard by college students.

Clichés churned out by journalists and pundits are therefore filling voids created by the absence of knowledge. As an editorial consultant to

a mass-circulation daily newspaper, I have participated in the daily routine of providing instant answers to the most intricate problems. This is
how they are dealt with at the 11 a.m. editorial conference: "Let's run a
'Topic of the Day' news analysis on why Saddam Hussein resembles
Hitler—10 questions, 10 answers, none longer than 40 words, deadline
4 p.m."

Clearly, more than 400 words can be said about the similarities
and differences between Saddam Hussein and Hitler. The editors know
that, and most of the paper's 11 million readers presumably know that
as well. However, the production and, respectively, consumption of
clichés has become a routine for editors and readers alike.

The journalist as an instant expert is, of course, another feature of
modernity. To dispense with the irksome and time-consuming task of
explaining enigmatic events or personages, a journalist delves into his or
her stock of clichés and finds seemingly appropriate phrases. For example, "Ho Chi Minh is an Asian Tito" or "When our forces liberate Bagh-
dad, there will be dancing in the streets" are clichés.[21] Such statements
are then parroted over and over again, often years or even decades later
when their absurdity has long been established.[22] As Zijderveld says,
"Repetitiveness is the core of [the cliché's] nature."[23]

For example, during the 1989 upheaval in China, U.S. television
commentators declared that the Old Guard in Peking had lost "the mandate of heaven." Western journalists like to dig up a similar phrase

21 Presumably, the Iraqis will dance like the French did in 1944 when Paris was liber-
    ated from German occupation. This ranks as one of the silliest clichés, given the
    staggering cultural differences between Europe and the Middle East.

22 Tito's distinguishing mark was that, though a Communist, he pursued a policy
    independent from that of the Soviet Union. Ho Chi Minh, by contrast, was known
    to have been a Soviet agent since the 1920s; he rarely wavered in his allegiance to
    Moscow. His successors, too, remained loyal to the USSR until its collapse. As the
    cliché will have it, Ho Chi Minh resembled Tito in that both fought a guerilla war
    against "foreign invaders" of their countries. While this was true in Tito's case, it
    did not apply to Ho Chi Minh. He started a guerilla war against the noncommu-
    nist part of his nation at a time when, except for a few military advisors, there were
    no foreign troops on Vietnamese soil. U.S. and other forces did not arrive in Viet-
    nam until the war had been in full swing for several years, and they did so at the
    request of an indigenous government that was certainly no less legitimate than Ho
    Chi Minh's.

23 Zijderveld, On Clichés, 36.

whenever an Asian government is in trouble. During the Vietnam War, the Saigon regime was alleged to have lost this divine commission while Hanoi supposedly received it.

When China's Old Guard politicians eventually regained control by means of a bloodbath and China went on to thrive economically, heaven's reckless handling of the "mandate" failed to become the subject of journalistic scrutiny. Most journalists do not have the time to read up on esoterica such as the original meaning of the phrase "mandate of heaven." Nor did journalists have time to wonder how the term would be received in Western societies that are inclined to view heaven as the dwelling place of God. The expression simply sounded sufficiently Eastern and seemed applicable to the conditions in China or Vietnam. And so it was employed—as a cliché.

Future scholars may ponder the impact that this cliché's frequent use had on subsequent developments. Did it, for example, contribute to the conviction of a majority of Americans that South Vietnam was not worth defending? If so, the cliché may have been partly responsible for the U.S. debacle in Indochina, including the autogenocide in Cambodia and the fate of the Boat People. In this sense, then, clichés are not just an irritating perversion of typification; they can become lethal weapons of the *Zeitgeist*.

If, as Zijderveld claims, there exists a strong affinity between clichés and modernity, the same applies to modernity and the term *Zeitgeist*. This expression is a child of early modernity, of the Enlightenment. Voltaire first coined this term. He said he considered it always his task to observe "the spirit of the times." As Voltaire saw it, this spirit directed all great world events.[24] Goethe defined the *Zeitgeist* thus: "When one side . . . asserts itself, takes control of the crowd and triumphs to the extent that the opposite side withdraws into a corner and must quietly hide for the moment, this disproportionate weight [of one side] is called the *Zeitgeist*."[25]

Thus the *Zeitgeist*, like the cliché, does not allow for potential relativizations. And like the cliché, it serves as a beacon in the vagueness

---

24 Karl Baur, *Zeitgeist und Geschichte* (Munich: Callwey, 1978), 14.

25 Johann Wolfgang von Goethe, "Schriften zu Literatur und Theater," in *Gesamtausgabe* (Stuttgart: Cotta, 1960), 15:896.

and uncertainty of modern society. The *Zeitgeist* gives individuals who are afloat in a sea of instability the "correct" position with which to orient themselves—for the time being.

THE CLICHÉ AS A "THING"

The one aspect of modernity that gives the "spirit of the times" its particular relevance is secularization. In the words of Dietrich Bonhoeffer, "when faith in God was lost all that remained was a rationalized and mechanized world."[26] In premodern times, man referred all things to God. To premodern man, "the world is what it is because the gods have so decreed it," writes Peter L. Berger.[27] Premodern man's world is one of fate, not choice (*hairesis*). But the modern world is one in which heresy has been universalized in the sense that choice, not fate, rules human reality.[28] Modernization has thus "brought with it a strong accentuation on the subjective side of human existence."[29] In this modern world, Arnold Gehlen writes, "art, law, even religion become subjectivized and weakened. 'Ideas' bud forth everywhere, and one can only deal with them by discussion, this being the appropriate form of external elaboration. This intellectualization and subjectivization of culture screened away from action is a novelty of our historical era; it is a component of the very air we breathe."[30]

"In changing the world, men have demolished the invisible supports of their own spiritual identity," states Gehlen.[31] It is the contention of this study that the *Zeitgeist* delivers a substitute support in the form of a crutch. The *Zeitgeist* provides society with a point of reference. But that point of reference is finite and fickle, in contrast to premodern society's infinite point of reference, which was God.

If Zijderveld links modern society's loss of tradition to cliché thinking, Walter Künneth connects its hostility to history with the *Zeit-*

---

26 Dietrich Bonhoeffer, *Ethics* (New York: Collier, 1955), 96.

27 Peter L. Berger, *The Heretical Imperative* (Garden City: Anchor Press/Doubleday, 1979), 14.

28 Zijderveld, *On Clichés*, 1.

29 Berger, *Heretical Imperative*, 14.

30 Gehlen, *Man in the Age of Technology*, 76.

31 Zijderveld, *On Clichés*, 68–69.

geist: "Having thrown the ballast of history overboard, a point of view hostile to history strives to bypass the past en route towards a new beginning for humanity. The historical dimension is to be replaced by an entirely new expectation: the vision for a history-free future of mankind."[32]

To Künneth, a theologian, this "escape from history" is an attempt to "flee from God," and "this tendency to reach beyond a given historical fate [*Geschichtsschicksal*] [also] resembles a dangerous play of fantasy the penalty for which is a loss of the sense of reality; but every day the realities of the historical world catch up [with this tendency], and these realities shatter utopian dreams."[33]

There exists a strong affinity between clichés and utopian dreams that also manages to avoid relativization brought about by reflection. Utopian aims are, of course, not an exclusive property of modernity. Yet sixteenth-century utopian movements have had a "decisive influence on modern development," according to Karl Mannheim, who has established the "structural link" between Reformation-era chiliasm and social revolution.[34]

Chiliasm expects the union of the anticipated millennium of Christ's rule with the present, Mannheim says.[35] In theological terms, it seeks to immanentize the *eschaton*. "Since the Christian message has lost its power," writes Joachim Fest, "the search is on for a substitute for God and a Hereafter which the utopias have transferred into this world."[36]

I shall return to utopianism later in this study. Here, I simply wish to point to the fact that as a result of the "escape from history" and the attempt to "flee from God" (Künneth), a secular religion catering to the *Zeitgeist* has emerged. Where faith in God has been lost, man's religious yearning focuses on causes no longer requiring sanctification by an

---

32 Walter Künneth, *Wider den Strom* (Wuppertal: R. Brockhaus, 1989), 98. Like Bonhoeffer, Künneth is a German Lutheran theologian who played a leading role in the church resistance against National Socialism. Unlike Bonhoeffer, he survived.

33 Künneth, *Wider den Strom*, 99.

34 Karl Mannheim, *Ideologie und Utopie* (Frankfurt: Vittorio Klostermann, 1985), 184.

35 Mannheim, *Ideologie und Utopie*, 189.

36 Joachim Fest, *Der zerstörte Traum* (Berlin: Siedler, 1991), 103. Fest is one of the publishers of *Frankfurter Allgemeine Zeitung*. In this volume, he proclaims the "end of the utopian era" after the collapse of Communism.

appeal to God.[37] Künneth names some of them: "The exuberant glorification of human rights," slogans calling for a radical renunciation of the use of force to attain world peace, the demand for a nuclear-free zone in Europe, and total disarmament. Künneth readily concedes that respect for human rights and love of peace are entirely biblical and represent the Creator's will. But when uttered without reference to a past that is marked by horrible acts of inhumanity and the implications such acts have for the present and the future, they become *Zeitgeist*-inspired clichés "leading to a dangerous labyrinth—a condition of enthusiastic blindness to historical realities."[38]

The *Zeitgeist* shares a property Zijderveld attributes to clichés: They become tyrannical because stereotypes are hard to avoid in a fully modernized society, and they are prone to become the molds of consciousness, while their functionality penetrates deeply into the fabric of sociocultural and political life.[39]

This conforms with Elisabeth Noelle-Neumann's notion of what she terms *Die Schweigespirale*, the spiral of silence: "*Schweigespirale* means: human beings don't wish to isolate themselves; they incessantly observe their environment; they register to the minutest detail what is gaining the upper hand and what is diminishing. He who sees that his own opinion is prevailing feels strengthened, speaks publicly, drops his caution. He who sees that his own opinion is losing ground, falls silent."[40] Noelle-Neumann then describes how society deals with small minorities daring to take an independent position: "Public opinion always has an irrational . . . component with moral as well as aesthetic values: he who thinks differently is not stupid but evil. It is from this moral element that public opinion draws its very force: its threat to isolate [those who differ]."[41]

---

37 Historically, it was the faithful who embraced causes such as the crusades or missions because such causes were sanctified by an appeal to the historically transcendent God. Today's causes are blessed by an imminent transcendence such as a classless society.

38 Fest, *Der zerstörte Traum*, 127.

39 Cf. Zijderveld, *On Clichés*, 26.

40 Cited in Jens Motschmann, *So nicht, Herr Pfarrer!* (Berlin: Ullstein, 1991), 29.

41 Cited in Motschmann, *So nicht, Herr Pfarrer!* 29.

Noelle-Neumann's description of the workings of the *Zeitgeist* thus matches Goethe's definition of this phenomenon. Working in tandem, the *Zeitgeist* and cliché thinking are incessantly pollinating one another. The *Zeitgeist* will spawn a cliché that in turn will propagate the *Zeitgeist*. It was the *Zeitgeist* of the late 1960s that sired the cliché that the South Vietnamese government had lost the "mandate of heaven." The cliché then kept popping up in countless newspaper articles, television debates, and, ultimately, dinner-party conversations, thus reinforcing, via public opinion, the *Zeitgeist*'s dictum that the South Vietnamese government was an ally not worth defending.

Clichés, Zijderveld says, have a reified nature.[42] "Reification is the apprehension of human phenomena as if they were things,"[43] Peter L. Berger and Thomas Luckmann write. Arnold Gehlen defines the term *reification* thus: "In our social capacities we often act schematically." This definition means that we enact habitualized, well-worn behavior patterns that unfold "by themselves."[44] This can be said not only of behavior of a practical, external nature but also (and primarily) of internal components of behavior. The formation of thoughts and judgments and the emergence of evaluative emotions and decisions are all things that are largely automatized.[45]

Gehlen goes on to say that "reified and automated operations of thought resist criticism and are immune to objections." Such invariance, "when applied to intellectual and emotional habits, is the condition of all reliable tradition . . . and thus constitutes a social cement of the greatest significance."[46]

Being "reified chunks of stale experience," Zijderveld suggests, clichés are things that can be collected like stamps or jokes. They can be used and recycled like tin cans. A tin can may be used in a variety of ways. In the Vietnam War, a "C" ration can of baked pork and beans, once emptied, might have become a soldier's cup and, later, part of the roof of a jungle hut.

---

42 Zijderveld, *On Clichés*, 15–16.

43 Peter L. Berger and Thomas Luckmann, *The Social Construction of Reality* (Garden City: Anchor Press, 1967), 89.

44 Berger and Luckmann, *Social Construction of Reality*, 145.

45 Berger and Luckmann, *Social Construction of Reality*, 145.

46 Gehlen, *Man in the Age of Technology*, 143.

Similarly, clichés may be used in multiple ways, reflecting a variety of vested interests.[47] Let us consider three purposes of the stereotype that will be developed in the following chapter—the cliché that Luther was somehow responsible for the Germans' subservience to Hitler:

1. In William L. Shirer's case, the function of the cliché was similar to that of the "mandate of heaven" formula decades later; it was simply a journalist's slick and instant answer to his readers' demand for an explanation of another nation's enigmatic comportment.

2. Lord Vansittart's motive was propagandistic. As Christabel Bielenberg explains: "The British, as a nation, did not go to war willingly, unless they had worked up a good, old hate."[48] Thus by portraying the Germans as a malignant nation whose evil roots go back to Luther, Vansittart strove to strengthen his countrymen's resolve to vanquish the enemy.

3. Thomas Mann's reasons may have resembled those of certain contemporary Americans castigating the United States: By pointing to the dark side in the national character of their own people, they appear to shoulder that burden; yet in reality, in recognizing those faults, they absolve themselves and become good guys. Of the three, Thomas Mann doubtless provides the best example of the *Zeitgeist* at work. His writings reflect the rapid and continuous shift of values and meanings, which, to Zijderveld, is a mark of modernization:

   • In the waning months of World War I, Thomas Mann opposed democracy as un-German. He thought that parliament and parties polluted "the life of the nation with politics."[49] He wrote: "Every

---

47 Berger and Luckmann, *Social Construction of Reality*, 123 and 204n. Here Berger and Luckmann discuss the link between vested interests and ideology. They acknowledge that the term *ideology* has been "used in so many different senses that one might despair of using it in any precise manner at all." But they retain it in a narrowly defined sense: "When a particular definition of reality becomes attached to a concrete power interest, it may be called ideology." Thus as the many uses of the Luther cliché are tied to vested interests, which in the final analysis are all power interests, they are ideological. In this narrow sense, then, ideology is a sibling of the cliché and the *Zeitgeist* because it excludes potential relativizations.

48 Christabel Bielenberg, *The Past Is Myself* (London: Corgi, 1984), 145.

49 Thomas Mann, "Betrachtungen eines Unpolitischen," in *Gesammelte Werke* (Berlin: Fischer, 1960), 12:260.

blockhead is a democrat these days,"[50] and he expressed horror at the thought of rule by the people.[51]

- When, at the end of World War I, revolutionary upheaval swept Germany, Mann rejoiced, confiding to his diary on March 24, 1918: "I am capable of running into the street shouting, 'Down with the western democracy and its lies! Long live Germany and Russia. Long live Communism!'"[52]

- A year later, Mann welcomed the extinction of revolutionary lunacy in Munich by military might: "Cleaning up according to martial law, certainly no cause for complaint. To my delight the red flags disappeared from the city. Military band played *Deutschland, Deutschland über alles* at the *Siegestor*. . . . I find that one breathes considerably more freely in a military dictatorship than under the rule of the crapulent."[53]

- In World War II, as an exile in the United States, Mann professed a "personal commitment to democracy,"[54] calling it "the political name for ideals . . . Christianity has brought to the world."[55]

- But in 1949, after a visit to East Germany, Mann had kind things to say about Communism: "I refuse to participate in the hysteria of the persecution of Communists . . . [a] future without Communist features has long become unimaginable . . . . The authoritarian state has its dreadful sides. But it has one blessing: Stupidity and impudence are finally constrained to shut their snouts."[56]

In the next chapter, we shall see how Mann's views of Luther underwent equally dramatic shifts. Here we only wish to establish that Mann was remarkably susceptible to the ever-changing spirit of the

---

50 Mann, "Betrachtungen eines Unpolitischen," 12:255.

51 Mann, "Betrachtungen eines Unpolitischen," 12:366.

52 Thomas Mann, *Tagebücher 1918–1921*, ed. Peter de Mendelssohn (Frankfurt: S. Fischer, 1979), 178.

53 Mann, *Tagebücher*, 227.

54 Mann, *Gesammelte Werke*, 11:853.

55 Mann, *Gesammelte Werke*, 11:670.

56 Thomas Mann, "Antwort an Paul Oberg," in *Gesammelte Werke*, 13:795–99.

times, a spirit sharing many of the properties of cliché thinking. Thus Mann's points of reference were finite. He was very much a representative of the modern era, an era that Zijderveld says has clichés as its very cornerstones.

We must now wonder whether from that point of reference, which in the final analysis is anthropocentric, if anyone can justly evaluate a premodern giant, such as Martin Luther, whose point of reference was strictly *theocentric*. Mann's dilemma may, in part, resemble the parable at the beginning of this chapter about watching a police chase and, blinded by cliché thinking, trying to ask the busy cop for directions.

Chapter Two

MARTIN LUTHER: THE VILLAIN

The cliché accusing Martin Luther of being a *Fürstenknecht*, a lackey of princes, is as old as Protestantism. Thomas Münzer, Luther's chief antagonist, first formulated this cliché during the controversy over the Peasants' War that took place from 1524–1525. The term *Fürstenknecht* encapsulates the stereotypical perception of Luther as a preacher of quietism in the face of absolute authority and as a supporter of the ruler's right to wield the sword with brute force. In our time, it has even caused individuals to blame Luther for some aspects of the Vietnam War.

In an otherwise undistinguished Luther biography, Richard Marius relates his tribulations as an antiwar activist:

> During these bitter years . . . I looked at Luther day after day and night after night with an almost devout intensity. I realized slowly and painfully that he had no word to speak to our time. And in my peregrinations around my state, speaking everywhere I could against the Vietnam War, I found my hostile audiences in the Christian churches that claimed to be heirs of the Reformation. Most pious Christians I met wanted to treat the Vietnamese as Luther treated the rebellious peasants: to destroy them without mercy as long as they were in resistance to our sovereign will as a nation.[1]

---

1 Richard Marius, *Luther* (Philadelphia: J. B. Lippincott, 1974), 11–12. Marius goes on to characterize the Reformation era thus: "[It] struck me not as an age of

As Gordon Rupp observed: "There has been the tradition of the Enlightenment, among modern left wing and liberal circles, which has always detested Luther."[2] Indeed, it was no less than leftist luminary Friedrich Engels who, in his book *The Peasant War in Germany*, repristinated the label *Fürstenknecht* in 1850.

During World War II, this kind of talk became commonplace among individuals who were either dyed-in-the-wool progressives or those who, like Thomas Mann, found it fashionable to align themselves with this group.

- Alexander Abusch, a German Marxist writer exiled in Mexico during the war, called Luther "the gravedigger of German freedom." He elaborated: "The Reformation began as a revolutionary fanfare in 1517, [but it ended with] Luther's call for the slaughter of the 'robbing and murdering hordes of peasants.' . . . For centuries Luther became the greatest spiritual figure of the German counterrevolution."[3]

- Dr. William Temple, the left-of-center archbishop of Canterbury, said, "It is easy to see how Luther prepared the way for Hitler."[4]

- The Very Reverend William R. Inge, the "gloomy" dean of St. Paul's, wrote: "There is very little to be said for this coarse and foulmouthed leader of a revolution. It is a real misfortune for humanity that he appeared just at the crisis in the Christian world. . . . We must hope that the next swing of the pendulum will put an end to Luther's influence on Germany."[5]

Inge also took Luther to task for his position during the Peasants' War: "Lutheranism declares that in all his outward social conduct the Christian owes unquestioning obedience to the temporal power. How far this dualism carried him is shown in Luther's

---

gallant heroes but rather as a generation of vipers, not one of the great stepping-stones of our civilization but rather a trauma like famine or plague that our ancestors barely survived."

2 E. Gordon Rupp, *Martin Luther: Hitler's Cause or Cure?* (London: Lutterworth, 1945), 13.

3 Alexander Abusch, *Der Irrweg einer Nation* (Berlin: Aufbau, 1946), 22.

4 *Malvern 1941: The Life of the Church and the Order of Society* (London: Longmans, Green, 1941), 13.

5 W. R. Inge, *Church of England Newspaper* (4 August 1944).

heartless encouragement of the princes in putting down the revolt of the peasants."[6]

- Peter F. Wiener, a friend of Inge's, triggered a wave of English polemics against Luther. In a pamphlet entitled *Martin Luther: Hitler's Spiritual Ancestor*, this emigré schoolmaster from Prussia claimed that Luther had said, "I am Christ." Wiener referred to himself as a "true Christian." And for "true Christians," he lectured his readers, "Christianity . . . is not a dogma . . . but a moral code which we ought to apply to all our actions and thoughts." Clearly, as far as Wiener was concerned, Luther did not measure up to those lofty standards. Wiener averred:

> [Luther] disliked and abhorred reason; he praised and advocated war; he encouraged absolutism, and gave the rulers a power they had never enjoyed before; he insisted on a brutal oppression of the common man . . . he produced a slave-mentality among his followers which even the Roman Catholic church had never forced upon its members; he preached and practiced a violent anti-Semitism and extermination of the Jews which would remain unsurpassed even by Hitler; he was the founder of modern nationalism in its most evil form.[7]

Wiener, who also labeled Luther "a supreme upholder of complete dictatorship,"[8] belonged to Lord Vansittart's circle of Germanophobes. As we have seen in the first chapter, Vansittart inferred from Luther's *alleged* abhorrence of reason that being unreasonable must be a quintessential German trait. I shall return to him later.

---

6 W. R. Inge, "Nationalism and National Character," *Quarterly Review* (July 1941): 133.

7 Peter F. Wiener, *Martin Luther: Hitler's Spiritual Ancestor* (London: Hutchinson, 1945), 69. This thin volume was one of Lord Vansittart's *Win the Peace* series of pamphlets. It is so full of falsifications of quotations and dishonest rhetoric that it cannot be taken seriously as a scholarly work. However, two reasons make it worth mentioning: (1) It led to a huge controversy in Britain at the end of World War II, a debate with repercussions even for contemporary Luther studies. (2) It provoked, in the words of Peter Clarkson Matheson, "one of the finest pieces of polemic seen in twentieth-century British historiography," Gordon Rupp's *Martin Luther: Hitler's Cause or Cure?* See Peter Clarkson Matheson, "Luther and Hitler: A Controversy Reviewed," *Journal of Ecumenical Studies* 17:3 (Summer 1980): 446.

8 Wiener, *Luther*, 51.

William L. Shirer, however, was the man whose condemnation of Luther became best known in the Anglo-Saxon world. Long after the war, this former foreign correspondent, who had witnessed the early years of National Socialism in Germany, wrote in his international best-seller *The Rise and Fall of the Third Reich*:

> This savage anti-Semite and hater of Rome . . . combined in his tempestuous character so many of the best and worst characters of the German—the coarseness, the boisterousness, the fanaticism, the intolerance, the violence but also the honesty, the self-scrutiny, the passion used for learning and for music and for poetry and for righteousness in the eyes of God—left a mark on the life of the Germans, both for good and bad. . . . Luther's siding with the princes in the peasant rising, which he had largely inspired, and his passion for political autocracy ensured a mindless provincial political absolutism, which reduced a vast majority of the German people to poverty, to a horrible torpor and a demeaning subservience.[9]

Shirer gave the reformer credit for creating the modern German language "through his magnificent translation of the Bible." But then he explained the "behavior of most German Protestants in the first Nazi years" as being determined by "the influence of Martin Luther." Shirer noted: "The great founder of Protestantism was both a passionate anti-Semite and a ferocious believer in absolute obedience to political authority. . . . The influence of this towering figure extended down the generations in Germany, especially among the Protestants."[10]

Shirer's book was first published in 1960, but every one of his allegations about Luther had appeared in print fifteen and seventeen years earlier. They had been written by Thomas Mann, who had come a long way from the utter admiration for Luther he expressed at the end of World War I.

In 1917, Mann saw Luther's Reformation as "an event of genuine German majesty . . . an event and a fact of the soul."[11] This reformation

---

9 William L. Shirer, *The Rise and Fall of the Third Reich* (New York: Simon & Schuster, 1960), 91–92.

10 Shirer, *Rise and Fall of the Third Reich*, 236.

11 Mann, "Betrachtungen eines Unpolitischen," in *Gesammelte Werke* (Berlin: S. Fischer, 1960), 12:514.

could neither be explained nor critiqued; thus it resembled "life itself."
But as an exile in the United States, Mann said that Luther:

- was "boisterous and coarse";[12]
- was "furiously nationalistic and anti-Semitic, but also deeply musical";[13]
- "formed the German language—his translation of the Bible was a literary feat of the first order";[14]
- was "a gigantic incarnation of the German character";[15]
- "did not understand . . . political freedom [which he found] . . . deeply repulsive";[16]
- "trained his people to submissiveness in the face of authority ordained by God";[17]
- "hated the Peasant Revolt . . . had the peasants beaten to death like mad dogs and called upon the princes to win the Kingdom of God by . . . slaughtering the peasants. Luther bears a great deal of responsibility for the sad ending of this first attempt at a German revolution, the victory of the princes with all its consequences."[18]

When I asked Shirer if he had known Mann personally, he replied, "He was a friend. We sometimes discussed my work. But I don't believe we discussed the [T]hird Reich book. By the time I began it, Mann had moved back to Europe."[19] Shirer added, however, that he had read *Doktor Faustus*, Mann's allegorical novel describing Germany's path to evil.[20] In this masterpiece, Luther is recycled as the boisterous, boorish, nationalistic theologian Ehrenfried Kumpf, who throws bread

---

12 Thomas Mann, "Die drei Gewaltigen," in *Gesammelte Werke* (Berlin: S. Fischer, 1960), 11:375. This essay, written in 1943, was first published in November 1949 in the Berlin monthly journal *Der Monat*.

13 Mann, "Die drei Gewaltigen," 376.

14 Mann, "Die drei Gewaltigen," 376.

15 Thomas Mann, "Deutschland und die Deutschen," in *Gesammelte Werke* (Berlin: S. Fischer, 1960), 11:1132. This was a lecture Mann gave in Washington in 1945.

16 Mann, "Deutschland," 1134.

17 Mann, "Die drei Gewaltigen," 375.

18 Mann, "Die drei Gewaltigen," 375.

19 In a letter to the author, March 2, 1989.

20 Thomas Mann, *Doktor Faustus* (Stockholm: Bermann-Fischer, 1947).

at the devil and is therefore marginally less violent against Satan than was Luther (who supposedly threw an inkwell).

Mann's opinions of Luther, as well as those expressed by Wiener, Inge, Reinhold Niebuhr, and many other writers and scholars, were essentially formed by Ernst Troeltsch,[21] the liberal Protestant theologian whom Mann knew personally. Troeltsch (1865–1923) viewed Luther as an adviser to advocates of territorial absolutism. Such absolutism, according to Troeltsch, is simply a repetition of medieval authoritarianism, encouraged first by Luther and then by his modern disciples.[22] "The way . . . Luther thought and the way his soul was shaped," Mann told a Washington audience in 1945, "[showed that] he was to a considerable extent a medieval man struggling with the devil all his life."[23] Troeltsch's assessment of the medieval nature of Luther and Lutheranism is reflected in Thomas Mann's portrayal of Kaisersaschern, an imaginary small town in Thuringia that provides the setting for the opening and closing chapters of *Doktor Faustus*.

In the second section of this chapter, I shall return to Troeltsch, for he played a key role in shaping the stereotype that is the principal theme of this study: the cliché that Luther's alleged "passion for political autocracy ensured a mindless and provincial political absolutism which reduced the vast majority of the German people to . . . a demeaning subservience."[24] Here, however, I must briefly address two charges, each of which warrant separate studies. The first charge is that Luther was "furiously nationalistic" (Mann), indeed, that he was "the founder of modern nationalism in its most evil form" (Wiener). The second charge is that Luther was a "passionate anti-Semite."[25]

---

21 Cf. Martin Doerne, "Thomas Mann und das protestantische Christentum," *Die Sammlung* 11 (1956): 409.

22 See Ernst Troeltsch, *Protestantism and Progress*, trans. W. Montgomery (New York: Beacon Press, 1912), 111–13.

23 Mann, "Deutschland," 1130.

24 Shirer, *Rise and Fall of the Third Reich*, 91–92.

25 For a detailed discussion of this particular charge, see Carter Lindberg, "Tainted Greatness: Luther's Attitudes toward Judaism and Their Historical Reception," in *Tainted Greatness: Anti-Semitism and Cultural Heroes*, ed. Nancy Harrowitz (Philadelphia: Temple University Press, 1994), 15–35.

Both claims are blatant clichés in Anton Zijderveld's sense of the word. They exclude vital relativizations:

1. The Nationalism Cliché

The necessary relativization is this: *Nationalism* is a concept that did not exist until 250 years after Luther.[26] "The moment of birth of modern nationalism," Dietrich Bonhoeffer stressed, came much later; it came with the French Revolution. "Whatever national consciousness existed earlier was essentially dynastic in nature."[27] Gordon Rupp commented, "We do not wish to deny that Luther was a patriot, and that he was not ashamed to love his country. But to pretend that he made a religion out of nationalism in any way comparable with that of Nazism could be refuted by a hundred facts: if this were even the main truth about his teaching, it could never have converted Finland, or Norway, or penetrated America."[28]

2. The Anti-Semitism Cliché

Relativizations that must be considered are the following:

a. The very term *anti-Semitism* implies a racial bias that was foreign to the sixteenth century. In his criticism of the Catholic prohibition against a Christian marrying a Jew, Luther made clear that he was not in the least bothered with what centuries later would be called "miscegenation" in the United States: "As I am allowed to eat, drink, sleep, go out, ride, speak and do business with a heathen, Jew, Turk or heretic, so I may also marry and remain in that

---

26 There exists a marked difference in the German and Anglo-Saxon definitions of the term *nation*. Anglo-Saxons often say "nation" but actually mean "state." For example, U.S. newspapers often referred to East Germany as a "nation." According to *Webster's Dictionary* this was correct; see *Webster's New World Dictionary* (New York: Simon & Schuster, 1984), 946. But in German, the vocable *die Nation* is only used to describe a community of people with a common culture and language. Thus in the German sense of the word, there was no "East German nation," but only a German one. If the term *Nation* is interpreted the German way, Luther may be considered a nationalist, for he loved his people's culture and indeed created a common language for them. But in the English—or French—interpretation of the word, nationalism was entirely alien to him.

27 Dietrich Bonhoeffer, *Ethics* (New York: Collier, 1955), 100–102.

28 Rupp, *Luther*, 82.

state, and do not worry about the stupid laws that forbid such things. You will find plenty of Christians . . . who in their secret unbelief are worse than any Jew, heathen, Turk or heretic. A heathen is just as much God's good creation as St. Peter, St. Paul, and St. Lucy, not to speak of a slack and spurious Christian."[29] Moreover, as much as Nazi propagandists tried to hijack Luther as the alleged precursor of their movement, their chief ideologue, the neo-paganist Alfred Rosenberg, declared it Luther's shortcoming that he "allowed" the "Hebraic" Old Testament to remain part of his canon.[30] In other words, Nazi "Christians" trying to "purge" Scripture of its Jewish roots followed in the footsteps of Marcion, the second-century heretic, but clearly not the path of Luther.

Nazi anti-Semitism, on the other hand, was a racist prejudice directed not only at practicing Jews but also against Christians or agnostics of Jewish descent. Indeed, as Karla Poewe shows in her remarkable study titled *New Religions and the Nazis*, leading Nazi ideologues and the SS went even further. They opposed Christianity as a whole precisely because it is rooted in Judaism. Poewe quotes Hitler: "Nothing will prevent me from eradicating, root and branch, all Christianity in Germany. . . . A German Church, a German Christianity, it is all rubbish . . . . One is either Christian or German."[31]

b. Luther was *theologically* anti-Jewish, and toward the end of his life, he expressed this sentiment in the most objectionable language. But, writes Gordon Rupp, "Luther was a small chapter in the large volume of Christian inhumanities toward the Jewish people. In the beginning Luther hoped great things from preaching the Gospel to them, since he held that there was some excuse for their being repelled by official Catholicism. But when it became clear that there was no hope of this converting them, he turned to polemic."[32]

---

29 WA 10/2:303.

30 Alfred Rosenberg, *Der Mythus des 20. Jahrhunderts* (Munich: Hoheneichenverlag, 1933), 129.

31 Karla Poewe, *New Religions and the Nazis* (New York: Routledge, 2006), 112.

32 Rupp, *Luther*, 75.

The cliché labeling Luther an anti-Semite ignores his 1523 treatise *That Jesus Christ Was Born a Jew*, in which he admonishes his fellow Christians: "If the apostles, who were also Jews, had dealt with us Gentiles as we Gentiles deal with the Jews, there would never have been a Christian among the Gentiles. Since they dealt with us Gentiles in such brotherly fashion, we in turn ought to treat the Jews in a brotherly manner in order that we might convert some of them . . . We should remember that we are but Gentiles, while the Jews are in the lineage of Christ."[33] Elsewhere in this treatise, Luther writes: "If I had been a Jew and had seen such dolts and blockheads govern and teach the Christian faith, I would sooner have become a hog than a Christian."

It is noteworthy that in the early twentieth century, the *Jewish Encyclopedia* made a clear distinction between the "two Luthers"—the pro-Jewish younger Luther and the anti-Jewish older Luther. In this remarkable publication, Gotthard Deutsch melancholically observed about Luther in 1906 that the "totally different attitudes which he took at different times with regard to the Jews made him, during the anti-Semitic controversies of the end of the nineteenth century, an authority quoted alike by friends and enemies of the Jews."[34]

Alas, it is true that in 1543, shortly before his death, Luther published his venomous book *On the Jews and Their Lies*, a work that was to cause great embarrassment to future centuries of Lutheran church leaders. In this book, he gave the "sincere advice" to burn down the synagogues, destroy the Jews' homes, take away their prayer books, forbid rabbinic teaching, abolish safe-conduct for Jewish travel, prohibit usury, and force Jews into manual labor.[35]

Johannes Wallmann has shown, however, that Luther's treatises against the Jews, though reprinted in the late-sixteenth and early-seventeenth centuries, had limited impact in the general population.[36] As the article in the *Jewish Encyclopedia* made clear, this and other

---

33 AE 45:200–201.

34 Gotthard Deutsch, "Martin Luther," *The Jewish Encyclopedia* (New York: Funk & Wagnalls, 1909), 213–15.

35 AE 47:268–72.

36 Johannes Wallmann, "The Reception of Luther's Writings on the Jews from the Reformation to the End of the 19th Century," *Lutheran Quarterly* n.s. 1:1 (1987): 72–78.

appalling texts did not resurface until the late nineteenth century. In fact, in a devastating critique of German Protestant attitudes in the Hitler years, Richard Steigmann-Gall writes: "Not only did racialist anti-Semitism find a warmer reception among liberal Protestants than among confessional Lutherans, in many ways, racialist anti-Semitism was born of the theological crisis that liberal Protestantism represented."[37] Liberal Protestantism is a child of the nineteenth century. According to Steigmann-Gall, it provided the platform for Nazi ideologues to develop such theories as the one that Jesus was an Aryan. In other words, Protestants who were theologically closest to Luther's teachings were more immune than liberals to one of the ugliest aspects of Nazism—racism. This observation could arguably also be made about deviant and sometimes lethal theologoumena that are currently rife in mainline churches in the United States and elsewhere in the West.

Still, reading the sickening and seemingly endless reams of the older Luther's anti-Jewish hyperbole has been one of the most exigent exercises during my research for this study. Einar Billing was right in 1909 when he wrote, comparing Luther with John Calvin: "At a distance . . . [Luther] undeniably possessed certain careless traits that we wish were not there and which found their way in even worse forms into the Lutheran Church. Yet who will hesitate to call him not only the richer, but the deeper, and more thoroughly cultivated culture [than Calvin]?"[38] In short, I agree with Gordon Rupp's statement: "I confess I am ashamed as I am ashamed of some letters of St. Jerome, some paragraphs in Sir Thomas More, and some chapters in the Book of Revelation, and must say that their authors had not so learned Christ, and that, thank God, this is not the major part of what they had to say."[39]

SOURCES OF A STEREOTYPE

The "monstrous myth" that Luther was completed by Hitler was first and foremost an invention of German Christians, notes Heiko Oberman. "Very likely, it weakened catastrophically an already weak will to

---

37 Richard Steigmann-Gall, *The Holy Reich: Nazi Conceptions of Christianity 1919–1945* (Cambridge: Cambridge University Press, 2003), 263.

38 Einar Billing, *Our Calling* (Rock Island, IL: Augustana Press, 1958), 37.

39 Rupp, *Luther*, 76.

resist Hitler,"[40] Oberman writes. Steigmann-Gall comes to a similar conclusion, making it clear, however, that he is not proposing a deterministic "Luther-to-Hitler" teleology anymore than scholars of the French Revolution would propose an "Athens-to-Paris" teleology because of the Jacobins' understanding of their republic as a revival of ancient Greece. What is revealing, rather, are the ways in which the Nazis—as the Jacobins before them—attempted to claim a certain past for themselves, to position themselves as inheritors of a venerable and vital cultural patrimony.[41] Thus on Reformation Day 1935, Professor Hermann Werdermann of the *Glaubensbewegung Deutsche Christen* exclaimed, "Hitler is today . . . what Luther was then, the tutor of the whole German nation."[42] Oberman traces the National Socialist veneration of Luther as the national hero back to the Bismarck era: "Luther's role as a symbol of national unity is well documented by the celebrations of his 400th birthday in 1883; a swelling tide which, I fear, few of his present-day critics would have been strong enough to resist."[43] Oberman makes the point that, after 1933, "a whole series of prominent Luther scholars" joined in conscripting Luther into the National Socialist cause, thus developing what Carl E. Braaten calls an "ideologically captive political theology."[44] Heinz Eduard Tödt states that "Emanuel Hirsch and Friedrich Gogarten, for example, seemed blind to the dangers National Socialism posed for the world community and the Christian churches. They used [Luther's] doctrine of the two kingdoms as a theological legitimation for a . . . peaceful coexistence of the Evangelical Church with the totalitarian state."[45]

Tödt laments the result of this legitimation, which is a world opinion that has since "associated Lutheranism with this 'dualistic'

---

40 Heiko A. Oberman, "The Nationalist Conscription of Martin Luther," in *Piety, Politics, and Ethics*, ed. Carter Lindberg (Kirksville: Sixteenth Century Journal Publishers, 1984), 71.

41 Steigmann-Gall, *Holy Reich*, 84–85.

42 Oberman, "Nationalist Conscription," 70.

43 Oberman, "Nationalist Conscription," 66.

44 Carl E. Braaten, *Justification* (Minneapolis: Fortress, 1990), 65.

45 Heinz Eduard Tödt, "Die Bedeutung von Luthers Reiche- und Regimentenlehre für heutige Theologie und Ethik," in *Gottes Wirken in seiner Welt*, ed. Niels Hasselmann (Hamburg: Lutherische Verlagshaus, 1980), 56.

and dichotornic doctrine." He calls for a return to the authentic doctrine of the two kingdoms and its theological and ethical application to
contemporary life. Below we shall see that "the Nazi Christians . . . rein-
terpreted Luther against his own intentions, [and] his own statements."[46]

But in the Anglo-Saxon world, "Nazi Christians" are not the principal source cited by Luther's detractors in support of their assertion
that he taught a "double morality" distinguishing between the official
morality of the world and the private Christianity of disposition. This
notion was advanced by Ernst Troeltsch,[47] who further argued that
Luther's thought fostered slavish obedience to authority and thereby set
the stage for absolutism.[48] Indeed, he even compared Luther to Machiavelli: "In the glorification of authority there were certain resemblances
to the doctrine of Machiavelli. . . . The only difference was this: Luther
lays the duty of the preservation of the law of reason upon the ruling
powers."[49]

Troeltsch's views were then simplified, intensified, and distorted by
theologians as well as by profane scholars and writers.

THE LEGACY OF ERNST TROELTSCH

For a long time, there prevailed an "almost exclusive American dependence upon Troeltsch in the interpretation of Luther," observes Carter
Lindberg.[50] To some extent, that dependence also existed in Britain, as the
previous chapter has shown. In fact, Robert Morgan writes: "Troeltsch has
been less popular in Germany than in the English-speaking world."[51]

---

46 Tödt, "Die Bedeutung von Luthers Reiche- und Regimentenlehre," 71.

47 Ernst Troeltsch, *The Social Teaching of the Christian Churches*, trans. Olive Wyon
(New York: Macmillan, 1931), 2:506ff.

48 See Troeltsch, *Protestantism and Progress*, 112.

49 Troeltsch, *Protestantism and Progress*, 532.

50 Carter Lindberg, ed., *Piety, Politics, and Ethics* (Kirksville: Sixteenth Century Journal Publishers, 1984), viii.

51 Ernst Troeltsch, *Writings on Theology and Religion*, ed. Robert Morgan and
Michael Pye (Atlanta: John Knox, 1977), 6. In the introduction, Morgan attributes
Troeltsch's lack of popularity in his own country to the fact that his contempo-
raries and successors were busy modernizing and glorifying Luther.

In Germany, "the melancholy image of Troeltsch as a theologian who lost his faith helped discredit his work."[52] Convinced that modern science had caused a "painful religious crisis,"[53] Troeltsch wrote: "Science has shaken the basic ideas Christianity has held so far. This applies both to historical elements, such as the wonderful tales of revelation and redemption, and its metaphysical contents of faith: the belief in providence and miracles, and in a divine being that descended [from heaven] and became man, the belief in revealed moral commandments, in heaven and hell, in the unconditional power of the Spirit over the body, a belief in ecclesial institutions and norms."[54]

Morgan portrays Troeltsch as a theologian who broke with orthodox Christianity: "Troeltsch believed passionately in God, and in the significance of Jesus of Nazareth, and he wished to hold the two together . . . [but] he saw no conceptual possibility, within a modern historical view of reality, of fusing belief in God with the traditional evaluation of Jesus—which is what the doctrines of the essential Trinity and the Incarnation are about."[55]

To Troeltsch, Jesus was a "cosmically irrelevant" figure who was "bound to time and space." He was "a symbol and a rallying point" but was not God. Troeltsch had convinced himself that Christianity, though the pinnacle of religious development thus far, was a "sinking ship" that must be kept afloat. Therefore, he proposed to throw overboard some of its dead freight. Among the "dogmata of secondary importance" that Troeltsch wished to discard were the following:

1. the divinity of Jesus Christ ("an error" because qualitatively Jesus is no different from the founders of other religions—He is on the same level as the Buddha);[56]

---

52 Troeltsch, *Writings on Theology and Religion*, 212.

53 Ernst Troeltsch, *Gesammelte Werke* (Tübingen: J. C. B. Mohr, 1912), 2:230.

54 Ernst Troeltsch, *Die wissenschaftliche Lage und ihre Anforderungen an die Theologie* (Tübingen: J. C. B. Mohr, 1910), 9.

55 Troeltsch, *Writings on Theology and Religion*, 212.

56 Cf. Gunnar von Schlippe, *Die Absolutheit des Christentums bei Ernst Troeltsch auf dem Hintergrund der Denkfelder des 19. Jahrhunderts* (Neustadt an der Aisch: Degener, 1966), 19.

2. the Trinity and incarnation (there is no place for them in a theology based on history);[57]

3. the concept of sin ("does not fit into the modern intellectual climate, is irreligious and unreasonable"[58]);

4. the notion that Christianity has been the "exclusive" recipient of supernatural revelation, whereas all other religions had to make do with natural revelation. To Troeltsch revelation was useless as a means to prove Christianity; it has no power of argument because it is incapable of leaving traces in history.[59]

As Bonhoeffer found out during his sojourn at Union Theological Seminary in 1930–1931, corresponding ideas were in vogue in the United States. Reinhold Niebuhr, who was Troeltsch's American disciple and a friend of Thomas Mann, defined religion as "the experience of the holy, transcendent experience of Goodness, Beauty, Truth and Holiness."[60]

Bonhoeffer missed in New York what Troeltsch had discarded in Germany—Christology: "In American theology, Christianity is essentially religion and ethics. But that means that the person and work of Jesus Christ had to retire into the theological background, and finally remain uncomprehended."[61] Bonhoeffer encountered Niebuhr at about the time when the U.S. theologian published *Moral Man and Immoral*

---

57 Troeltsch, *Writings on Theology and Religion*, 37–38.

58 Wolfhart Pannenberg, "The Basis of Ethics in the Thought of Ernst Troeltsch," in *Ethics*, trans. Keith Crim (Philadelphia: Westminster, 1981), 87.

59 Cf. Schlippe, *Die Absolutheit des Christentums*, 19.

60 Eberhard Bethge, *Dietrich Bonhoeffer* (New York: Harper & Row, 1970), 118. Here Bethge quotes Bonhoeffer's notes from one of Niebuhr's lectures.

61 Dietrich Bonhoeffer, *Gesammelte Schriften*, ed. Eberhard Bethge (Munich: Chr. Kaiser, 1965), 354. It is significant in the context of this thesis that at Union Seminary this most prominent Lutheran theologian, who sacrificed his life resisting Hitler, stood out for his orthodoxy. To John Baillie, Bonhoeffer was "as stout an opponent of liberalism as had ever come my way" (Bethge, *Bonhoeffer*, 117). Bonhoeffer criticized that "one of the characteristic features of church life in the Anglo-Saxon countries, and one from which Lutheranism had almost entirely freed itself, is the organized struggle of the Church against some worldly evil, the 'campaign', or . . . the 'crusade.' " He stressed that "it is necessary to free oneself from the way of thinking which sets out from human problems and which asks for solutions on this basis. Such thinking is unbiblical. The way of Jesus Christ, and therefore the way of all Christian thinking leads not from the world to God but from God to the world" (Bonhoeffer, *Ethics*, 356).

Society: A Study in Ethics and Politics.[62] Larry Rasmussen writes about this volume:

> Though very little Christology was to be found in its pages, there was considerable use of Marx. It was rallied in large part to demolish the liberalism of those who clung to the dream of social change through educational and evangelical means, and to press the case that justice could not be realized through the rigors of a more ethical religion, at least not apart from a vigorous alliance with countervailing power leveraged against economic privilege. For "there is no ethical force strong enough to place inner checks upon the use of power if its quantity is inordinate."
> . . . Marxism was demonstrably more adequate than Christian orthodoxy or secular liberalism in giving a coherent meaning to an entire age of storm and struggle. . . . Marxism could do so by generating, rather than abandoning, hopes for a more just social order, and this was above all Niebuhr's passion.[63]

Although Niebuhr rejected liberalism as "faith in man" and "soft utopianism," Rasmussen adds: "[He] retained many fundamental elements of German theological, and American religious and secular liberalism. With Ernst Troeltsch, who influenced Niebuhr far more than is commonly acknowledged, Niebuhr's theological starting point was that of Protestant liberalism: human needs, powers, and responsibilities."[64]

Niebuhr's Troeltschian stress on religiosity and ethics became evident in his dismay that Bonhoeffer based his work at Union Seminary on the theology of revelation and the doctrine of justification or eschatology instead of "realities,"[65] in other words, on Lutheran as well as Barthian essentials.[66] Rasmussen explains: "Bonhoeffer found Niebuhr

---

62 Reinhold Niebuhr, *Moral Man and Immoral Society: A Study in Ethics and Politics* (New York: Scribner's, 1932).

63 Larry Rasmussen, *Reinhold Niebuhr: Theologian of Public Life* (Minneapolis: Fortress, 1991), 10.

64 Rasmussen, *Niebuhr*, 25.

65 Cf. Bethge, *Bonhoeffer*, 118.

66 Karl Barth was probably Troeltsch's fiercest antagonist. However, where Luther's doctrine of the two kingdoms is concerned, Barth, too, accused the reformer of a fatal ethical dualism: "The German people suffer from the legacy of the greatest of all Christian Germans, from the mistake of Martin Luther regarding the relation of Law and Gospel, of temporal and spiritual order and power, by which the

too saturated with liberalism to be theologically compelling, just as Niebuhr found Bonhoeffer too taken with Barthianism to move from human moral experience into knowledge of God."[67]

Therefore, it is not surprising that Niebuhr took up Troeltsch's assessment of Luther. Niebuhr did so "uncritically," writes Carter Lindberg, and in fact intensified his condemnation of the reformer's "quietistic tendencies" and "defeatism."[68] Lindberg cites three quotations as examples:

> In confronting the problems of realizing justice in the collective life of man, the Lutheran Reformation was . . . explicitly defeatist.[69]

> Evidently [for Luther] no obligation rests upon the Christian to change social structures so that they might conform more perfectly to the requirements of brotherhood.[70]

> The weakness of the Lutheran position in the field of social ethics is accentuated to a further degree by its inability to define consistent criteria for the achievement of relative justice.[71]

Thus Troeltsch himself suffered the original thinker's fate of having his ideas reduced to a stereotype. This becomes even more apparent in

---

Germans' natural paganism has been ideologically clarified, confirmed, and strengthened rather than being limited and contained" (Karl Barth, *Eine Schweizer Stimme* [Zurich: TVZ, 1945], 113). He went on to state: "Lutheranism has to some degree paved the way for German paganism, allotting it a sacral sphere by its separation of creation and the Law from the Gospel. The German pagan can use the Lutheran doctrine of the authority of the state as a Christian justification of National Socialism, and by the same doctrine the German in Germany can feel himself summoned to recognize National Socialism. Both these things have actually happened" (Barth, *Eine Schweizer Stimme*, 122). I have found no evidence, however, that Barth's views, which were expressed in a letter to friends in the Netherlands in 1940, had influenced the attacks on Luther cited in chapter 3.

67 Rasmussen, *Niebuhr*, 12. Ironically, Karl Barth later denounced Niebuhr for his "primitive anticommunism." See Karl Barth and Johannes Hamel, *How to Serve God in a Marxist Land* (New York: Association Press, 1959), 46.

68 Carter Lindberg, "Reformation Initiatives for Social Welfare: Luther's Influence at Leisnig," *The Annual of the Society of Christian Ethics*, ed. D. M. Yeager (1987): 79.

69 Reinhold Niebuhr, *The Nature and Destiny of Man* (New York: Scribner's, 1964), 2:192.

70 Niebuhr, *Nature and Destiny of Man*, 2:193.

71 Niebuhr, *Nature and Destiny of Man*, 2:197.

William Montgomery McGovern's reduction of Troeltsch's attack on Luther's alleged quietism to a slick formula: "[Luther was convinced that] . . . princes . . . *must be blindly obeyed*."[72]

In England, High Churchman Dean Inge[73] twisted Troeltsch thus: "Lutheranism declares that in all his outward social conduct the Christian owes *unquestioning obedience* to the temporal power."[74] And Inge's friend Peter Wiener warped a Troeltsch quotation by means of malevolent omission: "Lutheranism provided a most favorable setting for the development of the territorial state. It smoothed the way for territorial absolutism. . . . Its only service to the actual modern state has been to encourage the spirit of modern absolutism."[75] What Wiener left out is one of Troeltsch's most significant observations about Lutheranism:

> It had *no theoretical tendency toward monarchism or absolutism at all*; this theory was only an invention of modern Conservatives. It was only because absolutism and the system of manorial estates arose in Central and North Germany that it there developed the loyal spirit which characterizes *Ostelbiertum*. In the Imperial towns it glorified aristocratic-republican rule. In Wurttemberg . . . it did not hinder bourgeois and peasant democratic ideas, but even fused itself with them. In the military national State of Sweden it justified the aggressive policy of Gustavus Adolfus . . . in Denmark and Norway a very firmly

---

72 William Montgomery McGovern, *From Luther to Hitler* (Cambridge: Riverside Press, 1941), 34 (*emphasis added*).

73 The urge to knock Luther does seem to be an industrial disease among some Anglican High Churchmen. Dom Gregory Dix provides a particularly distressing example. In a study on liturgy that has long been used in seminaries, Dix averred: "Luther furnishes curious parallels with Adolf Hitler—the same 'somnambulism'; the same sense of surrender to mysterious impersonal forces, 'grace' and 'nature' as he labels them, irresistibly thrusting the passive human soul to a predestined fate; the same rather frantic brand of oratory, glorying in antimonies and self-contradiction; the same contempt for reason and exaltation of intuition and impulse, which have proved able to stupefy the German mind in other periods also (cf. e.g. Caesar, *Gallic Wars*, I. 44)" (Gregory Dix, *The Shape of the Liturgy* [London: Dacre Press, Adam & Charles Black, 1964], 636). This study first appeared in January 1945, during World War II, and was reprinted repeatedly until 1964.

74 Inge, "Nationalism and National Character," 133 (*emphasis added*).

75 Wiener, *Luther*, 55.

established peasant democracy is today united with a sturdy Lutheranism . . . and in America the most orthodox Lutheranism one can imagine flourishes under the wing of democracy.[76]

What I have tried to establish thus far is that a specimen of honest scholarly analysis was perverted into a stereotype to fit personal or political agendas. This was accomplished by simplification, exaggeration, and by omitting Troeltsch's own relativizations.

Troeltsch presumably did not wish to slander Luther. He was a theologian whose belief in the infallibility of science tragically won out over his Christian faith. From that perspective, he could not share Luther's stress on *sola scriptura*, the Reformation principle that Scripture is the sole criterion of all true doctrine, including the Scripture-based Lutheran doctrines on secular authority.

Troeltsch's views were readily accepted by liberal Anglo-Saxon theologians such as Niebuhr or Inge, who stressed the ethical rather than the Christological aspects of Christianity. And their thoughts were then echoed by Luther's secular critics such as Mann, Shirer, Wiener, or Marius.

In the final analysis, Luther's alleged failure to highlight ethics is at the root of the *Fürstenknecht* cliché. Now, we must trace its lineage further back—to Luther's contemporary Thomas Münzer.

The Legacy of Thomas Münzer

Like Luther, Münzer was a Saxon. Like Luther, he had the Saxon penchant for rich hyperbole. Like Luther, he was endowed with the Saxon gift for creating ever-new derogatory labels for his adversaries. Like Luther, he understood the preacher's obligation "to look at the common man's snout."[77] In Luther's case, that amounted to being "foulmouthed," as far as Dean Inge was concerned. In just one tract, Müntzer called Luther "Flatterer of Princes," "Father Pussyfoot," "Brother Soft-Life," "Malicious Raven," "Doctor Liar," "Ungodly Flesh at Wittenberg," "Virgin Martin, the Chaste Babylonian Woman," "Flattering Scoundrel,"

---

76 Troeltsch, *Social Teaching of the Christian Churches*, 2:574–75 (*emphasis added*).
77 In Luther's words, "*dem Volk aufs Maul zu schauen.*"

"Doctor Ludibrii,"[78] "Cousin Steplightly," "Pope of Wittenberg," "Dear Flesh," and "Arch-Devil."[79] Luther had incurred Münzer's wrath by appealing to the princes to stab, beat, and strangulate "the robbing and murderous hordes . . . of peasants,"[80] whose demands Luther largely supported but whose insurrection he condemned. Münzer, on the other hand, was the spiritual leader of that rebellion. He played a pivotal role in the sacking of castles, monasteries, and churches. And he demanded that "godless rulers, monks and priests" be killed.[81]

Luther's theological reasons for opposing the uprising will be discussed in the next chapter. Here, it must be stressed that when Luther's twentieth-century critics refer to Münzer and the Peasants' War, they are aligning themselves with a totalitarian thinker and a revolutionary movement that, according to Karl Mannheim, was motivated "not by ideas but the murkier depths of the soul."[82]

It has been argued that this description of polluted motives also fits the Nazis. Joachim Fest reminds us of the many laudatory references to the Peasants' War in *Der Mythus des 20. Jahrhunderts,* a work written by National Socialism's principal ideologue—Alfred Rosenberg.[83]

The Communists are another set of utopian totalitarians tracing their ancestry to Münzer and the Peasants' War. Friedrich Engels wrote: "Heaven was to be sought in this life, not beyond, and it was, according to Müntzer, the task of the believers to establish Heaven, the Kingdom of God, here on earth. As there is no Heaven in the beyond, he asserted, so there is no hell in the beyond, and no damnation, and there are no

---

78 This is a pun on Luther's name. Ludibrium is the Latin vocable for "idle play."

79 See Thomas Müntzer, "Highly Provoked Defense and Answer against the Spiritless, Soft-living Flesh at Wittenberg, which Has Befouled Pitiable Christianity in Perverted Fashion by Its Theft of Holy Scripture," *Mennonite Quarterly Review* 38:1 (January 1964): 24–36.

80 See WA 18:357–61.

81 Thomas Müntzer, "Sermons before the Princes," in *Spiritual and Anabaptist Writers,* vol. 25 of Library of Christian Classics (Philadelphia: Westminster, 1957), 69.

82 Karl Mannheim, *Ideologie und Utopie* (Frankfurt: Vittorio Klostermann, 1985), 186.

83 Cf. Joachim Fest, *Der zerstörte Traum* (Berlin: Siedler, 1991), 63. Fest quotes Rosenberg as stating that much of what the rebellious peasants wanted "must today again be demanded by the [Nazi party's] program of renewal."

devils but the evil desires and cravings of man, Christ, he said, was a man as we are, a prophet and a teacher."[84]

Again, as in Troeltsch's case, an original thinker's complex ideas were twisted into clichés to fit into a modern ideology. It is true that Münzer had "devised a plan for the reorganization of the entire social order," writes Karl Holl.[85] It is also true that he was a Communist in the sense that he favored communal ownership of property[86]—to Luther an unbiblical notion.[87]

Indeed, states Holl, Münzer "introduced a modern sounding concept: religious reform is impossible without a corresponding social reform."[88] Power should be returned to the common people.[89] And in this respect, Münzer rather than Luther would appeal to the tendency in Anglo-Saxon theology much criticized by Bonhoeffer: "the idea that the Church has at her disposal, in principle, a Christian solution for all worldly problems."[90]

But it is certainly not true that Münzer questioned Christ's divinity or the existence of heaven and hell. Moreover, Münzer's chiliastic visions were more complex than those described by Engels; they require elaboration. Münzer ridiculed Luther's insistence on *sola Scriptura* by calling it *Affenglaube*, "the faith of apes." Münzer believed that at the moment of external dereliction, God's Word wells up within the elect, thus creating faith. Scripture's function is to relate to but not to originate such experiences. Those who are touched by the Holy Spirit

---

84 Friedrich Engels, *The German Revolutions* (Chicago: University of Chicago Press, 1963), 46.

85 Karl Holl, "Luther und die Schwarmer," in *Gesammelte Aufsätze zur Kirchengeschichte* (Tübingen: J. C. B. Mohr, 1929), 1:450.

86 Holl, "Luther und die Schwärmer," 453. Holl makes it clear, however, that Münzer did not favor *Produktionskommunismus*, i.e., the collective ownership of the means of production.

87 Martin Luther, "Wider die räuberischen und mörderischen Rotten der anderen Bauern," WA 18:358. According to Luther, the Gospel allows communal property only when voluntarily agreed upon. This was true in the case of the apostles and disciples as described in Acts 4.

88 Holl, "Luther und die Schwärmer," 454.

89 See Holl, "Luther und die Schärmer," 454

90 Bonhoeffer, *Ethics*, 354.

become God's church, a community of saints leading a life of asceticism.[91] Here again, the stress on ethics is rejected by Luther as a relapse into pre-Reformation works righteousness.

The elect are duty-bound to prepare for the coming of the kingdom by the power of the sword. "The godless person has no right to live when he is in the way of the pious,"[92] Münzer said, prompting Luther's sardonic retort, "It would follow that we are to put all non-Christians to death."[93]

The new kingdom would be brought about by a "new Daniel," a great prophet "after the Spirit of Elijah." Karl Holl makes it clear that Münzer did not see himself as that new Daniel.[94] But, writes Kurt Dietrich Schmidt, Münzer's bloody eschatological convictions "led him to the alliance with the peasants who also wished to establish a kingdom of absolute justice already here on earth."[95]

As I have stated above, Münzer's visions were those of a chiliast. It is the mark of a chiliast that he does not content himself with eschatological hope. To him the *eschaton* is not transcendent. It is historically imminent, and he seeks to make it immanent. He is thus what Paul Tillich deems a perilous creature—a utopian: "Utopianism, taken literally, is idolatrous. It gives the quality of ultimacy to something preliminary. It makes unconditional what is conditioned (a future historical situation) and at the same time disregards the ever-present existential estrangement and the ambiguities of life and history. This makes the utopian interpretation of history inadequate and dangerous."[96]

What makes the utopian interpretation of history so inadequate and dangerous is that it manages to avoid relativization brought about

---

91 Troeltsch considers this "the first instance of a pronounced opposition to the Protestant church type," in contrast to the "sect type" representing "the ethics of spiritual religion" (Troeltsch, *Social Teaching of the Christian Churches*, 1:753).

92 Müntzer, "Sermon before the Princes," 66.

93 Martin Luther, "Letter to the Princes of Saxony Concerning the Rebellious Spirit," AE 40:59.

94 Holl, "Luther und die Schwärmer," 456.

95 Kurt Dietrich Schmidt, *Kirchengeschichte* (Göttingen: Vandenhoeck & Ruprecht, 1984), 336–37.

96 Paul Tillich, *Systematic Theology* (Chicago: University of Chicago Press, 1963), 3:355.

by reflection. Hence utopianism, including its "soft," liberal variety, to use Niebuhr's term, is a sibling of the cliché—like the *Zeitgeist* that we examined in the previous chapter.

The *Zeitgeist* speaks of the liberation of man, which is the utopian dream of the Enlightenment and the French Revolution. Both of these events, according to Jurgen Moltmann, are Münzer's legacies. "For Bonhoeffer the French Revolution ushered in the age of revolutionary ideology that has dominated our century," writes Charles Ford. "He saw both the Nazis and the Communists as heirs to the legacy of the French Revolution."[97] Bonhoeffer thought that the French Revolution "was the laying bare of the emancipated man in his tremendous power and his most terrible perversity."[98] He was convinced that "the liberation of man as an absolute ideal leads only to man's self-destruction."[99]

It is time to rediscover Luther.

---

97 Charles Ford, "Luther, Bonhoeffer and Revolution," *Lutheran Forum* 25 (Advent 1991): 26.

98 Bonhoeffer, *Ethics*, 97.

99 Bonhoeffer, *Ethics*, 102.

Chapter Three

MARTIN LUTHER: NO VILLAIN AFTER ALL?

The number of relativizations that were omitted to create the Martin Luther cliché is astounding. The charge of quietism ignores his ceaseless admonitions to speak up in the face of governmental evil. The charge of warmongering neglects his unequivocal opposition to all wars of aggression—and his advice to soldiers to disobey orders that violate God's commandments.

The charge linking Luther to Germany's misdeeds in World War II ignores the Roman Catholic upbringing of National Socialism's worst Nazi villains, such as Adolf Hitler, Heinrich Himmler, Josef Goebbels, Julius Streicher, Arthur Seyss-Inquart, Ernst Kaltenbrunner, Auschwitz commandant Rudolf Hess, and the notorious Auschwitz doctor Josef Mengele. Furthermore, this charge conceals the fact that while more uniformly Lutheran countries, such as Norway, based their resistance to tyranny on Luther's theology, a primarily Roman Catholic Austria provided three-fourths of all extermination camp commandants.[1]

---

1 Cf. Elisabeth Pond, "Do Austrians Want to Forget—Or Confront?" *The Christian Science Monitor* (3 March 1988): 1: "Statistically, the Austrians constituted only 8.5 percent of the greater German population. Yet they would provide three-fourths of the commandants of extermination camps, and commit 40 percent of all war crimes, in the estimation of veteran Nazi hunter Simon Wiesenthal."

I would like to make it clear, however, that I am not implying that these Austrians acted in that manner because of their Catholic upbringing. Far be it from me to shift the responsibility for the crimes of National Socialism from Lutheranism to Roman Catholicism, especially as I agree wholeheartedly with Karla Poewe's assessment that "National Socialism was a national revolutionary movement determined to rid Germany of Jewish Christianity,"[2] including Roman Catholicism, which had remained faithful to the church fathers' condemnation of the Marcionite attempt to separate Christianity from Judaism as a heresy for eighteen centuries. Indeed, as Poewe and Richard Steigmann-Gall point out, the ex-Catholics in the top Nazi leadership rejected the Catholic faith of their childhood in favor of forms of religiosity that would not pass doctrinal review by theologians of any serious Christian denomination, with many, such as SS leader Heinrich Himmler, embracing a rabidly anti-Christian variety of neo-paganism.

I quote Elisabeth Pond's observation about Norwegian Lutherans and Roman Catholics in Austria simply to emphasize the absurdity of the charge that one Christian denomination's theology paved the way for genocide. In the twentieth century alone, former or nominal Protestants, Catholics, and Orthodox Christians perpetrated holocausts in Germany and the countries it conquered in World War II. Turkish Muslims, Orthodox Russians, and Cambodian Buddhists also perpetuated holocausts in their parts of the world. Yet nobody is linking Catholicism, non-Lutheran Protestantism, Eastern Orthodoxy, Islam, or the gentle *Hinayana* Buddhism of Southeast Asia with these crimes. The point of this study is to dissect a cliché, not to create a new one while attempting to answer one of the oldest questions of mankind: Why do humans at times behave inhumanly? Where that question is concerned, I bow to Helmut Thielicke's magnificent theological observation that "a fatality of guilt [*Schuldverhängnis*] is brooding over the world, over its continents and seas."[3]

Some of these and other relativizations will be discussed later in this chapter. But first I shall deal with the most important argument against the *Fürstenknecht* cliché, an argument by Carter Lindberg: "The

---

2 Karla Poewe, *New Religions and the Nazis* (New York: Routledge, 2006), 172.

3 Helmut Thielicke, *Das Gebet das die Welt umspannt* (Stuttgart: Quell, 1980), 109.

Reformers of the sixteenth century . . . did not understand themselves to be . . . ethicists, sociologists, politicians or economists, even though their contributions frequently involved all these fields. . . . The Reformers were . . . pastors and theologians—period! This is most certainly true of Luther."[4]

THE THEOLOGICAL IMPORTANCE OF ORDER

Modern critiques of Luther's views on governing authority often suffer from what Heinz Eduard Tödt terms a "fundamental flaw." They interpret his writings using twentieth- and twenty-first-century presuppositions and perspectives, which tend to be anthropological and are not sufficiently aware of Luther's decidedly theocentric orientation.[5] Luther gave his contemporaries "legal instructions [*Rechtsunterricht*] based on the Bible," writes Gerta Scharffenorth.[6] The question of justice was as perplexing in Luther's time as it is today. Luther's contribution was, in Tödt's words, "to exegete Scripture with reference to the concrete questions of life for his fellow human beings."[7]

One must keep in mind, however, that Luther's theological instructions generally do not possess the character of ecclesiastical

---

4 Carter Lindberg, "Luther's Critique of the Ecumenical Assumption that Doctrine Divides but Service Unites," *Journal of Ecumenical Studies* 27:4 (Fall 1990): 680. The extremely important consideration that Luther saw himself first and foremost as a theologian might also be employed to refute the charge of "furious nationalism" (Thomas Mann). There can be little doubt about two things: (1) Luther loved his country. (2) He must have realized that the Reformation was fragmenting Germany (the Peace of Augsburg, 1555, divided the country by confessions), thus weakening it in the face of external enemies. In the centuries that followed, the empire's enemies exploited this division repeatedly, with France frequently aligning itself with the Protestants against the Roman Catholic emperor. A "furious nationalist," anticipating this problem, would presumably have tried to forestall it by way of compromise. But as a theologian deeply committed to the Gospel, Luther did not have that option. Thus it can be argued that whatever "nationalistic" sentiment Luther might have had, he sacrificed it for the sake of God's Word.

5 Heinz Eduard Tödt, "Die Bedeutung von Luthers Reiche- und Regimentenlehre für heutige Theologie und Ethik," in *Gottes Wirken in seiner Welt*, ed Niels Hasselmann (Hamburg: Lutherisches Verlagshaus, 1980), 65.

6 Gerta Scharffenorth, *Den Glauben ins Leben ziehen* (Munich: Chr. Kaiser, 1982), 231–32.

7 Tödt, "Die Bedeutung von Luthers Reiche- und Regimentenlehre," 67.

doctrine.[8] In the words of Franz Lau, "the Lutheran church knows of no infallible Luther. [To Luther] a dogma of Luther's infallibility, even if not formally promulgated, would be worse even than the dogma of the Pope's infallibility. To place Luther's theology side by side with or even above Scripture would be the worst disavowal of Luther."[9]

Luther tries to help his fellow Christians manage the problems in their lives by making proper distinctions; he guides and advises them as they strive to make the right decisions. But he does not command them to follow him, the theologian. He simply tells them what the Bible says. Thus Gordon Rupp reminds us that "nobody can understand Luther's teaching about the office of the ruler who does not begin with the study of Romans 13."[10] I suggest, though, that to comprehend Luther we must first leaf all the way back to the beginning of the Bible, to the Book of Genesis.

Luther was an Old Testament scholar. For Luther, writes Gunnar Hillerdal, "Scripture was not just a collection of historical documents . . . but 'God's witness of himself.' "[11] Hence the creation story is God's *first* "witness of himself." It is the story of the transformation of chaos into an orderly world. Thus order corresponds to God's will, and the devil wants to destroy order.

---

8 Tödt, "Die Bedeutung von Luthers Reiche- und Regimentenlehre," 61.

9 Franz Lau, *Luthers Lehre von den beiden Reichen* (Berlin: Evangelische Verlagsanstalt, 1952), 94. However, Luther's doctrine of the two realms and governments, which will be discussed later in this chapter, figures prominently in the confessional writings of the Lutheran Church. Article XXVIII of the Augsburg Confession makes it clear that "ecclesiastical and civil power are not to be confused. The power of the church has its own commission to preach the Gospel and administer the sacraments. Let it not invade the other's function, nor transfer the kingdoms of the world, nor abrogate the laws of civil rulers, nor abolish lawful obedience, nor interfere with judgments concerning civil ordinances or contracts, nor prescribe to civil rulers laws about the forms of government that should be established. Christ says, 'My kingdom is not of this world,' and again, 'Who made me judge or divider over you?' " (Theodore G. Tappert, trans. and ed., *The Book of Concord* [Philadelphia: Fortress, 1959], 83). Furthermore, Luther deals with the two realms and governments in the Large Catechism, notably in his exegesis of the Fourth, Fifth, and Sixth Commandments and the Second and Fourth Petitions of the Lord's Prayer. See Tappert, *Book of Concord*, 379–95, 426–29.

10 E. Gordon Rupp, *Martin Luther: Hitler's Cause or Cure?* (London: Lutterworth, 1945), 37–38.

11 Gunnar Hillerdal, *Gehorsam gegen Gott und Menschen* (Göttingen: Vandenhoeck & Ruprecht, 1955), 18. Hillerdal is citing WA 50:282.7.

The result is a cosmic struggle in which man is the pawn. In an act of unfathomable grace, God created man in His own image, thus assigning man a special place within the order of creation.[12] But as the story of the fall shows, this God-likeness can be lost. Hillerdal notes: "A human being who is the devil's captive lacks the *imago Dei* and the disposition for it. No part of his being would be of higher origin distinguishing him from the rest of creation. Rather, having become subject of the devil's power, man takes on the devil's image."[13]

Luther makes it clear that man is incapable of taking on an image of his own: "Man must be an image either of God or of the devil. For on whomever [of the two] he orients himself, that one he resembles."[14] This is a point well worth remembering when we contrast Luther's theocentric thrust with the anthropocentrism so prevalent among his detractors.

God wants man to be His "cooperator,"[15] as Luther phrased it. Through this "cooperator," God wishes to act in this world, states Hillerdal.[16] And for man to become his "cooperator," God has installed various forms of order. One form of order is marriage, which assures procreation of life.[17] Another is secular authority, which acts, in Hillerdal's words, "as a wall against the devil's destructive powers."[18] It prevents chaos[19] and thus also prevents a return to a condition resembling that from which God's work of creation has rescued the world. Hillerdal adds: "In order to dissolve or even destroy secular rule, insurrection and war are provoked; indeed, even the powers of nature are employed [by the devil]. For the order created by God—even where its administrators are non-Christians—serves God's rule on earth."[20]

---

12 WA 42:51.19ff.

13 Hillerdal, *Gehorsam gegen Gott und Menschen*, 34.

14 WA 14:111.14–18 and WA 42:47.8–11.

15 Modern theologians, such as Philip J. Hefner, take this one step further. They see man's purpose as that of a cocreator, as God's partner in the ongoing process of creation.

16 Hillerdal, *Gehorsam gegen Gott und Menschen*, 84.

17 Lau, *Luthers Lehre von den beiden Reichen*, 32.

18 Hillerdal, *Gehorsam gegen Gott und Menschen*, 30.

19 Lau, *Luthers Lehre von den beiden Reichen*, 97.

20 Hillerdal, *Gehorsam gegen Gott und Menschen*, 30.

This is why Paul writes in Romans 13:1: "Let every soul be subject to superior authorities. For there is no authority except by God, and those which exist are ordained by God." To stress the rulers' importance in God's plan for the world, Paul assigns them a title he also claims for himself.[21] They are *leitourgoi gar Theou*, God's servants or agents. [22] In other words, Paul and pagan politicians[23] are colleagues.

Romans 13:1–7 and its corresponding pericope, 1 Peter 2:13–17, are the New Testament's only passages discussing political order on a broader scale. And this is why they formed the basis for more than Luther's political thinking. In fact, writes Gerta Scharffenorth,[24] these biblical texts shaped theologians' views on governing authority as early as the High Middle Ages. They thought that wherever there is power and might in this world, even when abused by man, it comes from God, the *rex regum et dominus dominationum*.

But the insight that secular power stems from God did not originate with Paul. He drew on the Old Testament and the Apocrypha, which affirm over and over again that God chooses the ruler for His people (Psalm 2:7; 1 Samuel 13:14; 2 Samuel 3:1; 5:1–3). Furthermore, Proverbs 8:15 reads: "By Me kings rule, and rulers decree justice," and Wisdom 6:3 stresses this point: "For your power was given to you of the Lord and your sovereignty from the highest." Finally, Jesus Himself pointed to the source of all secular power when He told Pontius Pilate, "You would not have any authority against Me had it not been given to you from above" (John 19:11).

THE TWO REALMS

The biblical statement that God is the one to whom secular rulers owe their authority is the centerpiece of Luther's doctrine of the two realms and governments,[25] which is a concept that has been woefully perverted

---

21 Romans 15:16.

22 Romans 13:6.

23 Paul referred to the authorities of the Roman Empire.

24 Scharffenorth, *Den Glauben ins Leben ziehen*, 206.

25 Also called the doctrine of the two kingdoms. I find this translation of the German term *Lehre von den beiden Reichen und Regimenten* misleading. It can be misconstrued to mean that there are two different kings lording over God's two realms. Luther made it clear that both are God's realms.

by pro-Nazi German Christians, malevolently misinterpreted by Luther's enemies, and sadly disavowed even by some Lutheran theologians who are embarrassed by its misuse. Luther himself attached the utmost importance to this complex doctrine, relates Tödt. And Luther was also immensely proud of his contribution: "I can in good conscience... pride[26] myself with having written as magnificently and usefully about secular authority as no other teacher before me, with the possible exception of Augustine."[27]

According to Luther, all Christians lead a double existence. They are citizens of two realms—the spiritual and the secular.[28] Luther is by no means alone in distinguishing between two realms. In *De Civitate Dei*, Augustine differentiated between the worldly state and God's state.[29]

Tödt calls Luther's doctrine of the two realms "a central instrument of Lutheran theology," but he insists that the term *doctrine* be understood in the way Luther defined it: "[It is] a means to grasp the *summa* of what really is divine... doctrine: Holy Scripture."[30]

Perceiving a discrepancy between the radical demands of the Sermon on the Mount and the structure of this world's orders, Luther attributes the following properties to the two realms:

(1) *The spiritual realm is infinite.* It is the realm of the *Deus revelatus*, the God who revealed Himself in Christ. It is the realm of the Gospel, of grace, of faith, and of love. It is a realm where God and Christ

---

26 Or "praise myself," in German, *rühmen*.

27 WA 30/2:110ff.

28 Non-Christians are subject to the secular realm only. But Christians must live in both realms until the end of the world.

29 Since Cain, the people of God had to coexist with the *civitas terrena*, the worldly state. This was the case with the Jews in Ashur and Babylon and with the early church in the Roman Empire. The secular state is marked by injustice, selfishness, and excessive self-love. The *civitas Dei*, God's world, is the church where Christ reigns. Its law is love for one's neighbor resulting from self-denial. In formulating his doctrine of the two realms, Luther borrowed from Augustine's concept but transformed it significantly. In the medieval interpretation of Augustine, the *civitas Dei* is the *visible*, organized Catholic Church on earth (it is also the eschatological kingdom). For Luther, the spiritual realm becomes a reality for Christians through faith. It is an *audible* realm because it reaches the believer through the Word. It becomes visible only in the Sacrament, the visible Word. Cf. Lau, *Luthers Lehre von den beiden Reichen*, 26–27.

30 Tödt, "Die Bedeutung von Luthers Reiche- und Regimentenlehre," 66–67.

rule and all humans are equal. This realm is a reality in this sinful world. It becomes a reality wherever the Word is proclaimed, the Sacraments are administered, and Christ forgives His followers' sins. The spiritual realm, which is the realm of the church, will not disappear but be gloriously completed in the *eschaton*. Then there will be no more sin and therefore no longer a need for forgiveness.[31] Until then, says Luther, it is the spiritual government's job to "direct the people vertically toward God that they may do right and be saved; just so as the secular government should direct the people horizontally toward one another, seeing to it that body, property, honor, wife, house, home, and all manners of goods remain in peace and security and are blessed on earth."[32]

(2) *The secular realm is finite.* It is the realm of the *Deus abscondi-tus*, the hidden God. This is the realm where He never reveals Himself.[33] Lau writes: "It is obvious that God conducts a curious masquerade in one of these two worlds [the secular one]; but that is a genuinely Lutheran thought. Luther has made it clear enough to us that God knows and uses ample means to make sure that his rule in the earthly world does not slip away from him."[34]

This means that God has not withdrawn from the secular realm but has delegated the "sword," which to Luther symbolizes secular power, to governing authority.[35] In this realm, which has superiors and subordinates and consequently no equality, man lives his temporal, biological life. It is the realm of the law that is from the hidden God. It is

---

31 Lau, *Luthers Lehre von den beiden Reichen*, 33.

32 AE 13:197.

33 But the secular realm is God's creation too. It must not be confused with the realm of Satan. In fact, the devil is its bitter enemy. See WA 23:514.32ff.

34 Lau, *Luthers Lehre von den beiden Reichen*, 95.

35 See WA 23:514.1–6. Here Luther defines the term *sword* thus: "By sword I mean everything that belongs to the secular government, such as secular laws and rules, customs and habits, gestures, estates, different offices, persons, clothes, etc." In his Table Talks, Luther called secular authority "a sign of divine grace, of the mercy of God who takes no pleasure in murdering, killing and strangling" (WATr 1:77). "Temporal authority was not instituted by God to break the peace and to initiate war, but to keep the peace and repress the fighters. As Paul says in Romans 13 [:4], the office of the sword is to protect and to punish, to protect the good in peace and to punish the wicked with war" (*Works of Martin Luther*, Philadelphia Edition [Philadelphia: Fortress, 1931–1943], 5:56).

governed by reason, which is a gift of God for this very purpose,[36] says Luther. In the realm of the world man lives, in Bonhoeffer's terminology, *etsi Deus non daretur*, "as if there were no God." As Bonhoeffer phrased it:

> God would have us know that we must live as men who manage our lives without him. The God who is with us is the God who forsakes us (Mark 15:34). The God who lets us live in the world without the working hypothesis of God is the God before whom we stand continually. Before God and with God we live without God. God lets himself be pushed out of the world onto the cross. He is weak and powerless in the world and that is precisely the way, the only way in which he is with us and helps us. Matt. 8:17 makes it quite clear that Christ helps us, not by virtue of his omnipotence, but by virtue of his weakness and suffering.[37]

In this realm, then, the rulers may be godless but still do God's work by limiting evil and warding off chaos and disorder. Although it is a sinful realm, the secular law is intended as a bastion against sin. Misdeeds are not forgiven; they are punished.[38] Luther has said repeatedly that this is not the realm of God, Christ, or the Gospel,[39] and secular rulers need not be saints. "It is sufficient for the emperor to possess reason,"[40] writes Luther. This applies to all levels of authority. Lau explains this beautifully:

---

36 As are wisdom, honor, and faith. See Scharffenorth, *Den Glauben ins Leben ziehen*, 302.

37 Dietrich Bonhoeffer, *Letters and Papers from Prison*, ed. Eberhard Bethge (New York: Macmillan, 1972), 360.

38 WA 18:369.19–26: "God's realm is a realm of grace and mercy, not of wrath and punishment . . . but the realm of the world is a realm of wrath and severity. There [you find] . . . punishment, prohibitions, judgment, and verdicts in order to constrain the wicked and protect the righteous. This is why it bears . . . the sword, and why Scripture (Is. 14:5) calls a prince or a lord God's wrath and rod."

39 Yet it is an *ordinatio divina*, ordained by God.

40 WA 27:417–18. Carter Lindberg comments: "Reason replaced the ecclesial legitimation of politics. This is easily misunderstood today if we think of reason in post-Enlightenment terms as autonomous reason. . . . For Luther, the essential characteristic for worldly rule is reason informed by wisdom and equity" (Lindberg, "Luther's Critique," 690).

The office obliges [its holder] not only to his superior, but also binds him to God. The father of a family, who faithfully does his duty, thus stands in God's service. His estate has God's Word, even if the man does not believe, and is not interested in God. A prince who administers his office with integrity and governs his subjects with justice is the executor of God's will, even if he is an agnostic or a Catholic, and even if his lifestyle is Epicurean. The subject who obediently does his duty outwardly obeys a man . . . but in the final analysis [he obeys] God who stands behind secular rulers, albeit in a hidden way.[41]

Both realms, though separate, exist for one another; they serve each other. In proclaiming the Gospel, the spiritual realm supports and protects the secular realm. The Gospel admonishes Christians to be obedient.[42] For Luther, it is the duty of all preachers to back the secular realm. The preacher's office must not subvert secular authority but strengthen it. On the other hand, the secular realm serves the office of the preacher, the proclamation, and thus the growth of the kingdom of God.[43] Secular authority enables the Gospel to be preached. In wild chaos, the Word would not be able to take its course.

But Luther insists just as emphatically that the two realms be meticulously distinguished, a distinction also noted in the Augsburg Confession.[44] This is a point all too frequently overlooked in this century—even by Lutheran churches. The German Christians' submission to National Socialist ideology of race and blood is one example; another is the invasion of theology by a vast array of anthropocentric "isms," such as feminism and other forms of "liberationism."

Luther warns: "We have to . . . learn that the spiritual and the secular governments are as far apart as heaven and earth."[45] For Luther, mixing the two realms is tantamount to opening the door to the devil:

Constantly I must pound in and squeeze in and drive in and wedge in this difference between the two kingdoms, even

---

41 Lau, *Luthers Lehre von den beiden Reichen*, 37.

42 WA 30/2:527.8–18.

43 WA 16:339.17–23.

44 AC XXVIII 12–13 (Tappert, *Book of Concord*, 83).

45 WA 47:284.12–14.

though it is written and said so often that it becomes tedious. The devil never stops cooking and brewing these two kingdoms into each other. In the devil's name the secular leaders always want to be Christ's masters and teach Him how He should run His church and spiritual government. Similarly, the false governments and schismatic spirits always want to be masters, though not in God's name, and to teach people how to organize the secular government. Thus the devil is indeed very busy on both sides, and he has much to do. May God hinder him, amen, if we deserve it![46]

Former bishop of Oslo Eivind Berggrav, who led the resistance of Norway's Lutheran state church against the pro-Nazi Quisling government, put this into a contemporary context:

When God made a sharp line of demarcation between the kingdom, which has to do with order and that which has to do with the soul, it was not just for the purpose of drawing straight lines. There is a deeper reason. Where this distinction is not maintained Satan stands to gain. He then sneaks in and rules in *both kingdoms.* Whenever civil authority assumes power over the souls of men, it presumes on God. Whenever the church desires worldly power, it becomes demon-obsessed. The danger is equally great for both. Both the pope and the emperor, the church and the state, can become servants of the devil![47]

"Power over the souls" and "presuming on God" are the key expressions here. It is the principal concern of the much-maligned doctrine of the two realms to free Christians from secular intrusions into their relationship with God. At the same time, this doctrine is meant to protect Catholics, schismatics, heretics, and non-Christians from persecution by secular authority. Luther insists: "The thoughts and beliefs of the souls cannot be known to anyone but God. Therefore it is futile and impossible to oblige anybody by force to believe this or that."[48]

Even heretics should be permitted to preach freely, as long as they

---

46 AE 13:194–95.

47 Eivind Berggrav, *Man and State,* trans. George Aus (Philadelphia: Muhlenberg, 1951), 305 (*Berggrav's emphasis*).

48 WA 11:264.

do not whip up unrest.[49] Luther notes: "Heresy is a spiritual matter; no iron can smash it, no fire can burn it, no water can drown it. God's word alone can deal with it, as Paul says in 2 Cor. 10:4, '[T]he weapons of our warfare are not worldly but have divine power to destroy strongholds.'"[50]

In an axiom that seems particularly poignant in the early twenty-first century, with its culture war resulting from religious fanaticism, Luther ridiculed secular authority for attempting to enforce doctrinal purity with violence but achieving the opposite of the desired effect: "Just look what fine, clever lords we have. They want to drive away heresy by attacking it, and so they strengthen the opponent, come themselves under suspicion, and justify the other side."[51]

As Carter Lindberg puts it:

> Luther's fundamental doctrinal commitment to justification by grace alone informed his rejection of all expressions of the *corpus Christianum*, whether of the medieval papacy or of the "radical" Reformers from Karlstadt and Müntzer to the Anabaptists. He saw in each of these expressions the claim that political criteria are relevant to determining who is and who is not the church and that political programs may be identified with the will of God. Luther's condemnations of . . . the Peasants' War . . . were consistent applications of his theological perspective that the Gospel stands against all "holy wars" and efforts to "baptize" politics.[52]

In trying to reestablish religious legitimation, Münzer became the Reformation-era reactionary, argues Lindberg.[53] He struggled for a return to the pre-Reformation blur in the relationship between the spiritual and the secular realms. Luther, on the other hand, was the revolutionary. Lindberg writes: "He hoped to free Christians for service in a world that is always shrouded in political and ethical ambiguity by

---

49 AE 40:57. In WA 18:299, Luther states: "Authority should not forbid anybody to teach or believe or say what he wants—the Gospel or lies. It is sufficient that authority fights the teaching of insurrection and unrest."

50 WA 11:268.

51 WA 11:269.

52 Lindberg, "Luther's Critique," 691.

53 Carter Lindberg, "Theology and Politics: Luther the Radical and Müntzer the Reactionary," *Encounter* 37:4 (1976): 371.

distinguishing between human, civil righteousness measured by justice and equitable laws and the righteousness before God that is a free, unmerited gift."[54]

Hence, the doctrine of the two realms is wedded to the doctrine of *sola gratia*, which de-ideologizes politics (Lindberg) and de-idolizes the state (Lau), which thus becomes "worldly in an honest sense of the word."[55] This is precisely what should make Luther's theology so attractive at our time when the world is beginning to take note of the nightmares triggered by the French Revolution and its hideous child, the deified state. This state was exemplified first by revolutionary France, then the Soviet, Nazi, Chinese, and Cambodian Communist systems, as well as their Third World emulators such as Sékou Touré's Guinea, Idi Amin's Uganda, Jean-Bédel Bokassa's Central African Empire, Robert Mugabe's Zimbabwe, and Saddam Hussein's Iraq, to name just a few. Lau notes: "It would be the greatest inversion of Luther's doctrine of the two realms if the totalitarian state, the Machiavellian state, Hitler's state, the state idolizing itself were to be considered the ideal state from Luther's point of view. . . . Whoever tries to base the idolization of the state on Luther, strangely misunderstands him. Luther wants exactly the opposite."[56]

Bishop Berggrav, the resister, thought likewise. In 1941, when Hitler's Norwegian puppet Quisling ruled his country, Berggrav lectured pastoral and parish meetings thus:

> When the state insists on being *totalitarian*, e.g., when it considers itself a philosophy of life and insists on forcing this view on others, then, according to Luther, the devil is on the loose. When a state acts in this way, then it claims for itself the glory which belongs to the holy and puts itself in God's place; in short, it has become antichrist. Only as long as the state is *under God* is it a power according to God's design.[57]

As we have seen above, Luther was the converse of what Ernst Troeltsch and Thomas Mann made him out to be. Rather than being

---

54 Lindberg, "Luther's Critique," 691.

55 Lau, *Luthers Lehre von den beiden Reichen*, 72.

56 Lau, *Luthers Lehre von den beiden Reichen*, 72.

57 Berggrav, *Man and State*, 305–6 (*emphasis added*).

stuck in the Middle Ages, he took the revolutionary step of liberating the church and the state from the medieval chains binding them together. Münzer wanted to chain them together again.

William Shirer's charge of "fanaticism and intolerance" notwith-standing, it was Luther who had freed the state from ideology and lib-erated men of other faiths from the fear of *Meister Hans*, the henchman. Münzer denied those of other faiths the right to live freely, as did assorted utopians following in his footsteps—Nazis, Communists, and Islamists are only the most recent examples.

Luther was appalled when the emperor reverted to the medieval idea of spreading the Gospel by the power of the sword. Luther told Chris-tians to avoid the crusaders' army like the devil, urged soldiers to desert,[58] and made a suggestion that sounds familiar to modern ears. He noted that the funds allotted for the crusade against the Turks would be better spent on building schools and educating children.[59] Münzer, on the other hand, was willing to shed blood to bring about the kingdom of God.

Thus Richard Marius, who in his peregrinations around Tennessee "looked at Luther day after day and night after night" for appropriate words about the Vietnam War and could not find them, clearly did not look hard enough. On the other hand, supporters of the U.S. role in Vietnam, Afghanistan, and Iraq might also have found comfort in Luther's writings about war and peace because he was only opposed to wars of aggression. So the application of Luther's teachings depends on whom one considers to be the aggressor.

But even for this dilemma, Luther has an answer that also addresses a highly topical question in the post-Nazi and post-Communist era: Must a Christian follow orders that to his knowledge clearly violate God's commandments? Luther says: Absolutely not! The Christian owes more obedience to God than to man and must refuse to execute evil com-mands even if that means risking his life and the loss of all worldly belongings.[60] On the other hand, a Christian commits no sin if he par-ticipates *in good faith* in a war which turns out to be an unjust one.[61]

---

58 WA 30/2:115.1–16.

59 WA 15:29–30ff.

60 WA 19:656.25–32.

61 WA 11:278.10ff.

When to Resist Authority

Why is Luther's teaching so vulnerable to the reduction to clichés in Zijderveld's sense of the term? Because it is rich in potential relativizations for cliché-mongers to omit. In other words, Luther's teaching is extraordinarily complex, but each of its component parts sounds plausible enough to make a good stereotype.

But if we are fair to Luther, we will find it impossible to "atomize" his theology in such a way "that far-reaching conclusions can be drawn from each individual sentence in and by itself."[62] This is because "Luther's speech is always dialectical." On the other hand, his language, the hyperbolic language of sixteenth-century Saxony, is plain enough to be understood by peasant, patrician, and nobleman alike. He is, after all, first and foremost a preacher.

This becomes especially clear as we consider Luther's views on whether, when, and how governing authority can or must be resisted. Did he really preach "unquestioning obedience" to rulers, as Dean Inge asserts? Did he teach "absolute obedience," as Shirer claims? Did he "train his people to submissiveness," as Mann charges? Was he the "quietist" Troeltsch and Niebuhr made him out to be?

Taken by itself, and read by twentieth-century Anglo-Saxons unfamiliar with the rich verbosity of medieval central Germany, Luther's appeal to the princes to "stab, clobber, and kill" the "robbing and murdering hordes of peasants" would suggest all of the above.[63] But if we want to prevent this from degenerating into cliché thinking, we have to ponder the relativizations:

1. The Language

Saxons practice the art of overstatement. They like to "let rip," assuming that their colorful remarks will be taken with a grain of salt by their audience. This is still the case today;[64] it was even more so in Luther's time.[65] A fine example is the reformer's much-quoted, though

---

62 Lau, *Luthers Lehre von den beiden Reichen*, 92.

63 WA 18:361.

64 I speak from experience; I am a native Saxon.

65 . . . and beyond. This was by no means an exclusively German phenomenon, to wit, the earthy and exquisitely direct style of Puritan sermons preached from seventeenth-century New England pulpits.

possibly apocryphal, advice to preachers that the best way to practice their craft is to "hang their teats over the pulpit for the congregation to suckle on." To a refined Englishman such as Dean Inge, that statement would be "coarse and foul-mouthed," but Saxons understand and love this kind of earthy talk—a style at which not only Luther but also his adversaries such as Münzer or the redoubtable Johannes Tetzel excelled.

This is not to say that Luther did not really think the rebels merited the death penalty. From his theological and legal perspectives, rebels are worse than ordinary murderers, for unlike a murderer, "a rebel grabs for . . . the sword[66] in order to use it in other ways than . . . ordained by God."[67] But for all his ranting, Luther did not ask for more than that the law take its course to prevent anarchy.

2. LUTHER'S EQUALLY HARSH CONDEMNATION OF THE PRINCES

Immediately before calling for a bloody suppression of the peasants' insurrection, Luther accused the princes of inciting that rebellion by their haughty behavior: "You . . . oppress and rake in money, you . . . lead a lavish and arrogant lifestyle until the ordinary man can and will no longer bear it. The sword is at your throat, and yet you believe you are firmly in the saddle . . . . You will see, your impertinence will break your necks. Beware of Psalm 107:40, 'He pours contempt upon the princes.' "[68]

This is not the language of quietists—neither is Luther's appeal to the rulers to be merciful to surrendering peasants nor the tongue-lashing he metes out to the princes after the war:

> Furious, raving, senseless tyrants who after the battle still don't have their fill of blood . . . I have feared both: Had the peasants become lords, the devil would have become an abbot; but if tyrants became lords, [the devil's] mother becomes an abbess. That is why I wanted so much to calm down the peasants and teach piety to authority. These [the peasants] did not want to listen; well then, they received their just deserves. But those [the lords] don't want to listen either; well then, they'll get their just deserves as well. Too bad for them that they were not murdered

---

66 Meaning, secular power.

67 WA 17/1:266.

68 WA 18:294.

by the peasants; this would have been mild punishment for them. Hell-fire, trembling, and clattering teeth will be their eternal reward if they do not repent.[69]

3. The Scriptural *No* to Insurrection

Luther supported many of the peasants' demands. But when they resorted to violence, when they set out to kill the lords and ransack their estates, they rebelled against a divinely established order that existed "since the beginning of the world."[70] They violated Christ's instruction, "Render to Caesar the things that are Caesar's,"[71] and Paul's admonition in Romans 13 to obey governing authority. By murdering and robbing, they disobeyed God's commandments in the most heinous way. They raised the sword against God's Word,[72] and they compounded their crimes by committing them "in the name of the Gospel" and calling themselves "Christian brethren." That was blasphemy.[73]

Does Luther expect us, then, to bow to everything a government does simply because authority is divinely established? Not at all, says Lau: "Luther does not teach silent obedience, but an almost foolhardy opposition against all governmental injustice. He raises his voice against the rape of the law in every respect and against godlessness. He grabs into the politicians' snout, but does not interfere with their craft."[74]

Berggrav concurs: "To put it in a nutshell—he who keeps silent shares the guilt. He fails God. It does not matter whether they [the oppressors] are stronger than we."[75] During the German occupation of Norway, Berggrav reminded his pastors of Luther's charge to Christians who were opposed by their ruler: "Let your mouth be the mouth of Christ's Spirit."[76] Rather than preaching quietism, Luther called quietist preachers unfaithful pigs: "There are many bishops and pastors in the

---

69 WA 18:400–401.

70 WA 11:248.

71 Matthew 22:21.

72 WA 18:360.

73 WA 18:359.

74 Lau, *Luthers Lehre von den beiden Reichen*, 88–89.

75 Berggrav, *Man and State*, 308.

76 WA 8:682.

ministry, but they do not 'stand' and serve God faithfully. On the contrary, they lie down or otherwise play with their office. These are lazy and worthless preachers who do not tell the princes and lords their sins. In some cases they do not notice the sins. They lie down and snore . . . like swine, they take up the room where good preachers should stand."[77]

Not only are clergymen duty-bound to speak up against unjust and merciless leaders, but ordinary citizens are also to question and petition them, albeit with all due respect. When the Beowulf (meaning the Antichrist) enters a village, Luther said that those who fail to speak against him will incur guilt.[78] God wants us to stand up for justice, for truth, and for our convictions. Showing moral courage is an indispensable obligation for every Christian.[79] But this is as far as Christians may go. They must then let God take action.[80] Luther bases this demand for verbal but peaceful resistance on John 18:23:

> [That Christ says to the officer:] "If I have spoken wrongly, bear witness to the wrong" must be understood in this way: There is a great difference between offering the other cheek, and punishing with words the one who hits us. Christ must suffer. But the word has been put into his mouth so that he may speak and punish what is unjust. . . . Even though somebody might slap me [in court] ten times over, I must not veer from the truth. . . . You are to separate the mouth from the hand. I shall not give up

---

77 AE 13:49.

78 According to Danish Bonhoeffer scholar Jørgen Glenthøj, Bonhoeffer acted true to this dictum by Luther. Cf. Jørgen Glenthøj, "Dietrich Bonhoeffers Weg vom Pazifismus zum politischen Widerstand," in *Dietrich Bonhoeffer aktuell*, ed. Rainer Mayer and Peter Zimmerling (Giessen: Brunnen, 2001), 48–51. Bonhoeffer's friend Eberhard Bethge relates that Bonhoeffer thought Hitler was the tool of the Antichrist. Eberhard Bethge, *Dietrich Bonhoeffer: Theologe, Christ, Zeitgenosse* (Munich: Christian Kaiser, 1967), 811.

79 Thus when Bonhoeffer, in his prison letters, bemoans "the dearth of civil courage," he displays an eminently Lutheran way of thinking. "Civil courage," he writes, "can grow only out of the free responsibility of free men. . . . It depends on a God who demands responsible action in a bond venture of faith, and who promises forgiveness and consolation to the man who becomes a sinner in that venture" (Bonhoeffer, *Letters and Papers from Prison*, 5–6). Bonhoeffer's own show of moral courage is very much rooted in his Lutheran theology.

80 WA 15:311.

my snout lest I consent to injustice. But the hand I shall keep still so that it may not avenge itself.[81]

This leads us to one aspect of Luther's teaching on the subject of resistance that Troeltsch finds particularly objectionable. While the Christian must act on his neighbor's behalf, he is not to fight for his own cause. This, to Troeltsch, is further proof for what he calls Luther's "double morality." But, in fact, Luther is only referring to Scripture. The "Christian law," which Luther deduces from Christ's example and the Sermon on the Mount, reads thus: Judge not, but suffer. That one cannot judge, sentence, and acquit oneself is, for Luther, a kind of basic law of the world. Where this basic law is violated through insurrection, everybody is called to become presiding judge and hangman. And if that happens, the very foundation of the world is threatened.

Furthermore, Luther's view is consistent with the theology of the cross. A Christian accepts suffering, follows the Savior, and will see God's glory. This is why Christians never struggle in their own behalf but endure injustice, humiliation, and pain like their Lord did on the cross. Hillerdal says: "When Christ steps in on behalf of a human being, misfortune and injustice matter little. The freedom and the joy of such a man are grounded in Christ and do not depend on temporal success, nor on the respect and the honor other humans may give or deny him."[82]

Because Luther rated most rulers as "fools and scoundrels," he thought it quite likely that a Christian's voluntary renunciation of force will result in suffering and oppression. But this, says Luther, is just the consequence the believer has to accept for advocating justice and truth. While the people are not obliged to follow their rulers in unjust actions,[83] their resistance must be passive, and they are not to rebel.[84] There are exceptions to Luther's opposition against armed resistance, and these exceptions will be discussed below. But insurrection can never

---

81 WA 28:283.19–32.

82 Hillerdal, *Gehorsam gegen Gott und Menschen*, 99.

83 WA 11:277.28–31.

84 This is a golden rule on which Luther and Calvin—as well as seventeenth-century Anglican doctrine—agree. It had clearly also inspired Martin Luther King Jr., whose nonviolent civil rights movement I covered as a foreign correspondent in

be countenanced, for it violates the *lex naturae*. Hillerdal says: "Luther's doctrine of the *lex naturae* expresses most of all the idea that God has written his law upon man's heart; therefore nobody can escape him. He who violates God's will stands accused by natural law. Furthermore, natural law serves as a source of cognition [*Erkenntnisquelle*]. [This source] does not provide a knowledge of God, but a kind of reason which tells man how to act in certain situations."[85]

Contrary to Lord Vansittart's interpretation of Luther, the importance of reason in Luther's theology can never be overrated. Reason, though under sin like everything in the secular realm, is "the head of all things"; when measured against other aspects of life, it is "the very best, yes, it is divine."[86] Reason is the force that maintains the order created by God at the beginning of time. "God made secular government subordinate and subject to reason," writes Luther. By reason man exercises his "jurisdiction over physical and temporal good, which God places under man's dominion, Genesis 2:8 ff."[87] Reason guides even heathen leaders.[88] Reason is "the heart and the empress of the laws; [it is] the fountain

---

the 1960s and found vastly more successful than the violent upheavals I witnessed in various parts of the world. I was in New York City during the Harlem riots in 1964 when King "warned Harlem negroes that violence would only exacerbate the problem and . . . beseeched them to follow his course on nonviolent resistance" (Stephen Oates, *Let the Trumpet Sound* [Harrisburg: New American Library, 1982], 302). On March 28, 1968, shortly before his assassination, King led a demonstration in Memphis, Tennessee. When some teenagers among the 6,000 demonstrators began smashing shop windows and looting, King announced, "I will never lead a violent march, so please call it off" (Oates, *Let the Trumpet Sound*, 477).

85 Hillerdal, *Gehorsam gegen Gott und Menschen*, 113.

86 WA 39/1:175.9–10.

87 AE 13:198. Luther makes it clear that secular government, and reason, have "no jurisdiction over the welfare of souls or things eternal."

88 AE 13:199: "Because God willed to give temporal dominion to the heathen or to reason, He also had to provide people who had wisdom and courage, who had the necessary inclination and skill, and who would preserve it. In the same way He always had to give His people true, sound, and faithful teachers who were able to rule His Christian Church and do battle against the devil. By these two groups, all sorts of books, laws, and teachings have been produced and preserved until the present day. The heathen, for their part, have their heathen books; we Christians, for our part, have the books of the Holy Scriptures."

whence all laws come and flow."[89] Reason enables man to live *etsi Deus non daretur* in this world where reason is "beautiful and glorious" and where it reigns.[90] "In temporal matters man . . . needs no other light than reason. This is why God does not teach in Scripture how to build houses, make clothes, get married, conduct war and the like . . . . [F]or all this the natural light is sufficient."[91]

Anything that is contrary to reason is even more contrary to God.[92] Hence Luther's statement: "Insurrection has no reason and in general hurts the innocent more than the guilty. This why no rebellion is right—even if the cause were justified. It always results in more damage than improvement."[93]

In a rebellion, the mob rules. For Luther, when the rabble tries to undo the divinely ordained secular order, their actions are "not Christian."[94] "The mob has and knows no bounds, and in every one of them more than five tyrants are hidden. Now, it is better to suffer injustice under one tyrant, e.g., governing authority, than under countless tyrants, e.g., the mob."[95]

There is, however, one exception to the rule that the Christian must obey governing authority: "Where a prince, king or lord should lose his mind, he should be deposed and taken into custody. For he who has lost his reason is no longer to be considered to be human."[96]

However, even in this case, the task to remove a ruler should not be left to the rabble. Walter Künneth explains an essential condition for the removal of a ruler by force: "[It can be done only by] personalities holding

---

89 WATr 6, no. 6955.

90 WA 16:261.29–32.

91 WA 10/1.1:531.6–16.

92 Cf. WA 8:629.31–630.1: "What is contrary to reason is certainly even more against God. How could something not be against divine truth if it conflicts already with human truth? As Christ divides truth in John 3:12 [into a secular and a heavenly truth] so you must say: 'If I have told you earthly things and you do not believe, how can you believe if I tell you heavenly things?' "

93 WA 8:680.18–21.

94 WA 17/1:149.23–25.

95 WA 19:639.22–25.

96 WA 19:634.18–20.

responsible positions in the structure of the state or are former office holders. . . . Depending on the circumstances, even the ordinary citizen can grow into such a position. . . . But it is vital that there be a recognizable organized . . . responsibility."[97]

Bishop Berggrav gave similar advice to Helmuth Count Moltke, who had asked him whether tyrannicide was theologically justified. According to Klemens von Klemperer, Berggrav answered in the affirmative but with one proviso: "The assassins must be able to kill Hitler and right away form a government capable of concluding peace." But at the time, in the spring of 1942, it was already too late for that, said Berggrav.[98]

WUNDERMÄNNER

Künneth and Berggrav are both touching on an important aspect of Luther's thinking on authority. On the one hand, the children of God "have to put up with their tyrants, [and] must also pray for them, wishing and doing everything good for them."[99] On the other hand, when tyranny becomes unbearable, God Himself interferes. He has a secret way of correcting such abominable inversions of His order. He punishes one scoundrel with another. He pushes the mighty from their thrones and raises the lowly. "This," writes Lau, "is God's secret order, the order of the magnificat."[100]

To repay tyrants who neglect their duty to protect the righteous and to punish the wicked, God will send fire or sudden death. Or He will send a *Wundermann*. This term sounds so odd that it is not much discussed in Anglo-Saxon theology. In fact, in the English-language version

---

97 Walter Künneth, *Das Widerstandsrecht als thelogisch-ethisches Problem* (Munich: Claudius, 1954), 14.

98 Klemens von Klemperer, "Glaube, Religion, Kirche und der deutsche Widerstand gegen den Nationalsozialismus," *Vierteljahreshefte für Zeitgeschichte* 3 (1980): 307. By and large, Moltke followed Berggrav's counsel. According to Peter Hoffmann, Moltke opposed his co-conspirators' assassination plans for two reasons: (1) Hitler must be kept alive and made to carry the entire responsibility for the catastrophe with his party. (2) A deeply religious man, Moltke rejected all force and brutality, even in countermeasures. See Peter Hoffmann, *The History of the German Resistance, 1933–1945* (Cambridge: MIT Press, 1977), 372.

99 AE 13:211.

100 Lau, *Luthers Lehre von den beiden Reichen*, 87.

of Luther's exegesis of Psalm 101,[101] where this notion is discussed in great detail, no satisfactory translation has been found for *Wundermann*. This vocable, peculiar even to modern German ears, is translated as "wondrous man," "extraordinary leader," or "outstanding man." A *Wundermann* owes his name to the divine miracle (*Wunder*) of his appearance. He is graced with a particular *afflatus*, a whiff of the Spirit. He is to the secular world what the prophet is to the spiritual realm. He is a special gift of God.

The collapse of the Soviet empire late in the twentieth century has fueled the discussion among East German and Baltic Lutherans whether or not Gorbachev was a *Wundermann* to whom Luther's words might apply: "It is a great gift if God gives an extraordinary leader whom He Himself rules."[102] Thus it is quite appropriate to take another look at what Luther meant by that term. Luther writes:

> Some have a special star before God; these he teaches Himself and raises them up as He would have them. They are the ones who have a smooth sailing on earth and so-called luck and success. Whatever they undertake prospers; and even if all the world were to work against it, it would still be accomplished without hindrance. For God, who puts it into their heart and stimulates their intelligence and courage, also puts it into their hands that it must come to pass and must be carried out; that was the case with Samson, David, Jehoiada, and others. He occasionally provides such men not only among his own people but also among the godless [*sic*] and the heathen; and not only in the ranks of nobility but also among the middle classes, farmers and laborers. For instance, in Persia He raised up King Cyrus; in Greece the nobleman Themistocles and Alexander the Great; among the Romans, Augustus, Vespasian, and others....
> I do not call such people trained or made but created; they are princes and lords directed by God.[103]

For Luther, his protector, "the sainted Duke Frederick elector of Saxony,[104] was [such a *Wundermann*] created to be a wise prince, to rule

---

101 AE 13:146–224.
102 AE 13:165.
103 AE 13:154–55.
104 Frederick the Wise (1486–1525).

and carry on his affairs in peace." But the mark of a *Wundermann* is not sainthood, as the example of David shows: "He fell into adultery, murder, and great sin against God."[105] No, the mark of a *Wundermann* is simply the extraordinary character of his divine commission, such as the call to destroy unjust authority. But as a *Wundermann* is only a tool of God, he must never derive personal benefits from the victory he has achieved. He has to act like a stranger who in a foreign country comes to the rescue of foreign people.

Yet it would be a very un-Lutheran thought that after God has raised and sent a *Wundermann* endowed with reason and wisdom to put things right, he will not allow that work to be reversed. Luther writes: "But so things happen in this world: If God builds a church, the devil comes and builds a chapel beside it, yes, even countless chapels. If God raises up an outstanding man [*Wundermann*], the devil brings his monkeys and simpletons to market to imitate everything. And yet it all amounts to monkey business and tomfoolery."[106]

As Bonhoeffer said, God lets Himself be pushed out of the world. But in the Lutheran way of thinking, this can never be the last word in God's drama acted out in the secular realm. Bonhoeffer continued: "I believe that God will bring good out of evil, even out of the greatest evil. For this purpose he needs men who make the best use of everything. I believe that God will give us the strength we need to help us to resist in times of distress. . . . I believe that even our mistakes and short-comings are turned to good account."[107]

When to Take up Arms against a Tyrant

Bonhoeffer was, of course, prepared to go beyond passive resistance to get rid of an evil ruler. Although theologically an orthodox Lutheran, Bonhoeffer eventually approved of attempts to assassinate Hitler. His friend and biographer, Eberhard Bethge, reports that this became clear during a meeting with anti-Nazi conspirators shortly before the outbreak of World War II: "One evening Bonhoeffer [was asked] what he thought about the New Testament passage 'all who take up the sword

---

105 AE 13:223.

106 AE 13:159.

107 Bonhoeffer, *Letters and Papers from Prison*, 11.

will perish by the sword' (Matt. 26:52). Bonhoeffer's reply was that the word was valid for their circle too—we have to accept that we are subject to that judgment, but that there is now need of such men as will accept its validity for themselves."[108]

Was Bonhoeffer, then, out of step with Luther? Not at all, says Bethge. In fact, Bonhoeffer explained himself with the quintessentially Lutheran imperative: "Sin boldly! [*pecca fortiter*]."[109] This advice to the citizens of the secular realm is often ripped out of context and then becomes a dreadful cliché to be used against Luther by those such as Peter F. Wiener. But when quoted in full, it really sums up how, according to Luther, a Christian should live in this world: "Be a sinner and sin boldly, but believe even more boldly and rejoice in Christ, who is victor over sin, death and world. We must sin as long as we are what we are; this life is not the dwelling place of righteousness[110] but we look, says Peter, for new heavens and a new earth in which righteousness dwells."[111]

In affirming the Christian's right to take up arms against an evil ruler, Bonhoeffer appealed to the *Gnesio*-Lutheran[112] tradition, which had a great influence on the Huguenot wars of the late sixteenth century. This tradition has its origins in the older Luther's change of heart on the subject of governing authority, which came about in connection with the Diet of Augsburg on June 30, 1530.

In his refuge at Coburg Castle, Luther fumed over the terms of the Recess that gave his side six months to accept the *Confutatio Pontificia*, the Roman Catholic reply to the Augsburg Confession. Proselytizing and religious publishing were to be prohibited in the Lutheran domains, and a common front was to be maintained against the Sacramentarians and Anabaptists. According to Martin H. Bertram,

---

108 Bethge, *Bonhoeffer*, 530.

109 Bonhoeffer said that the experience of evil under Hitler made him for the first time fully understand the value of Luther's famous dictum, *pecca fortiter*! Eberhard Bethge told me this in February 1991, during a conversation concerning whether an act of tyrannicide against Iraq's dictator Saddam Hussein was justified or not. Bethge felt that in Bonhoeffer's way of thinking it was.

110 Righteousness ontically understood!

111 WABr 2:372.

112 Literally, "true" Lutheran.

Luther viewed these terms as intolerable. . . . But if submission was impossible, one had to contemplate what would follow the expiration of the six-month period of grace. Luther, for one, viewed it as entirely likely that the emperor would turn to the use of force. . . . It was this conviction that moved Luther to issue the *Warning to His Dear German People*. On the peril of their souls, he warned, they should in no way collaborate in such an enterprise. The emperor's authority does not extend to lordship over spiritual matters. When the Gospel is at stake, one must obey God rather than men.[113]

In his *Warning*, Luther explicitly sanctions armed resistance to the monarch, thus departing from positions he had previously held:

If war breaks out—which God forbid—I will not reprove those who defend themselves against the murderous and bloodthirsty papists, nor let anyone rebuke them as being seditious, but I will accept their action and let it pass, as self-defense will direct them in this matter to the law and to the jurists. For in such an instance, when murderers and bloodhounds wish to wage war and to murder, it is in truth no insurrection to rise against them and defend oneself. . . . A Christian knows very well what to do—namely, to render to God the things that are God's and to Caesar the things that are Caesar's (Matt. 22:21), but not to render to the bloodhounds the things that are theirs.[114]

Luther thus laid the groundwork for a theology of defense against tyranny. Following the Augsburg Diet, Luther's support of the notion of resistance increased, as Cynthia Shoenberger observes.[115] At first he did so on legal grounds. For example, this was his reasoning when he signed the Wittenberg theologians' and jurists' brief that was formulated at their Torgau Disputation in October 1530. It states: "When we previously taught that authority should not be resisted, we did not realize that the right to do so was guaranteed by the very authority which we

---

113 Cf. Bertram's introduction to *Dr. Martin Luther's Warning to His Dear German People*, AE 47:5.

114 AE 47:13.

115 Cynthia Grant Shoenberger, "The Development of the Lutheran Theory of Resistance: 1523–1530," *Sixteenth Century Journal* 8:1 (April 1977): 64.

have always diligently instructed people to obey."[116]

Eight years later, Luther went even further: "If the emperor undertakes war, he will be a tyrant and will oppose our ministry and religion, and then he will also oppose our civil and domestic life. Here there is no question whether it is permissible to fight for one's faith. On the contrary, it is necessary to fight for one's children and family. If I am able, I'll write an admonition to the whole world in defense of such people."[117]

Richard R. Benert sees three levels of argumentation upon which Lutherans have since founded the right to resistance:

1. The highest level: Out of love for God, all are bound to stand on rare occasions in history against the legions of Satan.

2. The middle level: Natural law obligates all men to protect their families and neighbors, even against an emperor turned robber or murderer.

3. The lowest level: Positive law and the constitution offer the estates the right to resist when the emperor violates his agreements with them. This frees them from their obligations to him. Benert adds, "Feudal law combined with numerous Roman, canon, and Germanic laws allowed self-defense against authorities and public officials when they broke their faith or exceeded the limits of their office."[118]

Benert suggests a reassessment of the common view that only Calvinism injected political activism into the Protestant movement, while Lutheranism left its radical impress only in the realm of the Spirit. He especially draws attention to the sixteenth-century Lutheran concept of *untere Obrigkeiten*, or inferior magistrates.

Contrary to the widely held notion that the right and duty of inferior magistrates to resist tyranny by force of arms was first proclaimed by Calvinism, there is ample evidence to suggest that the idea was introduced to the Protestant movement by the Lutherans. According to

---

116 Heinz Scheible, ed., *Das Widerstandsrecht als Problem der deutschen Protestanten 1523–1546*, Texte zur Kirchen Geschichte 10 (Gütersloh: Gerd Mohn, 1969), 67.

117 AE 54:278–79.

118 Richard R. Benert, "Lutheran Contributions to Sixteenth-Century Resistance Theory," paper presented to the American Historical Association, 30 December 1970.

Oliver K. Olson, "Calvin did, indeed, recognize the obligation of lesser magistrates to shield their subjects from irresponsible exercise of power, but only by using measures which stopped short of armed resistance."[119]

It was Luther who extended this right and duty to all men, admonishing them to protect their families and neighbors. When attacked in the absence of a constituted authority, the private individual must act as a magistrate (*plebs est magistratus*).[120] The key passage supporting this idea can be found in a brief that Luther, Jonas, Bucer, and Melanchthon prepared for John Frederick of Saxony and Philip of Hesse in November 1538:

> And as the Gospel confirms the office of authority, it also confirms natural law. As Paul said, '*Lex est iniustis posita.*'[121] And there is no doubt that a father is beholden, to the extent of his ability, to protect his child against murder committed by public authority,[122] and there is no difference between a common murderer, and the emperor when he abuses his office to perpetrate a violent injustice, especially if he uses force officially and notoriously. For according to natural law, official violence dissolves all obligations between subjects and rulers.[123]

Luther and his collaborators thus formulated a legal concept that is as valid in the twenty-first century as it was almost 500 years ago. As conventional opinion will have it, the notion of the inferior magistrates' God-given duty to take up arms against "higher authority" under certain circumstances originated with Calvin. But that idea is wrong. In reality, argues Olson, this concept was formed before Calvin:

> [It] was articulated prior to the Schmalkaldic wars in conversations between the Wittenberg theologians and the electoral Saxon jurists and was transmitted at exactly the right moment by Calvin's successor in Geneva, Theodore Beza, to the monarchomachs, the publicists who were leading the Protestant oppo-

---

119 Oliver K. Olson, "Theology of Revolution: Magdeburg, 1550–1551," *Sixteenth Century Journal* 3:1 (1972): 59.

120 WATr 4:236–37.

121 1 Timothy 1:9: "the law is not laid down for the just."

122 "*Wider Offentlichen mord zu schützen.*" The word *öffentlich* has to be read as "public," in the sense of "public office."

123 Scheible, *Das Widerstandsrecht*, 93.

sition to the French king after the St. Bartholomew's [Day] Massacre and who needed a theoretical foundation for their agitation.[124]

The Magdeburg Confession

A crucial role in the transmission of the theory of resistance was played by Magdeburg, which was the first city in northern Germany to claim the Reformation faith. It became a model of Lutheran resistance. In fact, it was the last pocket of military defiance in the Smalcald War, which followed the failure of a series of attempts to reconcile the differences between the Roman Catholic and the Lutheran side. In this war, two powerful Protestant princes, Hans of Küstrin and Maurice of Saxony, joined the emperor. The causes for that conflict, which are highly relevant to our subject, will be discussed below.

At a time when the Protestants throughout the country faced almost certain defeat, it was Magdeburg's fierce opposition that turned the tide of the conflict and thus presumably preserved the Lutheran faith in Germany. This is how Olson describes the situation in the city in 1549 when it was under siege by the superior forces of the Saxon elector, who were fighting for the emperor's cause:

> The tense situation, in which it seemed that Luther's movement was about to be crushed, helped form an ecclesiastical party that in one guise or other has persisted within Lutheran tradition ever since, a party claiming to preserve Luther's true intent. Thus Melanchthon's observation that "these absurd persons consider themselves the only *gnesio* [true] Lutherans" had a kernel of truth.[125] Their convictions were expressed by the soldiers

---

124 Olson, "Theology of Revolution," 56.

125 Melanchthon and the *Gnesio*-Lutherans opposed each other over the question whether the terms of the Augsburg Interim should be observed, e.g., whether liturgical practices demanded of the Lutherans by the other side should be considered *adiaphora* (indifferent) and therefore observed. Melanchthon and his followers, the Philippists, favored this. The *Gnesios*, led by Matthias Flacius Illyricus, opposed it. Flacius, who had come to Germany from the area formerly called Yugoslavia, coined the famous phrase "*In casu confessionis et scandali nihil est adiaphoron*" ("When provocations demand an act of confession there is no such thing as an indifferent practice").

of the city's garrison. Outnumbered six to one, they defended Magdeburg as the Saxon elector, in a mopping-up operation after the Schmalkaldic War, mounted a siege against the city on the emperor's behalf. Under constant fire, they sang about themselves as the last faithful remnant of Luther's cause—modern Maccabees.[126]

Olson adds that "in 1550 Magdeburg theologians allied with Matthias Flacius Illyricus, the staunchest among the *Gnesio*-Lutherans, signed a 1550 *Confession, Instruction and Warning.*" It claimed not to be original but simply a rehearsal of Luther's own thought, now stripped of its cautious, pastoral, prewar ambiguity.

A key paragraph of this Magdeburg Confession[127] states clearly that subjects of authority, even children and servants, do not owe obedience to those rulers, parents, or employers "who want to lead them away from true fear of God and honorable living." Those authorities and parents "will become an ordinance of the devil instead of God, an ordinance which everyone can and ought to resist with a good conscience."[128]

The center of the lengthy document is a definition of four degrees of injustice and recommendations for appropriate responses to each of them. These are the degrees:

1. Authority, because of human weakness, has its vices and sin and often knowingly or deliberately does injustice in small mean things. At this point of the argument we do not want the lesser magistracy to use force to resist the superior magistracy. . . .

2. Authority does great and public violence and injustice to its subjects as when a prince, a town, the Emperor, attacks a prince who is innocent in an unjust war against his own oath, duty and law and wanted thus to deprive him of body and life, wife and child, his liberties or of his land and people. . . . In this case, just as we do not want to order anyone to defend themselves as in

---

126 Oliver K. Olson, "Matthias Flacius Illyricus," in *Shapers of Religious Traditions in Germany, Switzerland, and Poland, 1560–1600,* ed. Jill Raitt (New Haven: Yale University Press, 1981), 4.

127 I used an unpublished translation by A. M. Stewart of Aberdeen University, which is in my possession.

128 Olson, "Matthias Flacius Illyricus," 38.

accord with God's command . . . so too we do not want it to weigh on anyone's conscience if he does do so. . . .

3. When the lesser magistracy is forced by superior magistracy to certain sins, and when it can not tolerate such injustice without sin so it raises opposition and also bears its sword. . . . We have to pay careful attention here that . . . in resistance to public forces some higher law or command of God is not broken which would make the resistance unjust. . . .

4. When tyrants become so mad and crazy that they persecute with weapons and war not only the persons of the lesser magistracy and subjects in a legitimate case, but also (attack) in these persons the highest and most necessary rights and also our Lord God himself . . . if say a prince or emperor were to become so reckless or mad as to suspend the law of marriage and discipline and set up another law . . . permitting all sorts of shameful misbehavior . . . we and other Christians can resist with calm confidence.

This document helped provide the theoretical basis for one of the most celebrated events in the history of resistance—the fourth Huguenot war that began after the St. Bartholomew's Day Massacre of 1572 and ended in 1598 with the Edict of Nantes that guaranteed the French Protestants the freedom to practice their religion.

The St. Bartholomew's Day Massacre prompted Theodore Beza, who was then Calvin's successor as "Moderator of the Venerable Company of Pastors of Geneva," to formulate arguments in favor of armed uprising. Beza, who had repeatedly served as chaplain to Huguenot forces in France, completed his work in June or July 1573 and first distributed it with a title page that made it appear to be the Magdeburg Confession. The title read: *Of the Right of the Magistrates Over Their Subjects. A very necessary treatise in these times to advise the magistrates as well as their subjects of their duties: published by those of Magdeburg in the year 1550 and now revised and augmented by several reasons and examples.* The purpose of this cover was to bypass Geneva's municipal authorities, who feared reprisals from the king of France, according to Robert M. Kingdon.[129]

---

129 Robert M. Kingdon, introduction to Théodore de Bèze, *Du Droit des Magistrats* (Geneva: Droz, 1970), xxxi.

Beza had already shown great interest in the Magdeburgers. In his treatise *De haereticis a civili magistratu puniendis* (1554), he favorably mentioned their defiant attitude.[130] To be sure, *Du Droit des Magistrats* is anything but a copy of the Magdeburg Confession. Kingdon writes: "It is longer and more elaborate; its examples stem from different sources, and finally the reasons on which he bases the treatise, are markedly different."[131]

But the key phrase in Beza's treatise has a distinctly Magdeburg flavor. Chapter 10 carries a title that reads like a summary of the fourth degree of injustice[132] as described by the *Gnesio*-Lutherans: "*Si estant persecuté pour la religion, on se peut defendre par armes en bonne conscience*" ("If one is persecuted because of one's religion, one may in good conscience defend oneself with arms").[133]

Bonhoeffer's Bow to Flacius

Documentary evidence suggests that, in their resistance against Hitler, Bonhoeffer and his circle invoked Flacius. It is not by accident that a scholarly work about Flacius was published in Germany in 1940 at the beginning of World War II. Its author was Hans-Christoph von Hase, Bonhoeffer's cousin and close confidant.

As these two theologians maintained a constant exchange of manuscripts, it can be assumed that Bonhoeffer was familiar with von Hase's text and may even have influenced it because earlier writings by Bonhoeffer draw the analogy between events in his own and Flacius's times. The very publication of von Hase's book was an act of defiance. Opponents of totalitarian regimes often resort to history when they wish to make a point concerning a contemporary situation they could not tackle otherwise. That this was clearly the case with von Hase's text can be discerned from his preface. He wrote:

> The confusion in the evangelical camp was great. However, as a true pupil of Luther's there surfaced Matthias Flacius, who with unbending courage defended the freedom of the Lutheran faith against all papal might and who coined the term

---

130 Bèze, *Du Droit des Magistrats*, 69.

131 Kingdon, *Du Droit des Magistrats*, xiii.

132 Bèze, *Du Droit des Magistrats*, 69.

133 Bèze, *Du Droit des Magistrats*, 63.

casus confessionis to describe the situation. . . . Let us in our time prove, as did the brave Magdeburgers in their day, "that there are still the old and steady German hearts and minds who love God's word, their fatherland and their freedom."[134]

The historical situation described by the author was that of the Augsburg Interim of 1548, which was imposed on the German Protestants by Emperor Charles V. It established a truce between the Roman Catholic and Lutheran parties. Philip Melanchthon and his group of Wittenberg theologians accepted "out of fear," as they later admitted.[135] They gave in to some of the emperor's conditions, such as the wearing of vestments and a return to Catholic liturgical practices in Protestant services. The Wittenbergers bowed to these conditions, calling them *adiaphora*, "dogmatically indifferent."

Obviously with the sorry performance of church leaders in Hitler's Germany in mind, von Hase wrote:

> With one glance Flacius recognized that it was lack of faith that ailed Wittenberg's resistance. All those secret negotiations, the silence, and the yielding made it clear to him that one was no longer able to walk in Luther's ways. Flacius said, he (Luther) had risen from the safe nave of his church; his eyes fixed on the word alone, he rushed with a joyous face across the waves to Christ. He arrived at his goal. But now the others are scorning his merry kind of a sea voyage—and are beginning to sink.[136]

Von Hase left his fellow churchmen in no doubt as to how un-Lutheran their own way of dealing with such adversity was in his eyes. He quotes Flacius's statement: "What has pressed Peter into the sea, and what drowns us in our time in different ways . . . is that he did not want, and we do not want, to look in our faith to Christ alone, but gape with human wisdom all around us, to the wind, the sea, and the waves. That is the beautiful wisdom of the old Adam which angered Dr. Luther so."[137]

---

134 Hans-Christoph von Hase, *Die Gestalt der Kirche Luthers: Der Casus Confessionis im Kampf des Matthias Flacius gegen das Interim von 1548* (Göttingen: Vandenhoeck & Ruprecht, 1940), 4.

135 Hase, *Die Gestalt der Kirche Luthers*, 23. In quoting these words from a sixteenth-century theological brief, von Hase subtly alludes to the lack of courage displayed by their twentieth-century successors.

136 Hase, *Die Gestalt der Kirche Luthers*, 38

137 Hase, *Die Gestalt der Kirche Luthers*, 39.

The Wittenbergers' expression, *adiaphora*, was used in 1933 by the German Christians, the pro-Nazi wing of the German church, in reference to the Aryan Clause stipulating that pastors of Jewish descent must be removed from the ministry.[138] It affected an insignificant number of pastors, namely 29 of the 18,000 evangelical clergymen in Germany.[139] Yet Bonhoeffer, who had opposed anti-Semitism in church and society prior to Hitler's takeover, realized that ultimately not only a handful of ministers but all non-Aryan congregants were going to be barred from the church by this law.[140] On September 6, 1933, he sent the following telegram to the secretary-general of the World Council of Churches in Geneva: ". . . only Teutonic Christians admitted to National Synod, Aryan paragraph now in action, please work out memorandum against this and inform the press."[141]

To Bonhoeffer a "purely German" church from which members would be excluded on biological grounds was a theological absurdity.[142] In April 1933, only days after the Nazis had ordered a boycott of Jewish shops[143] and passed a law eliminating non-Aryans from the civil service, he said in a lecture,

> It is the duty of Christian proclamation to say: here, where Jew and German stand together under God's word, is the Church, here it is proven whether or not the Church is still Church. Nobody who feels unable to live in an ecclesial community with Christians of Jewish origin can be prevented from leaving that . . . community. But it has to be made clear to him with extreme seriousness that he is thus abandoning the place on which the Church of Christ stands.[144]

Bonhoeffer left no doubt that he based his convictions on Luther's own theology. He preceded his lecture with the reformer's statement of

138 Dietrich Bonhoeffer, *Gesammelte Schriften* (Munich: Chr. Kaiser, 1959), 2:68.
139 Wolfgang Gerlach, *Als die Zeugen schwiegen* (Berlin: Institut Kirche und Judentum, 1987), 61.
140 Gerlach, *Als die Zeugen schwiegen*, 11.
141 Bonhoeffer, *Gesammelte Schriften*, 2:70.
142 Bethge, *Bonhoeffer*, 206.
143 Anti-Semitism was anathema to the entire Bonhoeffer family. On April 1, 1933, Dietrich's 91-year-old grandmother, Julie Bonhoeffer, walked through the SA cordon in Berlin that was imposing a boycott of Jewish shops. See Bethge, *Bonhoeffer*, 3.
144 Bonhoeffer, *Gesammelte Schriften*, 2:53.

1523: "If the apostles, who were also Jews, had treated us the way we gentiles are treating the Jews, no gentile would have become a Christian." And Bonhoeffer ended with a commentary by Luther on Psalm 110:3: "As to who are the people of God and the Church of Christ no other rule or test applies but this one: [they are] a little band who accept God's word, teach it with purity and confess it against those who persecute it."[145]

Moreover, a document has survived proving beyond any doubt that Bonhoeffer's views on this subject were clearly and consciously *Gnesio*-Lutheran. This document is his personal copy of the Formula of Concord, which was strongly influenced by the Flacian circle, especially Article X of the Solid Declaration, which deals with "The Ecclesiastical Rites That Are Called *Adiaphora* or Things Indifferent." In this article, Bonhoeffer underlined the last words "Disagreement on fasting should not destroy agreement in faith." In the margins he wrote, *"DC's Judenpolitik ist Irrlehre!"* ("The German Christians' policy on the Jews is heresy").[146]

And in exactly the same way Matthias Flacius had published leaflets declaring that where the Confessions were concerned there could be no such thing as an *adiaphoron*, Bonhoeffer printed a leaflet stating: "The German Christians say: The Aryan clause is an *adiaphoron* which doesn't concern the confessions of the Church. We answer: . . . The substance of the Church and of the ministry, e.g. the Confession, is under attack."[147]

He thus established, like Flacius in the sixteenth century, a *casus confessionis* in which nothing can be considered indifferent and Christians are called upon to resist authority. And this was exactly what Bonhoeffer did when he joined the *Abwehr*, Germany's military intelligence service, which was one of the most powerful groups opposing Hitler. Bonhoeffer's involvement in the *Abwehr's* efforts to smuggle Jews out of the country ultimately led to his arrest and execution.

---

145 Bonhoeffer, *Gesammelte Schriften*, 2:53.

146 This document is in Eberhard Bethge's possession. On April 2, 1985, he sent a photocopy to Robert Bertram in St. Louis, Mo. Professor Bertram passed it on to me.

147 Bonhoeffer, *Gesammelte Schriften*, 2:68.

When the National Socialist state imposed itself on the Lutheran church government, a major crisis ensued within the confessing wing of that church. Lutheran theologians, even in the Confessing Church, claimed that the opposition to such state interference proved excessive "reformed" influence in the Confessing Church—from the Lutheran perspective such opposition was false doctrine.

Arguing from a clearly *Gnesio*-Lutheran perspective, and with direct reference to Flacius, Bonhoeffer stated that this kind of talk rendered "genuine [*sic*] Lutheranism a disservice."[148] In a brief distributed by the Council of Brethren of the Confessing Synod of Pomerania, Bonhoeffer wrote: "It is Lutheran as well as reformed doctrine that (church) orders must be tied to the confessions and that *in statu confessionis* not a single step may be yielded where such orders are concerned."[149]

Bonhoeffer elaborated:

> It is Lutheran doctrine that all offices and orders of the Church must be oriented solely on the Church's confession. Their conformity with the confession decides their ecclesial legality. Confession and order cannot be separated. It is Lutheran doctrine that the congregation is free to determine its order of service in the proclamation (of the word), but *in statu confessionis*, e.g. when the Church is under external attack, the orders of the Church are part of its confessional package from which nothing must be yielded.... Thus, what is *adiaphoron* inside the Church, is not *adiaphoron* in relation to the outside but belongs to the confession. *In statu confessionis* the Church's confession and order are one.[150]

This is unadulterated Flacian diction. But Bonhoeffer went even further in his *Gnesio*-Lutheran approach to the question of church order. Referring to the relevant sections in the Solid Declaration, which he underlined in his own copy of the Formula of Concord, Bonhoeffer wrote: "It is indicative that here the Lutheran, Flacius, stresses 'popular missionary' point of view: The poor people look mainly at the ceremonies, for those fill the eyes, but doctrine cannot be seen.... The peo-

---

148 Bonhoeffer, *Gesammelte Schriften*, 2:264.

149 Bonhoeffer, *Gesammelte Schriften*, 2:275.

150 Bonhoeffer, *Gesammelte Schriften*, 2:270.

ple recognize the inroad of false doctrine by the surrender of the order!"[151]

Without mentioning the issue of church order directly, Bonhoeffer's cousin Hans-Christoph von Hase gave his fellow German ministers some deft Flacian rhetoric to ponder in their predicament: "The greatest fool is he who believes that one can avoid war and destruction by pacifying godless people who are but dirt and feces. This angers God, the almighty and stern judge."[152]

The Danish expert on Dietrich Bonhoeffer, Jørgen Glenthøj, attributes Bonhoeffer's rejection of any kind of compromise with the Nazis to his view that, by Luther's standards, Hitler was the Antichrist.[153] In the hymn "A Mighty Fortress Is Our God," Luther defined the Antichrist as the one who takes "*den Leib, Gut, Ehr, Kind und Weib*" ("life, goods, fame, child, and wife").[154]

It was in this spirit that Bonhoeffer accepted the unusual roles as an *Abwehr* agent and a co-conspirator against Hitler. It was in this spirit, too, that he told the Secretary-General of the Provisional Council of Churches, W. A. Visser't Hooft, "I pray for the defeat of my own country, for I think that this is the only possibility of paying for all the suffering that my country has caused in the world."[155] And it was in this spirit that he went to Norway in 1942 ostensibly as a military intelligence agent but in reality to strengthen the resolve of the Norwegian Lutherans in their resistance against Prime Minister Quisling, Hitler's stooge.

When Bishop Berggrav was arrested, German occupation officers belonging to the Lutheran Michael fraternity, a high-church group, as well as to the secret Kreisau Circle opposing the Nazis, had alerted

---

151 Bonhoeffer, *Gesammelte Schriften*, 2:271.

152 Hase, *Die Gestalt der Kirche Luthers*, 39.

153 Jørgen Glenthøj, "Die Eideskrise in der Bekennenden Kirche 1938 und Dietrich Bonhoeffer," *Zeitschrift für Kirchengeschichte* 96:4 (1985): 390. During his secret meeting with Bishop Bell of Chichester in the summer of 1940 in Stockholm, Bonhoeffer said, "If we claim to be Christians, there is no room for expediency. Hitler is the Anti-Christ. Therefore we must go on with our work and eliminate him whether he be successful or not" (Bethge, *Bonhoeffer*, 627).

154 Body, wealth, honor, child, and wife.

155 Bethge, *Bonhoeffer*, 648.

friends in *Abwehr* headquarters in Berlin. The *Abwehr* sent two emissaries to Oslo. One of them was Bonhoeffer. Bethge explains:

> Officially, they were sent to examine the church struggle as a danger to the German occupying troops; secretly, the intention was to advise them not to deviate one step from the way that they had taken. . . . Of course, Bonhoeffer was keenly interested in the Norwegian church struggle, because he saw here suddenly accomplished what he himself had proposed, though without response, in 1933—pastors' strike, laying down of office, and church resignations. The advice that he gave was authoritative; he warned the Norwegians from his own experiences not to give way now.[156]

As Gordon Rupp reminds us, the Norwegian Lutherans explicitly paid tribute to the German church struggle as they resisted the Quisling regime. And when their clergy resigned *en masse* in a heroic act of protest, they appealed to the man whom Münzer, Engels, Troeltsch, Inge, Wiener, Temple, Mann, and Shirer presumed to be a lackey of princes:

> Like Luther, we tried to be loyal to the authorities so far as the Word and the commandments permitted. As it came to Luther, so to us has come the moment when we must be loyal to our beliefs and assert the justice of the Church against the injustice of the state. Forms of government may change, but the Church knows—as did the Father of the Church—that against that which Luther calls tyranny stands God Himself in His word and in the strength of His Spirit. Woe to us if we did not obey God rather than man.[157]

To sum up, elements of an immensely complex theology were ripped out of context to forge a stereotype that is haunting Lutheranism to this day. The cliché-mongers ignored some of the key aspects of Luther's doctrine on the two realms: that he was neither a politician nor a sociologist or ethicist, but a theologian giving advice entirely based on the scriptural idea of a secular order ordained by God; that he unceasingly stressed the rule of reason in the secular realm; that his doctrine was revolutionary in that it freed Christians from religious bounds "for

---

156 Bethge, *Bonhoeffer*, 658.
157 Cf. Rupp, *Luther*, 68.

service in a world that is always shrouded in political and ethical ambiguity" (Lindberg); that far from being a quietist he implored Christians to speak up against governmental injustice; that unlike the church of Rome or Protestant utopians, he condemned governmental intolerance of heretics, schismatics, and non-Christians; and finally, that the Lutheran church knows no infallible Luther. Luther never declared himself infallible—quite the contrary. On the issue of armed resistance against tyranny, he quite unabashedly reversed himself.

As a result, when faced with a Hitler or a Stalin, a Lutheran has two Luthers to appeal to. Neither countenances insurrection and mob rule. But the younger Luther teaches that only passive and verbal resistance is permissible. The older Luther says that under certain circumstances the Christian must take up arms against an evil ruler—never to fight for his own cause, but in defense of his faith and his family.

Bonhoeffer eventually followed the older Luther. So did Eugen Gerstenmaier, another Lutheran pastor in the resistance who later became the speaker of West Germany's lower House of Parliament. And Father Alfred Delp, a Jesuit priest, agreed with both of them that Hitler had to be physically eliminated.[158] In the next chapter, we shall see how Dr. Carl Goerdeler, the civilian head of the resistance, acted in a way the younger Luther would have approved.[159]

In either case, Luther is shown to be a teacher of great moral courage and fortitude.

---

158 Cf. Hoffmann, *History of the German Resistance*, 371–72.

159 Although they differed over the means of Hitler's removal, Bonhoeffer was fond of Goerdeler, whose overwhelming optimism he admired. According to Bethge, Bonhoeffer had Goerdeler in mind when he put one of his most famous insights to paper: "The essence of optimism is not its view of the present, but the fact that it is the inspiration of life and hope when others give in; it enables a man to hold his head high when everything seems to be going wrong; it gives him strength to sustain reverses and yet to claim the future for himself instead of abandoning it to the opponent. . . . [T]he optimism that it will for the future should never be despised, even if it is proved wrong a hundred times" (Bonhoeffer, *Letters and Papers from Prison*, 15). Bethge adds that Bonhoeffer felt akin to Goerdeler in that respect; see Bethge, *Bonhoeffer*, 638.

Chapter Four

MARTIN LUTHER VINDICATED
(I): CARL GOERDELER

Zwingli thought that authority hostile to God should be top-
pled. This has heavily influenced Calvinism. Hence: Christian
tyrannicide, Christian revolution, Christian civil war! The
result has always been disappointing.[1] Active disobedience and
rebellion have no place in Luther's doctrine of the two realms,
even if the government is tyrannical and hostile to the Gospel.
He who thinks that he can justify a "Christian" right to revolution should in all fairness not appeal to Luther.[2]

When Franz Lau wrote the above shortly after World War II, presumably he had the younger Martin Luther in mind. Lau more or less
sums up the attitude to resistance that was internalized by some of the
leading Lutheran laymen in the German opposition during the Hitler
years. For example, Helmuth Count Moltke,[3] Hans-Bernd von

---

1   As a former Vietnam War correspondent, I feel that the disastrous consequences
    of the 1963 murder of President Ngo Dinh Diem of South Vietnam support Lau's
    argument rather powerfully.

2   Franz Lau, *Luthers Lehre von den beiden Reichen* (Berlin: Evangelische
    Verlagsanstalt, 1952), 86.

3   In his final statement before the Nazi "People's Court," Moltke defiantly recited
    the fourth stanza of Luther's "A Mighty Fortress Is Our God": "Were they to take
    our house / Goods, honor, child or spouse / Though life be wretched away / They

Haeften,[4] and particularly Carl Goerdeler all shared a similar view.[5] Goerdeler, the former mayor of Leipzig, was the civilian head of the bourgeois-military opposition. His military partners were Colonel-General Ludwig Beck, the army chief of staff, and Beck's successor, Colonel-General Franz Halder. Goerdeler was one of the first to warn the world of the evils of National Socialism, but he was not listened to. He was slated to become German chancellor, had plans to overthrow Hitler succeeded. Instead, Goerdeler was hanged on February 2, 1945. A lawyer by training, Goerdeler was an eminently practical man who, according to his daughter Marianne Meyer-Krahmer, "probably never once in his life stopped to think: How would Luther have wanted me to act in this or that particular instance?"[6] In this respect, he certainly differed from the theologian Dietrich Bonhoeffer. Meyer-Krahmer commented, "Theologians have Luther in their heads; my father had Luther in his blood."[7] But this makes Goerdeler all the more interesting for our

---

cannot win the day / The Kingdom's ours forever!" (American Committee to Aid Survivors of the German Resistance, "Our Allies inside Germany." Karl Adler Collection, Leo Baeck Institute, NY).

4 Diplomat von Haeften objected to tyrannicide primarily on religious grounds and talked his brother, Werner, out of shooting Hitler, saying, "Gangster methods should not be used even against gangsters" (Peter Hoffmann, *The History of the German Resistance, 1933–1945* [Cambridge: MIT Press, 1977], 330).

5 I should like to make it absolutely clear that it is neither my place nor indeed the intention of this study to take sides in an agonized dispute over whether or not it would have been morally and theologically justifiable to assassinate Hitler. The purpose of this study is to expose the cliché that Luther turned his followers into a subspecies of cowardly quietists. This charge was disproved in World War II by the comportment of courageous Lutherans on both sides of the tyrannicide argument. To some, Goerdeler's position that tyrannicide violates God's will seems to be supported by the astonishing fact that no assassination attempt against the
• world's bloodthirstiest rulers of the twentieth century succeeded. Hitler survived at least forty such attempts before taking his own life. Vladimir Ilyich Lenin, Joseph Stalin, Mao Zedong, Pol Pot, Jean-Bédel Bokassa, and Idi Amin all died peacefully in their own beds. Had it not been for the U.S.-led invasion of Iraq, Saddam Hussein would presumably still be torturing and slaughtering his subjects and others by the tens of thousands, effectively evading potential assassins by sleeping in a different palace every night.

6 Interview with the author, April 1989.

7 Interview with the author, April 1989.

study to investigate a cliché about internalized, not academically acquired, Lutheran attitudes.

Carl Goerdeler (1884–1945) should be seen as an archetype of a Prussian patrician. He was well-educated, had high moral standards, was an advocate of economic liberalism, but was also politically conservative. He embodied a class that was in the vanguard of the German resistance against National Socialism—the traditional elite made up of high-ranking civil servants, landowners, clergymen, and "old school" military officers. Their ideas, writes Klemens von Klemperer, were mainly conservative and rooted in Germany's imperial past:[8] "[T]he affirmation of the created order was an essential mark of European conservativism, but it must be remembered that this is to be understood as order *created by God*. Thus conservativism was the rediscovery of the religious dimension and its translation into the political realm."[9]

The eminently Lutheran desire to preserve and, later, to restore order guided Goerdeler's actions throughout his life. When he was deputy mayor of Königsberg and then mayor of Leipzig, his scrupulous insistence on order in public finances earned him the reputation of being one of the most outstanding municipal officials in Europe. His sense of order made him an early opponent of National Socialism. In very Lutheran terms, Goerdeler called the anti-Semitic outrages of the Hitler regime an "unbearable offense to civilization and a manifestation of mob rule." Driven by his own motto, *omnia restaurare in Christo*,

---

8 Klemens von Klemperer, "Der deutsche Widerstand gegen den National-sozialismus im Lichte der konservativen Tradition," in *Demokratie und Diktatur, Geist und Gestalt politischer Herrschaft in Deutschland und Europa*, ed. Funke et al. (Bonn: Bundeszentrale für Politische Bildung, 1987), 266. These conservatives were allied with trade unionists and Social Democrats, Wilhelm Leuschner, for example. But they, too, were conservatives in the sense that their values were traditional, especially with regard to law and order.

9 Von Klemperer, "Der deutsche Widerstand," 267 (*emphasis added*). Von Klemperer does not neglect to mention the other side of the story, though: "National Socialism came to power with the help of the German conservative social and . . . political groupings. With the exception of a few sensible people, the German elite, the grande bourgeoisie as well as the nobility, the 'establishments,' the 'national parties,' and assorted neo-conservative circles succumbed to the temptation of National Socialism in that they expected from [that movement] a national renaissance and a reliable bulwark against Bolshevism" (Von Klemperer, "Der deutsche Widerstand," 268).

Goerdeler strove to topple Hitler in an "orderly fashion," that is, not by way of rebellion but by having the dictator arrested in a military coup d'etat and tried before a court of law. It was because of his sense of order that Goerdeler opposed attempts to assassinate Hitler. His reasons were twofold, his daughter Marianne Meyer-Krahmer, explained: "He was loath to violate the Fifth Commandment, 'Thou shalt not kill,' but even more important, he feared that an assassination would create among the German public a 'stab in the back myth' and lead to civil war and therefore chaos. My father thought that this would be prevented if Hitler's crimes were brought to the attention of the public in an orderly trial."[10]

Most significant, though, Goerdeler and his partners followed the principle: Whatever you do, consider the consequences of your action. This becomes clear as we consider their plans for the removal of Hitler at the height of the Sudeten crisis in 1938. Gerhard Ritter notes: "It is indicative of the profoundly unrevolutionary character of the bourgeois-military opposition movement in Germany that at that point none of its leaders planned a murderous act. Halder thought of overwhelming and arresting the tyrant in a military coup d'état, and to unmask him before the German people as a wanton adventurer."[11]

Ritter goes on to say that by Halder's standards, which were also Goerdeler's, military disobedience is only permissible where an obvious criminal gives the orders. This is, of course, exactly what Luther said, as we have seen in the last chapter. Ritter pursues this notion, saying: "Only when Hitler stands exposed before the entire world as such [a criminal] would there be any hope of a cooling down and possibly a sudden reversal of the general . . . enthusiasm for Hitler. The leaders of the *Wehrmacht* . . . should not be seen as traitors and saboteurs by the nation, but rather as its saviors."[12]

This represented precisely Goerdeler's way of thinking, says Marianne Meyer-Krahmer:

It is simply not enough just to act; one must prepare for the

---

10 Interview with the author, April 1989. Like many Christian laymen of his period, Goerdeler erred in his interpretation of the Fifth Commandment. Its original Hebrew text says, "Thou shalt not murder," using an entirely different verb.

11 Gerhard Ritter, *Carl Goerdeler und die deutsche Widerstandsbewegung* (Stuttgart: Deutsche Verlags-Anstalt, 1956), 192.

12 Ritter, *Goerdeler*, 192.

next step and the next and the next. This idea, which after all amounts to none other than responsible action, occupied at least 50 percent of my father's thoughts. That is why he drew up cabinet lists and wrote a detailed program for a government led by himself in the event of Hitler's overthrow. That is why he asked Leo Baeck, the Jewish leader, to write a plan for the role and status of Jews in a post-Nazi Germany. That is why even on death row he developed a program for the reconstruction of the German cities destroyed by air raids. And that is why in the darkest hour of Europe he drafted a blueprint for a European Economic Union that included a European foreign ministry, a European economics ministry, and even a European army.[13]

I shall return to some of these plans later. Here, I would like to make two points. First, Goerdeler's insistence on thinking and planning beyond a coup against Hitler squared fully with Walter Künneth's and Eivind Berggrav's theological ideas on this subject, ideas I cited in the last chapter. Second, by coolly trying to calculate the outcome of his actions and making the proper arrangements, Goerdeler allowed himself to be guided not just by emotions, however commendable, but by what Luther called the "empress" of the secular realm—by reason.

Gerhard Ritter sees in Goerdeler's "high degree of faith in the . . . power of reason, chiefly moral reason," a strong affinity to Baron Karl vom und zum Stein, the celebrated Prussian statesman whom Goerdeler, as well as most other prominent members of the resistance, endeavored to emulate.[14] Meyer-Krahmer, who under her father's influence made vom Stein the subject of her doctoral dissertation, draws one significant parallel between Goerdeler and the baron. Both bemoaned the Germans becoming "increasingly evil, cringing, and ignoble under the rule of despots."[15] Baron vom Stein (1757–1831) reformed the

---

13 Interview with the author, March 1992.

14 Ritter, *Goerdeler*, 48.

15 Marianne Goerdeler, *Die Reichsidee in den Bundesplänen 1813/15 und ihr geistiger Hintergrund* (Weida: Aderholt, 1943), 35. In her thesis, Marianne Meyer-Krahmer, nee Goerdeler, cites vom Stein's August 1813 memorandum. Vom Stein was referring to the Germans' behavior under Napoleonic rule. It was vom Stein who, with his reform programs, prepared Prussia's liberation from the Bonapartist yoke. During Napoleon's occupation of Prussia, vom Stein was outlawed and lived in exile, first in Russia and then in Austria.

Prussian administration, giving autonomy to municipalities and liberating the rural population from serfdom. It was vom Stein who surmounted the Enlightenment's idea of the state, which was absolutist, and emphasized the responsibility of the individual citizen. Furthermore, by granting freedom to the citizens and protecting their lives and property from the arbitrariness of the princes, vom Stein strengthened their attachment to the state. And this, according to Erich Foerster, amounts in its ethical dimension to a renewal of the Lutheran concept of state.[16] It is a concept that stressed the accountability of the ruler as well as the "lesser magistrates" such as the mayor, the councilman, and even the head of the family. According to Franz Schnabel: "The character of that Prussian period [of reform] was shaped by devout Protestants. . . . The crucial point was that the leader of the reformers [vom Stein] was a devout Christian who never saw his task in any other way than in the spirit of Christianity: In Baron vom Stein, more than in any other figure in German history, the Evangelical-Lutheran statesman became reality."[17]

In evaluating Goerdeler's Lutheranism, we must bear in mind, though, that he was very much a Lutheran of the nineteenth-century liberal mold, according to his daughter. He saw the existence of God as a "given," she says. Ritter relates: "All his life Goerdeler considered himself a convinced Christian." And under the impression of Nazi godlessness Goerdeler's religious fervor increased. He regularly attended church with his family, said prayers at mealtimes, and kept the Bible by his bedside and read it diligently.[18] But, writes Ritter, "[Goerdeler's Christianity] was essentially only the belief in Christ's commandment to love your neighbor. [It was] . . . an ethic of the noblest kind."[19]

Thus Goerdeler's Christology was as inadequate as Troeltsch's, and this was to cause him horrible theodicy problems as he awaited his execution. In his nineteenth-century understanding of the Christian faith,

---

16 Erich Foerster, *Die Entstehung der Preussischen Landeskirche unter der Regierung König Friedrich Wilhelms des Dritten* (Tübingen: J. C. B. Mohr, 1905), 126.

17 Franz Schnabel, *Deutsche Geschichte im 19. Jahrhundert* (Freiburg: Herder, 1937), 4:309.

18 The same was true for most members of the German resistance.

19 Ritter, *Goerdeler*, 444.

there was no room for Luther's doctrine of the hidden God whose secret the human mind is not capable of deciphering, there was no place for Paul's harsh admonition, "Who are you, man, that you presume to judge God?" (See Romans 9:20.) Ritter, a fellow prisoner in the waning weeks of World War II, gives a moving account of Goerdeler's torpor:

> The prisoner [Goerdeler] struggles with Augustine's statement that even the sinner will be blessed. But he can neither grasp it nor approve of this, for it violates reason. He sees only three possibilities: Either God is not good, and human beings don't matter to him, or there is no God, or there is a just God who himself keeps the laws he has given nature and humanity but leaves it to us to handle them as we see fit. . . . Maybe he punishes the whole German people, even innocent children, for having allowed the Jews to be exterminated without lifting a finger. But would that be a loving, merciful God—or simply a philosophical power which wants to force us to moral progress but walks over piles of corpses . . . in the process.[20]

In his farewell letter to his family, Goerdeler exclaims:

> No, reason cannot find a way out. [Reason] must shout at God the words of the Psalmist: Stop! Don't you see that these sufferings of the innocent can no longer be comprehended? That they inevitably will result in dull submission, rebellious indignation, and taunting induration? That hard punishment will set man back in his efforts to reach out to you? You have forbidden [man] to kill . . . and therefore seen to it that the assassination [attempt against Hitler] failed; but in doing so you have sentenced millions of innocent people to death. . . . And yet I seek through Christ the merciful God. I have not found him. O Christ, where is truth, where is comfort?[21]

It was Goerdeler's real tragedy that, because of his roots in nineteenth-century Protestant liberalism, he lacked the theological tools to put this sense of dereliction into its proper Christian context. As William P. Mahedy writes:

---

20 Ritter, *Goerdeler*, 442. What made matters worse was the lack of pastoral care. No chaplain was allowed to see Goerdeler, relates Ritter.

21 Ritter, *Goerdeler*, 443.

No Christian image is more subversive or troublesome than the cross. When Jesus confronted evil, He lost. When he faced sin, it overcame Him. Though He desired to be spared suffering, He was not. Like all of us, He protested the approach of death, but even He yielded before it. . . . The worst of it is that Jesus, too, underwent not just the physical agony of crucifixion but spiritual anguish as well. The primordial "dark night" experience was His. When death approached, Jesus cried out, making his own the words of the psalmist, "My God, my God, why have you forsaken me?" (Mark 15:34).[22]

But as we know from Max Weber, what we internalize is not doctrine but the ethos and attitude emanating from it.[23] It is in this sense, then, that Goerdeler must be seen as a Lutheran *par excellence*. In his case, this Lutheran ethos manifested itself in a multitude of ways: (1) in his love of good order and abhorrence of mob rule; (2) in his scorn for governmental persecution of Jews; (3) in his rejection of wars of aggression; (4) in his fearless verbal attacks on the regime's evil nature; and (5) in his willingness to risk his life defying that tyranny, albeit nonviolently.

One of the most cherished products of this internalized Lutheran ethos has been the tradition of integrity in Prussia's civil service, an integrity National Socialism and subsequently Communism set out to destroy. Goerdeler pointed out: "The Prussian public servant has been trained to obey his superior; but he was also obligated to express his opinion undauntedly in front of that superior. Officials daring to do that today . . . have to be sought with a torch. And this undermines the public administration."[24]

Meyer-Krahmer recalls how distressed her father was over the spinelessness of senior public officials, such as the presiding judge and other justices of the German Supreme Court (*Reichsgericht*), which was based in Leipzig:

My father used to say that these men possess an *Informationsvorsprung*, a head start on information, which should have

---

22 William P. Mahedy, *Out of the Night* (New York: Ballentine, 1986), 165.

23 See Max Weber, *Gesammelte Aufsätze zur Religionssoziologie* (Tübingen: J. C. B. Mohr, 1920), 1:12ff.

24 See Marianne Meyer-Krahmer, *Carl Goerdeler und sein Weg in den Widerstand* (Freiburg: Herder, 1989), 121.

compelled them to denounce the criminal character of the National Socialist regime. He considered their opportunism a disgusting violation of the German civil service tradition to resist evil ordinances. He deemed it the duty of senior officials to see to it that the state does not fall into the hands of gangsters.[25]

Fred Grubel, the head of the Leo Baeck Institute and former secretary of Leipzig's Jewish congregation, recalls how the Prussian mayor of Leipzig, a Saxon metropolis, displayed that kind of moral courage at a time when Hitler's takeover of Germany was imminent, though not carried out: "In the summer of 1932 we traveled together by train to Berlin. . . . To our great astonishment he explained in front of fellow-passengers—total strangers—that Germany could only be saved if the Reich government dissolved the N.S.D.A.P.[26] and locked up Hitler and his entire *entourage*. We were amazed to hear the mayor, who was politically on the right, express such a radical opinion in public."[27]

In letters to Meyer-Krahmer, Jewish ex-citizens of Leipzig told her of her father's show of moral courage immediately after the Nazis had come to power. Hermann Scharfir wrote: "In early 1933 the S.A.[28] arrested me and brought me to the *Volkszeitung*,[29] which had been occupied by an S.A. troop from Hamburg. On the third day mayor Dr. Goerdeler showed up with four policemen and got us out . . . . Dr. Goerdeler has saved my life."[30] And Henry Rosedale reported, "[When the Nazis staged a boycott of Jewish shops] your father donned a black suit or even a morning coat . . . and a top hat and came to the Brühl[31] to visit several Jewish fur shops in order to express his abhorrence."[32]

Goerdeler's active resistance to the Hitler dictatorship began in November 1936 when, during his absence, the Nazis removed the

---

25 Interview with the author, April 1989.

26 Acronym for *Nationalsozialistische Deutsche Arbeiter-Partei* or National Socialist German Workers' Party (the Nazi Party).

27 See Meyer-Krahmer, *Goerdeler*, 69.

28 Storm troopers, or brown shirts.

29 Leipzig's Social Democratic daily newspaper.

30 Meyer-Krahmer, *Goerdeler*, 73.

31 A Leipzig street, which was the world's traditional fur center.

32 Meyer-Krahmer, *Goerdeler*, 73.

Mendelssohn monument that stood in front of the *Gewandhaus,* Leipzig's famed concert hall. Leipzig loved Felix Mendelssohn-Bartholdy, and well it should, for it owed much to him. As *Gewandhaus* conductor, the Jewish-born composer literally rediscovered Johann Sebastian Bach, who had been virtually forgotten, even in Leipzig where he had lived and worked for twenty-seven years. Moreover, in 1847 Mendelssohn started the Leipzig Conservatory, which is still one of the world's finest. The Nazis destroyed the monument while Goerdeler was on an official visit to Finland and Sweden. He immediately resigned in protest. Later, he was to write in his death cell: "I . . . was not prepared to assume the responsibility for this outrage against civilization. . . . To deny Mendelssohn would have been cowardly and ridiculous. . . . My resignation was a protest before the entire world. And this is exactly how it was understood [by the whole world]."[33]

After his resignation, Goerdeler was immediately financed by Stuttgart industrialist Robert Bosch,[34] a practicing Lutheran and an ardent democrat who spent vast sums of money for anti-Nazi causes. He funded the emigration of Jews persecuted by the regime, supported theology students of the anti-Nazi Confessing Church, and aided the pan-European movement of Count Coudenhove-Calergi. Through his

---

33 See Meyer-Krahmer, *Goerdeler,* 93. On the same page, Goerdeler's daughter cites journalist Fritz Barsch's description of how the Leipzig public reacted to this step: "When Goerdeler shortly after his resignation entered the *Gewandhaus* to attend one of its [regular] Thursday concerts, the enthusiasm and applause of Leipzig's citizenry [for him] was boundless. This was one of the most embarrassing acts for Leipzig's National Socialists."

34 Bosch's company manufactured electrical equipment for automobiles, such as spark plugs and ignition systems. It invented the fuel injection pump and is today probably the world's most respected manufacturer of automotive electronics. In our interview in May 1989, Marianne Meyer-Krahmer raised an interesting point pertaining to the principal subject of this study, which is cliché thinking. She said that Bosch's story defies the familiar cliché that all German industrialists and capitalists were Nazi collaborators. In truth, Bosch is one of the unsung heroes of the German resistance. That his important role is almost unknown in Germany and abroad must again be attributed to cliché thinking. Postwar historians adhering to the left-wing orthodoxy at many universities had a hard time coming to terms with the historical fact that the majority of the most powerful figures in the resistance were not men of the left, though the "group of counts" within the Kreisau Circle of anti-Nazi conspirators harbored "Christian social" utopian dreams. Bosch was an old-fashioned Swabian liberal.

company's representatives abroad, Bosch maintained foreign contacts for the German opposition. He sent Goerdeler on extended trips to the United States, Canada, France, and Britain to warn foreign leaders: "The world must expect every conceivable act of violence and every horror of human fate. This . . . will be all the more dreadful as National Socialism has masterfully managed to deceive, at times, eighty percent of the German people, and indeed the entire world."[35]

This was the central message of Goerdeler's political testament, which he deposited with Friedrich Krause, a Leipzig editor who had fled to New York, during a 1937 visit to the United States.[36] In repeating these words over and over again, Goerdeler pursued a threefold purpose, his daughter relates. His purpose was (1) to tell the world that there was another, dignified Germany whose honor he labored to defend; (2) to implore the world's leaders to stand up to Hitler; (3) to convince them that, contrary to the assumptions of many, Hitler was no bulwark against Bolshevism—quite the contrary:

> The blindness of some economic leaders will have a bitter price. What those who know Hitler's state of mind and moral character have predicted is coming to pass: Nazism will fade into Bolshevism; indeed, under German conditions it will be even more effective because all its cruelties are being shamelessly camouflaged by the old ideals of the German people: God, nation, freedom, socialism.[37]

---

35 Carl Goerdeler, "Das politische Testament," in *Goerdelers politisches Testament*, ed. Friedrich Krause (New York: Krause, 1945), 43.

36 Upon his return from this trip, Goerdeler voiced a complaint about the U.S. media that sounds familiar to modern ears. According to his daughter, he was "embittered over the inability of the American press to grasp the intensity of evil that had befallen his country. He felt that American newspapers treated events in Germany in stereotypical terms—as if traditional conservative forces were running the show."

37 Carl Goerdeler, "Zur Lage," unpublished (July 1939), 13. Manuscript in Marianne Meyer-Krahmer's possession. This document was probably written in Turkey and forwarded to the governments of Britain, France, the United States, and presumably other countries. Meyer-Krahmer believes that Goerdeler's equating National Socialism with Communism was at the root of the animosity postwar intellectuals harbored toward him. Until the demise of Communism, there prevailed on both sides of the Iron Curtain a myth that left-wingers monopolized what little bona fide anti-Nazi opposition there was.

Hitler was determined to destroy three enemies, Goerdeler informed his readers. These enemies were, first, the Jews, then the Christians, an assessment confirmed by Karla Poewe's research six decades after Goerdeler's death at the gallows.[38] Ultimately, though, Hitler intended to destroy capitalism, according to Goerdeler. He explained:

> Hitler's socialism . . . differs little or not at all from the wild dreams of the original, absolute Socialism. But Hitler knows that his brutal methods will not produce new values. He simply wants to destroy the old [values]. . . . The man who has enunciated the doctrine of the totality of the party . . . cannot tolerate another God besides him. . . . His furious acts of violence are mainly directed against religion. Judaism has . . . inflamed his hatred with its doctrine of the one God who affects man's entire life with his laws and commandments. Next [Hitler's] hatred will turn on the Christian religion.[39] Humility and charity render him rabid . . . the secret of life makes him wild [with anger]. To [Hitler] the notion that man as a child of God is directly connected to [God] is a frightening heresy. . . . To the extent that in his appalling lack of education he knows Christianity at all, Hitler puts himself in the place of Christ.[40]

The warning that Hitler was intent on destroying Judaism, Christianity, and capitalism was Goerdeler's *cantus firmus* in his meetings with the British industrialist Arthur Primrose Young, who maintained contact with him on behalf of Sir Robert Vansittart, the permanent

---

38 Karla Poewe, *New Religions and the Nazis* (New York: Routledge, 2006), 112.

39 One fiendish aspect of Hitler's anti-Christian thrust is often overlooked, but was constantly stressed by Goerdeler and his friends: National Socialism had an enormous power of temptation "because it preached the self-idolization of the nation," Ritter writes, adding, "Only genuine faith, or at least a moral-political conviction rooted in genuine religion could stand up to this pseudo-religion" (Ritter, *Goerdeler*, 16). These convictions rooted in the Christian faith motivated Goerdeler and his co-conspirators, Ritter argues. Thus what occurred in Germany in the 1930s was a conflict between "idolatrous utopianism" (Tillich) and a brave group of men and women. As we have seen in the last chapter, Luther's doctrine of the two realms was meant to de-idolize the state. This is worth remembering as we ponder the cliché linking Luther to Hitler.

40 Goerdeler, "Zur Lage," 10–13. Although this was written in 1939, it sums up what Goerdeler told foreign leaders during his peregrinations following his resignation from his position as Leipzig's mayor.

undersecretary in the British Foreign Office. Young, an acquaintance of Robert Bosch, first met Goerdeler in England in 1937. This is what he wrote about that first encounter:

> Goerdeler impressed all of us with his forceful, humorous and likeable personality; and his superb moral courage dominated the man. He left no doubts in our minds about the evil things that Hitler and his associates were doing and would continue to do with increasing speed if no check were applied. He . . . pleaded most earnestly for a *firm* policy in dealing with Hitler as being the only one to . . . retard his evil purposes.[41]

At Vansittart's behest, Young secretly met Goerdeler five more times in Germany, Switzerland, and Britain. He came to view Goerdeler as a "man of supreme spiritual qualities." Goerdeler, though unfamiliar with Luther's theology of the cross, sensed that the cross was waiting for him, as Young observed:

> [In Goerdeler's view] Hitler was . . . the incarnation of evil. Goerdeler felt this so strongly in every fibre of his being, that he had to resist this evil power with all the forces at his command. The greatest of these [forces] was his Christian faith and courage, which led him, unflinching, along the road to crucifixion . . . after our first secret talk at Rauschen Dune [in East Prussia] . . . his parting words were: "Remember, if anything should happen to me, you may maintain contact with my brother who knows everything." The tone of Goerdeler's voice still rings in my ears. He was telling me that in his heart he knew what lay ahead.[42]

The highest officials in the British Foreign Office and Prime Minister Neville Chamberlain read Young's records of these rendezvous, as did the U.S. Secretary of State Cordell Hull and the president's wife,

---

41 A. P. Young, *The "X" Documents*, ed. Sidney Aster (London: Deutsch, 1974), 24 (*Young's emphasis*). The "X" in the title stands for Goerdeler. In his secret reports to the British Foreign Office, Young used the "X" as a code name for Goerdeler, and Bosch was designated as "Y."

42 Young, *"X" Documents*, 203. Fritz Goerdeler, city treasurer of Königsberg, was executed for connivance in the plot against Hitler. The news that his beloved brother had been sentenced to death drove the incarcerated Carl Goerdeler "nearly out of his mind" (Ritter, *Goerdeler*, 443).

Eleanor Roosevelt. Young noted: "Mrs. Roosevelt was also informed, and it is reasonable to assume that the gist of the "X" Document was also made known to the President himself. Certainly the subsequent speeches of both Roosevelt and Cordell Hull made one hope that Goerdeler's reasoned plea for a firm policy in dealing with Hitler as the 'only way' had made some impact on the two leaders in command of American foreign policy."[43]

Toward the end of this chapter, I shall return to this vital detail because it was to become one of those potential relativizations whose exclusion from policy considerations suggests a lethal case of cliché thinking in the White House. But first we must consider some key remarks by Goerdeler as memorized by Young, remarks ignored by Prime Minister Chamberlain with dire consequences to the world:

> With terrific emphasis he [Goerdeler] said . . . that [the Nazi leaders] are criminals—a set of gangsters who recognize no law but their own. . . . The world must recognize this and immediately adapt its technique of dealing with the Government of Germany to the requirements of this gangster type in mind.

> [Goerdeler said] that Hitler has reached the stage where he feels he is a god—in fact he is mad.

> [I]n thinking of Hitler we must constantly realize that we are dealing with an abnormality who has soared to his present position of power through an uninterrupted series of successful ventures. A dictator . . . must, if he is to maintain his position, move from one spectacular success to the next.[44]

> In a nutshell, Germany is now dominated by some 100,000 of its worst elements, men of low character, lacking in any moral sense.[45]

> He was greatly perturbed that there is not yet in evidence any strong reaction throughout the democracies, in the Press, the Church, and in Parliament, against the barbaric, sadistic and

---

43 Young, *"X" Documents*, 73. According to Karl-Heinz Janssen, Roosevelt's last-ditch appeal for peace in 1939 "was rooted in the 'X' documents" (Karl-Heinz Janssen, "Auf Goerdeler zu spät gehört," *Die Zeit* 30 [21 July 1989]: 32).

44 Young, *"X" Documents*, 76–77.

45 Young, *"X" Documents*, 78.

cruel persecution of 10,000 Polish Jews in Germany. These poor creatures are driven like wild animals, with machine guns behind them, over the Rhine into Switzerland and over the Polish frontier. Ten thousand of these people are in despair. Never, since the persecution of the Christians by the Roman Emperors, have Christians been so persecuted as is now happening in Germany.[46]

Chaim Weizmann, then president of the World Zionist Congress, tried in vain to persuade Chamberlain to listen to Goerdeler. In his memoirs, Weizmann tells the story:

> [T]hrough secret channels I had received an extraordinary German document and was urged to bring it to the attention of the Prime Minister. It was written and forwarded by Herr Goerdeler at great risk to his own life. . . . The document was a detailed expose of events in Germany and ended with the urgent plea to Chamberlain not to be deceived and to make no further concessions when he met Hitler in Godesberg and Munich. I showed this document to one of my friends in the cabinet and asked him to persuade Chamberlain to read it; he did not succeed. Then I went to Sir Warren Fisher whose office at Downing Street was next door to Chamberlain's. I showed him the document. . . . Sir Warren unlocked his desk and showed me an exact copy of the document. He said, "For ten days now I have tried to get Mr. Chamberlain to take a look at it—to no avail."[47]

Tragically, Chamberlain considered Hitler to be "a man of honor," indeed, "almost a decent, modest man."[48] So he traveled to Munich to agree with Hitler "in principle" that the Sudetenland must be separated from Czechoslovakia. In truth, writes Young, Chamberlain and his group of appeasers "were a selfish crowd . . . more concerned with the protection of their possessions than with the preservation of 'the eternal moral code'— advocated by Goerdeler."[49] Young stated:

---

46 Young, "X" Documents, 139.

47 Chaim Weizmann, Memoiren: Das Werden des Staates Israel (Zurich: Phaidon, 1953), 600–601.

48 Janssen, "Auf Goerdeler zu spät gehört."

49 Young, "X" Documents, 204.

Goerdeler's mission was to strengthen the resistance of the democracies to the evil growth of Hitlerism and thereby create a situation in which the German generals—who were desperately afraid of war on two fronts—could dethrone Hitler. The partnership between Goerdeler and the generals was at the zenith of its power on September 15, 1938, poised for action at the very moment when the British Prime Minister . . . rushed ignominiously to Germany to see Hitler. The appeasers won their greatest victory, and Goerdeler's efforts to hold the peace were defeated. His plan was to establish a new German government, with himself as Chancellor, which recognized—in words he so often repeated to me—"the eternal moral code." After the signing of the Munich agreement on September 30, 1938, Hitler was astride on the world, having demonstrated that the British and French democracies were of no account. It was one of the tragedies of history that a British Prime Minister raised Hitler to the peak of power, thereby making war inevitable.[50]

Could Goerdeler's plan have succeeded? His daughter is not so sure, neither is Klemens von Klemperer.[51] But Young felt there was a chance. In September 1938, the British Parliament was in recess. Goerdeler suggested—and opposition leader Clement Attlee requested—that it be recalled to discuss the Sudeten crisis. Young comments:

A free discussion of the great issues would have caused the right answers to emerge, leading to a firm pronouncement to Hitler: "Thus far and no further." In the changed world atmosphere created by the sudden and dramatic assembly of the British parliament at that point of time—something for which Goerdeler had pleaded so passionately—Goerdeler's plan of action would have been implemented and war avoided. Before the bar of history, the Prime Minister and those who thought like him will be condemned for crushing the voice of the people at a critical

---

50 Young, "X" Documents, 10. Prior to Chamberlain's and French Prime Minister Daladier's betrayal of Czechoslovakia, Goerdeler had told Young: "[I]f the British Government decided to assemble Parliament and decided to make an announcement [of firmness] . . . there would be no war. Either of two things would happen: (a) Hitler himself would abandon his present plan and hold the peace; (b) if Hitler was still determined on war, then the generals would stop him from putting his plan into action" (Young, "X" Documents, 82).

51 They voiced their doubts in telephone interviews with the author in March 1992.

moment in their history, thereby opening the floodgates to a cruel and unnecessary war. Britain suffered untold agonies, and more than 30 million people were killed before peace came— including 6 million Jews at the hands of Hitler's henchmen, and 22 million of Russia's finest sons.[52]

Ritter takes a similar view. Reminding his readers that "most German generals opposed war and many Germans could not understand why Hitler wanted war,"[53] Ritter writes: "Only this one time could it have been possible to bring the entire officers' corps of the army to take joint action—an action for peace which nobody could have called treasonous."[54]

Goerdeler's failure to convince England to stand up to Hitler did not stop him from continuing his mission. He informed the British government that the Germans were listening increasingly to English and French broadcasts because they no longer trusted their own government-controlled radio stations. He spoke of "terrible tortures and torments to which those in the internment camps in Germany are daily subjected" and averred that the German people would "physically revolt against the Nazi regime" if only they knew the whole truth. He reported a "deep disapproval [by the public] of the . . . cruel and senseless persecution of the Jews [which was being] deeper and deeper resented."[55]

Goerdeler made it known that Hitler personally ordered the pogrom on November 9–10, 1938—the *Kristallnacht*. According to Young,

> X spoke with great feeling of the way in which many German citizens, at great risk to themselves and their dependents, had given individual assistance to the Jews in their terrible plight. He spoke with burning indignation of two terrible features of this pogrom. Little children were driven from their homes, clad only in thin nightshirts, into the streets to suffer the agonies of hunger and cold. Jewish virgins were violated by the young Nazi gangsters who carried out the pogrom. He cited the case of a Jewish virgin, known to him, who only escaped this terrible fate

---

52 Young, *"X" Documents*, 205.

53 Ritter, *Goerdeler*, 199.

54 Ritter, *Goerdeler*, 202.

55 Young, *"X" Documents*, 160.

by telling those that would violate her that she was suffering from syphilis.[56]

Moreover, Goerdeler passed on to the British an early warning that Hitler and Stalin were about to conclude the nonaggression pact that would allow Germany to invade Poland without the risk of having to wage war against the Soviet Union. Although the source of that information was Captain Fritz Wiedemann, Hitler's personal adjutant, Vansittart was quite relaxed about it.[57] "Don't worry," he said to Erich Kordt, an emissary of the German resistance, "*we* shall most certainly conclude a treaty with the Soviet Union." And Goerdeler's repeated warning that Hitler intended to absorb Belgium, the Netherlands, and Switzerland was at first ignored because it did not accord with the general trend of British intelligence at the time.[58]

Doubtless, Goerdeler's failure to interest the British government in the planned coup against Hitler must be attributed to a combination of reasons. But the most important reason was stereotypical thinking in London. Sir Montagu Norman, the governor of the Bank of England, chided Goerdeler for denouncing his own government; that was not the way a patriot was supposed to act.[59] Sir Orme Sargent, assistant under-

---

56 Young, *"X" Documents,* 177. In his memorandum "Zur Lage," Goerdeler elaborated: "[Hitler] personally ordered all these cruelties, murders and tauntings [of Jews]. He approved all these measures in every detail, and prohibited any form of criticism. He ordered that the synagogues be set on fire, that Jewish morgues be desecrated, Jewish shops be looted, and Jewish property of any kind be handed over to the mob and the most brutal among the Hitler Youth leaders. . . . These orders were phrased in such a way that perverted people even drove naked children from Jewish orphanages into the cold of the night, until Christians took them in. It is important to know that in the face of this infamy many German families displayed a powerful spirit of neighborly love, protecting their persecuted fellow-citizens and giving them shelter. On the other hand, the average German never hears more than fragments of what is going on in the concentration camps" (Goerdeler, "Zur Lage," 20).

57 Wiedemann was Hitler's company commander in World War I. Goerdeler maintained close contacts with this officer, who shared his apprehensions about Hitler's policies.

58 Cf. Sidney Aster, "Carl Goerdeler and the Foreign Office," in Young, *"X" Documents,* 238–39.

59 Cf. Meyer-Krahmer, *Goerdeler,* 115. This was mild compared with the way Chamberlain reacted to warnings from Ewald von Kleist, another prominent

secretary of state in the British Foreign Office, commenting on Goerdeler's plea with the British government to take a firm line and strengthen the radio propaganda in Germany, responded, "It is a pity that Dr. Goerdeler tries to curdle our blood by overstating his case."[60] Only Young understood fully that Goerdeler's moral outrage was motivated by his Christianity, which was Lutheran. Young also understood this Prussian conservative's inner conflict: "He courageously faced . . . the challenge between two basic ideas—loyalty to the state and loyalty to a higher spiritual conception which he consistently expressed as 'the eternal moral code.' In a well organised [sic] and enlightened society, there would be no clash between these two ideas. [But] Hitler was the unique and towering exception in all history. He was the incarnation of evil."[61]

The Militarism Cliché

Vansittart did not comprehend this. Although he opposed Chamberlain's policy of appeasement and initiated Young's clandestine meetings with Goerdeler, Vansittart ultimately turned against the Germans. He harshly called Goerdeler to task for suggesting the "treasonous act" of a military coup.[62] And when Goerdeler said that a post-Hitler government

---

conservative opponent of the Nazi regime. Von Kleist had come to London "with a rope around the neck," as he put it, to inform the British government that there was not just a "danger" of Germany's going to war against Czechoslovakia; in fact, Hitler had definitely decided to conduct that war. Chamberlain disdainfully wrote to Lord Halifax that von Kleist was a "blind, rabid enemy of Hitler." Chamberlain compared him to the Jacobin exiles from England during the reign of King William III. See Ritter, *Goerdeler*, 185–86. But even this is benign compared with the curious Dutch "gratitude" shown to Colonel Hans Oster. A pastor's son, this devout Lutheran was the deputy head of the *Abwehr*, Germany's military intelligence service. He loathed Hitler and his warmongering to such an extent that he gave the Dutch military attaché in Berlin, Major G. J. Sas, the precise date on which Hitler planned to invade the Netherlands. He said: "People may say that I am a traitor but . . . I regard myself as a better German than those who are trotting along behind Hitler. It is my purpose and my duty to liberate Germany, and with her the world, from this plague." General Hendrik Winkelman, commander-in-chief of the Dutch forces, termed Oster a "miserable fellow" (Hoffmann, *History of the German Resistance*, 172).

60 Young, *"X" Documents*, 138.
61 Young, *"X" Documents*, 203.
62 See Ritter, *Goerdeler*, 171.

would negotiate—but never go to war for—a reversal of some aspects of the Versailles Treaty that were particularly odious to the Germans,[63] Vansittart wrote scathingly: "I have . . . for some time suspected that [Goerdeler] was the stalking horse for . . . the expansionist ideas of the German army as contrasted with those of the Nazi Party. There is really very little difference between them. . . . Do not trust Goerdeler except as an occasional informant. . . . He is quite untrustworthy, and he is the wrong kind of person and mind because his own mind is wrong."[64]

This statement could stand as a model of cliché thinking in Zijderveld's sense of the word, for it excludes several potential relativizations:

(A) Goerdeler thought on two levels: the moral and the political. His moral and religious convictions told him that evil in an unprecedented concentration had befallen his country and had to be stopped lest the whole world slide into a catastrophe. From a political point of view, Goerdeler was convinced that Germany had been wronged by the terms of the Versailles Treaty, that the rise of National Socialism was to a major extent the result of that injustice, and that Germany's grievances must be redressed. Failing that, no post-Nazi government would be able to gain the trust of the German public. Good order and spiritual calm, so cherished by conservatives of Goerdeler's persuasion, would not be brought about. To be sure, some of Goerdeler's demands, such as his call for a return of Germany's colonies, may sound outrageous to modern ears. But they could not have seemed alien to Vansittart, who had served under Lloyd George, one of the most strident among Britain's imperialists. In Goerdeler's and Vansittart's days, colonial empires were still considered a normalcy; thus Goerdeler demanded no more for his country than equality with the other European powers. In fact, Aaron Goldman writes:

> Until late 1936 Vansittart was willing to consider concessions to the dictators [Hitler and Mussolini] in the hope that they might be brought into a general European agreement. Believing that the Versailles treaty was indefensible, he advocated handing

---

63 For example, the Polish Corridor. Goerdeler also felt that the Sudetenland was German and should join Germany. But he made it clear that this should never be accomplished by military action.

64 Young, "*X*" *Documents*, 234.

over British colonial territory to Germany and Italy in order to curb their explosive energies, which he feared might otherwise be unleashed in war. . . . It is worth considering the intriguing possibility that Vansittart's later vehemence in denouncing pre-war appeasers and his uncompromising attacks on Germans during the war reflected a desire to compensate for his earlier advocacy of accommodation with the Hitler regime.[65]

(B) There was, writes Ritter, this "fateful cliché of the German generals' immortal militarism."[66] Not Nazism but militarism was the real menace, Vansittart wrote in World War II.[67] This was a stereotypical *idée fixe* he shared with Winston Churchill and, as we shall see below, with Franklin D. Roosevelt. It willfully ignored the deeply religious character of the "old-line" officers who were Goerdeler's friends: Beck, Halder, Oster, and von Witzleben, for example. From reading the "X" documents and listening to Goerdeler, Vansittart must have known the intense distress of these men over Hitler's warmongering. Vansittart surely knew that they abhorred wars of aggression, and he no doubt knew their apprehension over the new breed of officers spawned by National Socialism—former Hitler Youth leaders intensely loyal to the *Führer*.

The militarism cliché warrants a closer look because it is at least partly responsible for the West's failure to take seriously the German conservative resistance both before and during World War II. Therefore, it is partly responsible for the odious Casablanca formula demanding Germany's unconditional surrender, a formula extinguishing whatever chance there may have existed for a coup against Hitler before the Holocaust. Furthermore, the militarism cliché is partly responsible for the subsequent division not only of Germany but also of the whole of Europe and the subjugation of the eastern half by the Soviet Union.

---

65 Aaron Goldman, "Germans and Nazis: The Controversy over 'Vansittartism' in Britain during the Second World War," *Journal of Contemporary History* 14:1 (1979): 159. Significantly, Vansittart would later write: "The Treaty of Versailles has little to do with this war" (Robert Vansittart, *Lessons of My Life* [New York: Alfred Knopf, 1943], 34).

66 Ritter, *Goerdeler*, 325. Significantly, none of the old-school officers in the German resistance, all World War I veterans, ever considered replacing the National Socialist regime with a military dictatorship; see Ritter, *Goerdeler*, 155.

67 Vansittart, *Lessons of My Life*, 255.

The militarism cliché formed the cornerstone of what Frank Owen, the editor of the *Evening Standard*, considered a racist interpretation of Germany's behavior: "In this matter Vansittart is a kind of Nazi inside out."[68] Vansittart's racist view held that Britain was not at war with Hitler but with an "accursed race" of which 80 percent are "the moral scum of the earth."[69]

Ritter writes that Adam von Trott zu Solz, an anti-Nazi diplomat, Rhodes scholar, and devout Christian with excellent connections in both London and Washington, "was deeply troubled by the . . . grotesque notions of German militarism and irrepressible desire for conquest he saw incessantly reappear in the English media, in war literature, and also in speeches by British statesmen."[70]

In Vansittart's eyes, Luther had a lot to do with the Germans' degradation:

> Luther, whom Fichte considered the German *par excellence* . . . denounced the Jews in the wildest terms, and urged the foulest measures against them. . . . He hated reason, "the devil's greatest whore." His views on women were narrow and brutal. He was a propagandist, who excused lying on the ground of utility or even convenience. He practiced what he preached. . . . He altered the translation of the Bible to suit the cardinal point of his doctrine, and shouted down objections like a *Führer*. "I declare with utmost certainty every doctrine to be anathema which differs from my own."[71]

"Vansittartism," as this way of thinking came to be known, contended that the German "race" had been impregnated with militarism for more than a thousand years. In his pamphlet *Black Record*, which caused a violent debate in Britain during the war, Vansittart insisted that the British were not only fighting Hitlerism but also the entire German people, who had always been bloodthirsty. He calls Germans a "brazen Horde" who had remained "savages at heart." Vansittart states:

---

68 Frank Owen, "This Man Makes More Nazis," *The Evening Standard* (24 February 1942): 2.

69 Goldman, "Germans and Nazis," 160.

70 Ritter, *Goerdeler*, 385.

71 Vansittart, *Lessons of My Life*, 221–22.

German barbarism first crushed Latin civilization at the battle of Adrianople in the year 378, as it has again crushed Latin civilization in France today . . . . War was again the passion of the great Charlemagne, too conquest and expansion as usual. . . . By the time they got to their famous warmonger, Frederick Barbarossa, in the twelfth century, the only bone of contention was not whether they should remain in peace, but which race they should conquer and dominate—should it be Italians or Slavs? . . . These fierce characteristics showed themselves to the full in the Thirty Years War in . . . which Bohemia was overrun, and the Czech population subjected to a persecution almost equal to that of 1939.[72]

Vansittart keeps up this line of argument for fifty-five pages, bypassing anything that might slow its thrust. For example, he ignores that Charlemagne was also the ruler of what today is France, which by implication escaped the "militarist" temptation. One wonders what the Hundred Years War, the conquests of Louis XIV, and Napoleon's march to Russia were all about. Similarly, Vansittart skips some of the most important facts of the Thirty Years' War. For example, he overlooks the involvement of Spanish, French, Swedish, and assorted other forces in the destruction of Germany, whose population was, by some estimates, reduced from sixteen million to less than six million and whose commerce, manufacturing, and intellectual life were annihilated.[73] To Vansittart, the roots of Nazism go deep: "Impregnate a race with militarism, imbue it with a sense of its own superiority, convince it of its mission to enslave mankind for the good of mankind, persuade it that this end justifies any and every means however filthy; and you produce a race of hooligans which is a curse to the whole world."[74]

Vansittart's statements sound so outlandish that one would like to assume that no man shared them, and indeed there were some strident anti-Vansittartites. They included George Bell, the valiant bishop of Chichester, who maintained contact with Dietrich Bonhoeffer and

---

72 Robert Vansittart, *Black Record* (London: Hamish Hamilton, 1941), 20–22.

73 Cf. Williston Walker et al., *A History of the Christian Church*, 4th ed. (New York: Scribner's, 1985), 534.

74 Vansittart, *Black Record*, 12.

other members of the German opposition and courageously tried to convince the British government that there was another Germany. Many anti-Vansittartites, however, were to be found on the left of the political spectrum. As a curious irony will have it, most of them had been strongly anti-Nazi in the 1930s, when Vansittart was still prepared to make concessions to Hitler. They included Michael Foot, Victor Gollancz, Kingsley Martin, and Herbert Morrison. But the general population proved increasingly responsive to Vansittart's objurgations. Goldman noted: "Although anti-German feelings in Britain were never as strong as they had been after the First World War, as the war developed both the public and higher officials became more hostile to the German people." Polls taken during the war indicated that Vansittart spoke for many in Britain. In the spring of 1943, 43 percent of those questioned by Mass-Observation either hated or had no sympathy for the German people. By February 1945 this had increased to 54 percent.[75] Goldman goes on to say: "The hard line which makes less of a distinction between Germans and Nazis won support in the British cabinet and press as well as at the BBC where it was decided that, since it was no longer possible to make a useful distinction between party and people, the term 'Nazi' should be excluded from news bulletins. . . . Opinion was now crystallizing into a distinctive doctrine similar to Vansittart's."[76]

There were times when Winston Churchill sounded even more harsh than Vansittart.[77] In 1941, he spoke in a world broadcast of "sev-

---

75 Goldman, "Germans and Nazis," 156–57.

76 Goldman, "Germans and Nazis," 161. The public "dehumanization" of the Germans as a whole is being continued by Hollywood and the television industry. Although many feature films deal with the resistance in German-occupied Europe, no major movie has even hinted at the German resistance. It took an Israeli woman, Hava Kohav Beller, to produce a superb documentary on this subject. Her film, *The Restless Conscience*, was nominated for an Academy Award in 1992. But it did not receive the Oscar.

77 With great sadness, Ritter remarks that Churchill clearly had no idea how much he was admired by the German opposition and how much hope Goerdeler, who had met Churchill before the war, placed in him. See Ritter, *Goerdeler*, 325. I can affirm that in my childhood in Leipzig this sentiment was prevalent in bourgeois circles. In the middle of the war, as we were being bombed by British aircraft, my parents and relatives, though politically inactive, praised Churchill as *the* outstanding political figure in Europe and expressed the hope that he would ultimately lead the continent. My father, a blind World War I veteran, strove to

enty million malignant huns—some of whom are curable and others killable."[78] Goldman links the indiscriminate air raids on German cities to this intrusion of Vansittart's views into the thinking at the highest levels of Allied policy makers:

> At the beginning of the war the British chiefs of staff and the government announced that enemy civilian populations would not be attacked from the air with the aim of causing demoralization. Gradually, however, the government retreated from this position, claiming the Germans had set the example and would have to suffer accordingly. Thus the justification for air attacks on enemy civilians was that the enemy was evil. Unknown to the British public, indiscriminate (and ineffective) bombardment of Germany began in 1940. By the autumn of that year the war cabinet agreed to bombing concentrations directed against single German cities. The war cabinet always tried to convince the British public that the bomber offensive was directed against strategic targets and that German civilians were being killed by accident.[79]

Goldman thereby infers that this killing of some 600,000 German civilians, mainly women and children, was at least in part the result of racism—a singularly vile form of cliché thinking that generalizes by attributing base characteristics to an entire "race" deemed inferior or "accursed," to use Vansittart's term.[80] At the same time, racism excludes

---

improve his English so he could understand Churchill's speeches. The BBC was our main source of information. Listening to enemy broadcasts was considered a capital crime. At my elementary school, our class was occasionally visited by Nazi Party officials humming to us the opening bars of Beethoven's Fifth Symphony, the BBC's call sign. They would ask if we had ever heard this at home. But our parents had instructed us to answer this question in the negative, lest they be arrested by the Gestapo. Thus we said, "No."

78 Cf. Goldman, "Germans and Nazis," 165.

79 Goldman, "Germans and Nazis," 165–66. Here Goldman also cites a singularly callous remark by Churchill, who suggested that Germans could escape the destruction brought by British bombing raids by leaving the cities where munitions were being made, "abandon their work and go out into the fields and watch their home fires burning from a distance."

80 Under no circumstances do I intend to equate or even compare this kind of racism with the National Socialist extermination of the Jews. Racist discrimination and genocide are not identical. Churchill was not planning a "Final Solution."

relativizing qualities from the assessment of that "race." The genesis of what Victor Gollancz termed "Vansittart's . . . savage appeal to primitive blood lust and a base propaganda of hatred and revenge against the German people"[81] is a case in point.

Vansittart's stereotypical view that "militarism is the manifestation of German morality," that "German militarism was endemic and incurable," and that "the average German must . . . first learn to feel" is evidently rooted in his experiences as a student in Germany at the turn of the century.[82] That was a time of considerable ill feeling between the British and the Germans over two issues: the Boer War and the Kaiser's ambition to challenge England's domination of the world's seas by building up his own fleet to match the Royal Navy.[83]

Vansittart's sojourn in Germany strikes one as a baffling interlude. He was a highly cultured young man who spoke and wrote many languages, including Arabic, French, and German. He was the future author of fine novels, poetry, and plays, one of them in French. By all accounts, he should have had a wonderful time in a country that, at the time, had the most educated population in the world, a country that was replete with superb artists, writers, scholars, and scientists. But evidently he encountered mainly uninformed Anglophobes and almost comical militarists: "For some time a general explosion of Anglophobia had been in full blast. It was unpleasant, sometimes painful, to be in a theater or restaurant. It was worse to be at home. The headmaster's daughter used to pursue me about the house, even into my bedroom, cursing England, foretelling our destruction and the rise of Germany on our ruins. The other inmates joined in her pastime with gusto and venom."[84]

The most unpleasant "militarist" he encountered was a Captain Flesch, with whom he played tennis at Bad Homburg:

---

81 Cf. Victor Gollancz, *Shall Our Children Live or Die?* (London: Gollancz, 1942), 62–74.

82 Vansittart, *Lessons of My Life*, 182.

83 It is worth noting that during that period Anglophobia was by no means an exclusively German phenomenon. Practically all non-British publications at the time—French, German, Russian, and Italian—were strongly Anglophobic because of British behavior toward the Boers, particularly the internment of Boer civilians (including women and children) in "concentration camps."

84 Vansittart, *Black Record*, 34.

I was a beginner, and got a big handicap; and so it came about that I was still plodding along in the handicap singles, just when the two tennis heroes of all our youths, the brothers Doherty, were playing the final of the open doubles in the next court. My opponent was a champion duelist, called Captain Flesch. . . . The few points that I scored unluckily coincided with outburst of applause round the Doherty's court. Flesch thereupon challenged me to a duel, on the ground that I packed a court.[85]

Vansittart declined. His biographer Norman Rose tells the end of the story: "As it was obvious his welcome in Germany was wearing thin, he packed his bags and left for the more congenial atmosphere of Vienna."[86]

Rose reveals what may well have been the true reasons for Vansittart's relentless dislike of Germany:

[A]t Bad Homburg . . . he fell in love for the first time. In later life he was extremely reticent about this affair. One does not know how it began, how it ended, or even with whom it was conducted. In all probability his romance followed a pattern all too painfully familiar to young men of his class and education who have just been thrust out alone into the world. No doubt his first major encounter with the opposite sex left his ego bruised, his self-confidence in question, his pride shaken. But unless there was a basic flaw in his emotional makeup, he would certainly have looked upon this episode with a mixture of smug satisfaction and nostalgic regret.[87]

Vansittart's subsequent display of spite against the entire German "race," including such brave anti-Nazis as Goerdeler, suggests that there may indeed have been a "basic flaw in his emotional makeup." Did Vansittart's ordeal as a young man in Germany grow stale in his mind? Did it warp into a cliché, a "container of old experiences," as Zijderveld would phrase it? We shall never know for certain; Vansittart is dead. But a frightening thought lingers: Trivial incidents may have contributed to a misreading of Germany's opposition. Such incidents may, therefore, have been partly responsible for the confusion in Britain concerning the identity of the real enemy. Such incidents may have caused policy

---

85 Vansittart, *Black Record*, 41.

86 Norman Rose, *Vansittart* (London: Heinemann, 1978), 14.

87 Rose, *Vansittart*, 13.

decisions that precluded the last chance of toppling an evil government in Germany before the onset of the Holocaust. They may also have resulted in the destruction of hundreds of thousands of innocent lives in Germany. And for our purposes here, these factors, rather than a gross misunderstanding of and simplistic attack on Luther, may have determined the course of history.

Cliché Thinking in the White House

On the other side of the Atlantic, President Franklin D. Roosevelt shared Vansittart's view of Germans. During World War I, Roosevelt came to view Germany as a "monstrous nation," according to his biographer Frank Freidel.[88] During World War II, Roosevelt convinced himself that "the German character had to be totally reformed."[89] Like Vansittart, he formed his opinion of Germans and Germany in his adolescence. Like Vansittart, Roosevelt had spent a considerable amount of time in Germany toward the end of the nineteenth century. Like Vansittart, he spoke German; he had had a German governess by the name of Fräulein Reinhardt. At his school in Groton, New York, Roosevelt was an "A" student in German. Almost every year, his parents took him to Germany, where his mother "took the waters" at Bad Nauheim and Sankt Blasien, both spas. Once he even attended an elementary school in Bad Nauheim for six weeks.

But the Roosevelt family's willingness to fraternize with natives clearly had its limits: "By the way, Mama struck against feeding in com-

---

88 Frank Freidel, *Franklin D. Roosevelt: The Apprenticeship* (Boston: Little, Brown, 1952), 333. For good measure, Roosevelt was equally uncomplimentary about France, a country whose language he spoke. Robert Nisbet relates how, during the Teheran summit meeting with Stalin and Churchill in November 1943, the U.S. president and the Soviet dictator railed against the French. They decided that "France deserved nothing out of the war, given its collaboration under Vichy with the Nazis and its general unreliability in western Europe." Throughout a summit banquet, "Stalin railed against France . . . declaring it deserved dismemberment and other devastations with Germany when the war was over." Nisbet goes on to denounce Roosevelt's "support of Stalin's position on France. . . . Repeatedly [Stalin] told Roosevelt that France . . . must be . . . reduced to third class status in western Europe" (Robert Nisbet, *Roosevelt and Stalin* [Washington: Regnery Gateway, 1988], 47, 51, 73).

89 Warren F. Kimball, ed., *Churchill and Roosevelt: The Complete Correspondence* (Princeton: Princeton University Press, 1984), 133.

pany with German swine. So we have a separate table to ourselves," James Roosevelt wrote to his son Franklin on June 9, 1897, from their hotel in St. Blasien.[90] Like Vansittart, Roosevelt came to see Germans as hopeless militarists, though he does not trace that trait as far back in history as the Englishman:

> [I] went to school in Germany under the old emperor William I. The railroad employees were not in uniform. The school children were not in uniform and did not march all the time. It was not a military-minded nation then. That was back in 1888 . . . . The young Kaiser came in 1889. At the time I left Germany, the railroad employees all over Germany were in uniform. The school children were in uniform. They were taught to march. . . . German family life was a decent life. Gradually they got militaristic.[91]

To Roosevelt, it was indicative of that "militaristic" training of German children that since the reign of William II they were taught to read maps. Freidel writes that "F. D. R. was able to describe them in detail as an example of German planning for aggression."[92]

As we have seen above, Roosevelt knew the "X" documents and was therefore informed of the efforts by Goerdeler and his military friends to topple Hitler. He also knew that these efforts were frustrated by Britain's policy of appeasement. Roosevelt knew that the resistance continued even after war had broken out. Peter Hoffmann wrote:

> In November 1942 Allen Welsh Dulles, later Director of the CIA, was sent to Berne for the express purpose of establishing permanent contact with the German opposition. He informed

---

90 James to Franklin D. Roosevelt. Family Papers, Box 3, Folder 4 (1864–1904), Franklin D. Roosevelt Library, Hyde Park, NY.

91 Press conference minutes, 1944–45, page 560. Franklin D. Roosevelt Library. A splendid example of cliché thinking! Roosevelt neglected to say that schoolchildren throughout Europe were wearing uniforms, even after World War I. In Britain they still do. School uniforms are not symbols of "militarism," but they equalize rich and poor, the nobles and the commoners, which is why they are being employed again in places as diverse as New York City and France. As for the railroad officials, they must be identifiable—for the benefit of the passengers. That is why there is no major country in the world, including the United States, in which train crews and station attendants are not in uniform.

92 Freidel, *Roosevelt*, 33–34.

his masters of all developments and Washington had a vast amount of information on the resistance in Germany. Viewed from Washington, however, the United States was not merely fighting the Nazi regime but a people permeated by an illiberal inhuman ideology who had learned nothing from a fearful defeat in another similarly imperialist war.[93]

Louis B. Lochner, chief of the Associated Press bureau in Berlin, tried in vain to enlighten Roosevelt, whom he knew, concerning the German opposition. Its leaders charged him in November 1941 to do so. Lochner was to see the president on behalf of Prince Louis Ferdinand of Prussia, who was involved with the resistance. The prince, who until his death in 1994 was pretender to the German and Prussian thrones, had been on very friendly terms with the Roosevelts. "I hope you will be able to come back and see us in Washington or Hyde Park where a hearty welcome awaits you," Roosevelt had cabled him on March 23, 1939.[94] But clearly Roosevelt did not want to hear from the Kaiser's grandson in 1942. Hoffmann wrote:

[The opposition leaders] requested Lochner, who was shortly due to return to the United States, to tell the President at once and in the greatest detail of the opposition's compositions, aims and activities. He was also to ask the President to say something on the form of government America would prefer for a Germany liberated from Hitler. . . . When he finally returned to the United States he immediately sought an audience with President Roosevelt, saying that he had personal and confidential messages from Prince and Princess Louis Ferdinand of Prussia and secret information on resistance groups in Germany which he might not confide to anyone else. All attempts to obtain an audience with the President failed, however; he wrote from Chicago but received no answer. Finally, through

---

93 Hoffmann, *History of the German Resistance*, 215.

94 Cf. Correspondence with Louis Ferdinand and Prince Frederick of Prussia, File 110. Franklin D. Roosevelt Library. Louis Ferdinand knew America well. In the early 1930s, he had worked as a car mechanic at the Ford Motor Co. in Dearborn, Michigan. This was in keeping with a tradition of the royal house of Prussia that all princes were required to become proficient in three fields—military, academic, and craft. In the area of academics, the prince was a legal and economics scholar whose doctoral thesis focused on a contemporary theme—immigration theory.

the Washington office of the Associated Press, he was informed that there was no desire to receive his information and he was requested to refrain from further efforts to transmit it.[95]

To all intents and purposes, the German opposition was thus declared a nonevent. How deeply ingrained this attitude was in the White House can be discerned from the fact that it even transcended Roosevelt's death and Germany's defeat. One of the most astounding examples of this stance is Eleanor Roosevelt's vitriolic reaction to Pastor Martin Niemöller's visit to the United States in 1946–1947. As we have seen above, Mrs. Roosevelt had received ample information on the German opposition well before the war. It came from Goerdeler in form of the "X" documents sent to her by A. P. Young, documents that included a detailed description of Niemöller's plight. After Niemoller's liberation from the Dachau concentration camp, where he had spent five years in solitary confinement, he toured the United States as a guest of the Federal Council of the Churches of Christ in America. And wherever he went, wrote the *Detroit Free Press*, "he was hounded by the parlor pinks of the press who seem to delight in misrepresenting him. He has been so misquoted and misrepresented that he has deliberately limited his interviews, feeling that what he has to say can best be told to those who are interested from the platform."[96]

The most prominent writer to hound him was Eleanor Roosevelt, who since before the war authored a syndicated column entitled "My Day." In her column on December 4, 1946, she complained:

> I see by the papers that Pastor Martin Niemoeller, German Lutheran churchman who was jailed, has arrived in this country and is scheduled to make a lecture tour. I understand that Dr. Niemoeller has stated that he was against the Nazis because of what they did to the church, but that he had no quarrel with them politically. . . . I am sure he is a good man according to his lights, but his lights are not those of the people of the United States.[97]

---

95 Hoffmann, *History of the German Resistance*, 214–15.

96 Malcolm W. Bingay, "Good Morning," *Detroit Free Press* (27 January 1947): 6.

97 Eleanor Roosevelt, "My Day," *United Feature Syndicate* (4 December 1946).

On December 21, 1946, she wrote to Bishop G. Bromley Oxnam of the Methodist Church, president of the Federal Council of Churches:

I am perfectly willing to meet Pastor Neimoeller [sic] though I am not very anxious to see him. I think you have missed the reason why I do not think the Federal Council of the Churches of Christ in American [sic] should not have had him come to speak in this country. After the last war we succeeded as a people in making ourselves believe that the leaders in Germany were to blame and not the people and we brought on a Second World War. The kind of thing of having Pastor Neimoeller [sic] come over here and air his view before American audiences will lull them into sleep again. I want us to be vividly aware of the fact that the German people are to blame, that they committed horrible crimes. Therefore I think you are doing something, which is stupid beyong [sic] words in bringing this gentleman here.[98]

On February 2, 1947, Eleanor Roosevelt wrote to the Reverend Albert A. Ziarko: "If Pastor Neimoeller [sic] had been consistently anti-Nazi, I doubt if he would be alive today. . . . I think in this country we have to remember and not be too soft hearted about the Germans. They started two wars."[99]

And on February, 21 1947, she again railed in her column against the Council of Churches:

Sometimes I wonder what has happened to the religious groups in this country that all of a sudden they must bring representatives from Germany over here. First, the Federal Council of . . . Churches . . . brought over Pastor Martin Niemoeller. Now a group of the Catholic clergy are sending Cardinal von Preysing of Berlin around the country. . . . I am simply wondering if our people are aware of the fact that, when we bring these gentlemen here, they naturally create sympathy for Germany—a country, which twice has plunged the world into war.[100]

---

98 From the collection of Eleanor Roosevelt's papers. Franklin D. Roosevelt Library.

99 From the collection of Eleanor Roosevelt's papers. Franklin D. Roosevelt Library.

100 Eleanor Roosevelt, "My Day," *United Feature Syndicate* (21 February 1947). On the other side of the Atlantic, the redoubtable Peter F. Wiener even surpassed Mrs. Roosevelt in lambasting Niemöller: "He, the good Lutheran, *did* quarrel with Hitler in the end [sic]. But it was on no question of faith or religion. It was a Church conflict—a quarrel about the administration of the Church. . . . I am, indeed, more than sympathetic towards anybody who is in Hitler's prison. But my

This American variety of Vansittartism, making light of the German resistance, became official U.S. policy in occupied Germany, as Louis Lochner's son Robert was to find out. On November 8, 1948, Volkmar von Zühlsdorff wrote to his friend Hermann Broch:

> You ask me why in Germany nothing is written or said about the heroes of the resistance? I have been fighting for it since our return [from exile in the United States]. Recently I spoke about this with young Lochner who heads Radio Frankfurt [as Chief Control Officer on behalf of the U.S. Military Government] and shares our opinion. The reason for the silence? There exists an ordinance [by the Military Government] that the 20 July must not be mentioned; and this ordinance is still in force. Why? Because all Germans are Nazis, and if one mentions the 20 July people might get the idea that there were a few who were not Nazis, and that is not permissible.[101]

If ever there was a prime example for the willful exclusion of potential relativizations, here it is. A cliché was to be maintained that an entire race of people was evil at worst, quietist at best. As Vansittart wrote, "God would have spared Lot[102] for just ten good men—all were out."[103]

The "20 July" von Zühlsdorff is referring to was, of course, the day in 1944 when the German resistance made its last desperate and futile attempt to get rid of Hitler by assassination, an event disdainfully dismissed by Churchill: "The highest personalities in the German Reich are murdering one another, or trying to."[104]

---

sympathy goes rather to the Jews and Socialists, Communists and pacifists who suffer for their conviction—and not to people like Niemöller, who encouraged all these atrocities from the pulpit for many years" (Wiener, *Martin Luther: Hitler's Spiritual Ancestor* [London: Hutchison, 1945], 77–78). This is another prime example of a deliberate creation of a cliché. Wiener's pamphlet was part of Vansittart's *Win the Peace* campaign. Vansittart knew from Goerdeler and others of Niemöller's courageous fight against National Socialism.

101 Paul Michael Lützeler, ed., *Hermann Broch: Briefe über Deutschland, 1945–1949* (Frankfurt: Suhrkamp, 1986), 126. During the war, von Zühlsdorff and Broch both lived in exile in the United States. Von Zühlsdorff went home after Germany's surrender.

102 Vansittart is confused; Lot was spared, Sodom was not. See Genesis 18:33–19:30.

103 Vansittart, *Lessons of My Life*, 4–5.

104 Before the House of Commons, 3 August 1944, cited by Goldman, "Germans and Nazis," 173.

In his prison cell, Goerdeler interpreted the assassination attempt's failure as a sign that God reserved for Himself the right to judge Hitler.[105] Ritter speaks of an "enigmatic dispensation of Providence that the tyrant has time and again been spared a swift end."[106] Roosevelt knew little of the tremendous moral and religious scruples that plagued not only Goerdeler and Ritter but also virtually the entire German opposition. But the information was available. The Office of Strategic Services (OSS) was well aware of the caliber of these men and women. Reports describing the anti-Nazi activities of both Protestant and Roman Catholic Christians reached Roosevelt's office, and prominent German exiles in the service of the OSS, including historian Hajo Holborn, political scientist Franz Neumann, and sociologist Herbert Marcuse, urged the president to work with the resistance.[107] From his station in Berne, Allen Dulles "observed with increasing understanding and sympathy the efforts by the German resistance movement" to replace the Nazi government.[108]

---

105 Carl Goerdeler, "Im Gefängnis Weihnachten 1944" [unpublished], 4. Here he also expressed confidence that "God will justify us [the resistance], for we wanted to topple a government which has soiled Germany's shield: 1. with the brutal, indeed bestial murder of one million Jews (children before their mothers' eyes and vice versa); 2. with murder, theft and corruption in the occupied territories, 3. with the inhuman expulsion of hundreds of thousands from their farms and hearths in Poland, Slovenia and the Balkans, 4. with a regime of blood and snoops in Germany and the occupied lands." These handwritten notes, as well as Goerdeler's detailed plans for the future of Europe and the reconstruction of Germany, were smuggled out of jail by a sympathetic Gestapo warder; that, too, existed in Germany. The papers are in the possession of the Goerdeler family. I own a carbon copy of the transcript.

106 Ritter, *Goerdeler*, 250.

107 See Bernd Faulenbach, "Schicksalsgeschichte—Deutsche Historiker in der Emigration," *Frankfurter Allgemeine Zeitung* (16 December 1988): 36. Also cf. Alfred Schickel, "Von der F.-D.-Roosevelt-Library bis zur Kongress-Bibliothek," *Amerika-Woche* (15 October 1988). OSS reports on this subject are declassified and available at the Franklin D. Roosevelt Library. One report entitled "The Service of the Church Within the Framework of the Resistance Movement against the National Socialist Regime in Germany" reveals to what stunning extent Washington was familiar with the most prominent Christians in the German resistance. However, that report was sent to the White House in October 1944— after the last coup attempt against Hitler. An OSS memorandum dated March 20, 1944, informed Roosevelt that "all Swedes informed about Germany agreed that the doctrine of unconditional surrender . . . had resulted in uniting everyone in Germany behind Hitler."

108 Ritter, *Goerdeler*, 382.

One of its most valiant members, Adam von Trott zu Solz, kept stressing to Dulles the West's "pharisaical failure to understand the movement's precarious situation in a totalitarian system."[109]

But Roosevelt, who was more impressed with Stalin's Christianity,[110] clearly did not want to know. According to Ritter, Roosevelt "self-righteously"[111] formulated the demand for Germany's unconditional surrender, a demand so radical that it has no parallel in history, at a luncheon with Churchill on January 23, 1943, in Casablanca. The "Casablanca Formula," as it came to be known, was intended to destroy the National Socialist *Weltanschauung*. But, writes Günter Moltmann, "it ignored any other option for an overthrow of the Nazi government: [It] ignored the possible existence of Germans who [were] independent of the ruling regime and were prepared and in a position to negotiate a just peace. It fully identified ... National Socialism with the attitude of all Germans. ... [I]t smacks of a collective discrimination of an entire people."[112]

Thus it excluded relativizing factors and therefore qualifies, by Zijderveld's standards, as cliché thinking. Robert Nisbet shows how frivolously this formula was conceived: "FDR suddenly said 'unconditional surrender' out loud, and followed with, 'Of course, it's just the thing for the Russians. They couldn't want anything better.' 'Unconditional surrender,' he repeated, thoughtfully sucking his tooth, 'Uncle Joe might have made it up himself.' "[113]

Calling the Casablanca Formula "a monumental discouragement to resistance groups working inside the enemy's lines," Nisbet then tells his readers that Stalin was not at all pleased with it either:

> Stalin didn't like the doctrine on the ground that it would prevent the Allied nations from using any possibility of negotiating

---

109 Ritter, *Goerdeler*, 382.

110 Cf. Nisbet, *Roosevelt and Stalin*, 26. In a cabinet meeting in early 1945, Roosevelt spoke of Stalin's early preparation for the Orthodox priesthood and averred: "I think [this] entered into his nature of the way in which a Christian gentleman should behave."

111 Ritter, *Goerdeler*, 330.

112 Günter Moltmann, "Die Genesis der Unconditional-Surrender Forderung," *Wehrwissenschaftliche Rundschau* 6 (1956): 108.

113 Nisbet, *Roosevelt and Stalin*, 43. Nisbet is quoting Elliott Roosevelt, the president's eldest son.

with the German leaders for an earlier surrender. "Speaking about unconditional surrender, Stalin said," as Eden reported to London the following day, that "he thought this bad tactics vis-a-vis Germany" and suggested that the allies work out "terms" together and make these known to the German people. Eden added that Churchill "agrees that this is a better suggestion."[114]

Peter Hoffmann asserts, however, that in reality Britain's intentions did not differ from those of the United States:

> The Powers allied against Germany and Italy . . . intended to impose on Germany an unconditional surrender, Britain apparently from the very start of the war. Their public statements indicated that the terms would be more severe than those imposed at the end of the First World War. Unconditional surrender in 1941 and 1942 would have implied the evacuation by Germany of vast occupied territories in the Soviet Union, in northern, eastern, and southeastern Europe, and in Africa, and the cession of German territory; in 1943 and 1944 it would have meant most likely also the occupation of Germany by the Red Army, while the Western Allies had not yet established the Second Front and were making only slow process in Italy. An occupation of Germany by the Red Army was unacceptable to the German patriots, particularly in view of Russian actions in Poland, the Baltic states, and in Finland after the outbreak of war in 1939.[115]

According to Hoffmann, in January and April 1944 Roosevelt was ready to issue an encouraging proclamation to the German people. Hoffmann believes that this might have been in response to German resistance contacts, which had reached the president through the OSS. The intelligence agency urged the president to "limit the doctrine of 'unconditional surrender' to 'Hitlerite Germany.' No matter how undesirable, it

---

114 Nisbet, *Roosevelt and Stalin*, 44. The quote is taken from Martin Gilbert, *Winston S. Churchill*, vol. 7 *Road to Victory 1941–1945* (Boston: Little, Brown, 1986), 581.

115 Peter Hoffmann, "Peace through Coup d'État: The Foreign Contacts of the German Resistance 1933–1944," *Central European History* 19:1 (March 1986): 6. Hoffmann is citing the "Agreement between His Majesty's Government in the United Kingdom and the Government of the Union of Soviet Socialist Republics providing for Joint Action in the War against Germany" (with protocol), Moscow, 12 July 1941, cmd. 6304 (London, 1941).

is made necessary by the fact that Stalin has already done this . . . . keep Germany oriented to the West and prevent her from turning east."[116]

Moreover, Roosevelt probably realized that the Casablanca Formula had strengthened the Germans' resolve to continue fighting. Hoffmann wrote: "Churchill and Stalin vetoed Roosevelt's intention. It might have been prejudicial to war aims, and it might have disposed the German population more favorably to the Americans, while Europe was demanding revenge, as Stalin wrote. . . . Again, the German Resistance, unlike all other anti-Nazi resistance movements, remained without any encouragement."[117]

In June 1944, Adam von Trott zu Solz met a member of the British Legation in Stockholm. Hoffmann describes the meeting thus:

[The British official] said that "cooperation" of the Resistance with the Allies to end the war more quickly would enable the Allies to spare many bombing targets in Germany. Trott answered that a modification of the unconditional surrender formula was a condition for cooperation—recognizing that his British contact was looking only for treasonous collaboration. It was politically impossible, of course, for the Resistance to cooperate with the Allies if it meant the substitution of Allied arbitrariness for Nazi despotism, the denial of self-determination to the German people, the amputation of German territory, the enslavement of German workers and soldiers, the prevention of German courts of law from prosecution of Nazi criminals.[118]

Christabel Bielenberg, an Englishwoman who spent the war years in Germany as the wife of a prominent member of the opposition, relates how distraught Trott was when he returned from Sweden: "I don't know if I could have done more to persuade outsiders that there is another Germany. . . . From now on this is a German affair. We must rid ourselves of this regime by ourselves."[119]

Two months later Trott was dead—hanged by the Nazis for his

---

116 John C. Wiley, "Comments on the Moscow Manifesto to Germany," OSS memorandum to President Roosevelt, 11 August 1943. Box 167, Franklin D. Roosevelt Library.

117 Hoffmann, "Peace through Coup d'État," 38.

118 Hoffmann, "Peace through Coup d'État," 39.

119 Christabel Bielenberg, *The Past Is Myself* (London: Corgi, 1970), 146–47.

part in the attempted coup against Hitler. Bielenberg commented:

> [T]he demand for "unconditional surrender," which was per-
> haps the biggest blow ever delivered to the opposition in Ger-
> many, was so superbly timed, coming as it did just after Stalin-
> grad, handed to the wily Dr. Goebbels the very weapon he
> needed to rant and flail, cajole and spur on the flagging spirits
> to fight to the end. . . . It was incomprehensible to me that the
> British, that the Americans, had not been able to see that they
> had nothing to lose, and perhaps months of warfare and thou-
> sands of lives to save, by encouraging an opposition to Hitler
> within Germany.[120]

Trott's end was swift. Goerdeler lingered five months in jail, endur-
ing horrendous mental and probably physical tortures as well. Condemned to death, he proved eminently Lutheran as he made plans for a
future he knew he was not going to live to see. "And if I knew that the
world would come to an end tomorrow, I would still plant my little
apple tree today," Luther is supposed to have said. This quotation frequently cited by Germans is at best apocryphal. Nobody has ever succeeded in tracing it to any of the reformer's writings or Table Talks.[121]
But Lutheran it is, for it includes Luther's eschatological expectation as
well as his belief that until the *eschaton* man is expected to do his duty
in the secular realm of which he is also a citizen. This is the doctrine of
the two realms in a nutshell, a doctrine Goerdeler probably never wasted
a moment's thought on but whose ethos he had internalized.

Just a few weeks before he was led to the gallows, he appealed to
the very statesmen he had unsuccessfully warned of Hitler's evil designs:

> I beg my friends abroad not to carry out their announced plans
> of destruction. . . . Remember the harm the Versailles Peace has
> caused. . . . You need not punish the German people. You, too,
> are responsible for their degeneration, for . . . you placed might
> over justice. Now this seed has ripened to a gruesome harvest.
> Believe me, before the eyes of God the German people are not
> evil; when treated justly and decently, they are kindhearted and
> helpful. Only a small minority of them know the horrible mis-

---

120 Bielenberg, *Past Is Myself*, 144.

121 Cf. Martin Schloemann, "Luthers Apfelbäumchen," in vol. 7 of *Wuppertaler Hochschulreden* (Wuppertal: Peter Hammer, 1976), 8.

deeds that have been committed in their name since 1934. They have been committed behind their backs, and if they were told . . . they would not believe them. These are the crimes of individual, perverse, and violent characters. The German people are severely punished: four to five million men dead and as many wounded or crippled, all large cities and many medium-sized towns destroyed. . . . Almost half of all dwellings and places of work wiped out or severely damaged. Leave it to God to be their judge; do not sit in judgment yourselves, lest you be judged![122]

A VICTIM OF THE *ZEITGEIST*

Why did Carl Goerdeler and his partners in the German resistance fail in their efforts to persuade the West to stand up to Hitler? Why were they ignored, viewed with suspicion, belittled, and vilified as they sacrificed their lives in their attempts to rid the world of what they perceived to be the Antichrist? Why were they, Christians all, not given a chance by statesmen who called themselves Christians? From what we have seen in this chapter so far, the answer is clear: The German opposition's endeavors were frustrated by cliché thinking and its sibling, the *Zeitgeist*. The spirit of the time, being finite, has no place for theological insights such as this one:

> In our time we have come far too much in contact with demonic powers, we have sensed and seen much too clearly how mysterious and abysmal forces have seduced people and entire movements and steered them [in a direction] they themselves did not desire; we have all too often observed how an alien spirit has taken hold of people who had perhaps been quite nice and reasonable before; [we have seen] how [that spirit] was able to transform their very substance, how it made them commit acts of cruelty and [drove them into an] ecstasy of power and madness of which they had thought themselves incapable; we have seen how from year to year a poisonous atmosphere enveloped our globe.[123]

Helmut Thielicke said this toward the end of the war in one of his powerful sermons on the Lord's Prayer. He knew what he was talking

---

122 From Goerdeler's prison notes, Christmas 1944.

123 Helmut Thielicke, *Das Gebet das die Welt umspannt* (Stuttgart: Quell, 1964), 140.

about. He fought Hitler's regime from the beginning. Although Roosevelt maintained close contact with forty-nine theologians, it probably never occurred to him to think of evil as a very real force "brooding over the world, its continents and seas," to paraphrase Thielicke.[124] That explains why the president, "craving for Stalin's approval and friendship,"[125] could not see the close similarity between Hitlerite Germany and the Soviet Union,[126] a likeness stressed repeatedly in Goerdeler's memoranda to Western leaders. Roosevelt thought Stalin behaved like a Christian gentleman.[127]

In chapter 2, I have tried to show that the *Zeitgeist*, like the cliché, serves as a beacon in the vagueness and uncertainty of modern society. It serves modern society with a point of reference, albeit finite and fickle. It gives individuals who are afloat in that sea of instability the "correct" position with which to orient themselves—for the time being. But *Zeitgeist*-inspired clichés lead to what Walter Künneth terms "a dangerous labyrinth—a condition of enthusiastic blindness to historical realities."[128] The historical reality in this case was that evil had manifested itself with unprecedented immensity, and modernity with its penchant for quick-fix anthropological answers to every problem was not equipped to cope with this kind of wickedness.

Zijderveld sees a strong affinity between modernity and clichés. And clichés work in tandem with the *Zeitgeist*—they are its weapons and its tools. Like the *Zeitgeist*, these tools are inadequate to deal with what theologians know to be demonic powers, especially as the *Zeitgeist* proves time and again to be vulnerable to such demonic powers. In the 1930s and 1940s the *Zeitgeist* was racist. For our analysis here, it excludes the valid relativization that there existed another Germany whose representatives risked everything to fight an enormous evil with a magnitude they recognized but were unable to impart to their U.S. and British interlocutors.

---

124 Thielicke, *Das Gebet*, 109. Thielicke speaks of a *Schuldverhängnis*, "fatality of guilt," brooding over the world, etc.

125 Nisbet, *Roosevelt and Stalin*, 49.

126 Nisbet, *Roosevelt and Stalin*, 12.

127 See Nisbet, *Roosevelt and Stalin*, 26.

128 Walter Künneth, *Wider den Strom* (Wuppertal: R. Brockhaus, 1989), 127.

Did the Roosevelts really believe that World War II with all its horrors was the result of some ethnic deficiency on the part of the Germans? Did they believe their own clichés? Eleanor Roosevelt's astonishing correspondence with church leaders concerning the Niemöller visit suggests that she did. And the president's blindness to Stalin's totalitarianism leaves little doubt that he was no stranger to thinking in clichés either.

But what of Vansittart? He was a highly cultured man who ostensibly knew every nuance of European history and civilization. For years before the war, he received a steady stream of data about the Nazi menace—from anti-Nazi Germans and especially from Goerdeler. What made this man of letters, this linguist, this career diplomat, suddenly descend to base racism to give an instant answer to one of history's most troubling problems? Why did Vansittart link virtually all Germans of all generations—including Charlemagne, Luther, and Frederick the Great—to a genocide in the twentieth century? Why did he thus lower himself to the level of the Nazis, who justified the extermination of Jews, Gypsies, Poles, and others with a corresponding rhetoric? Was Vansittart still smarting from whatever happened to him in his youth in Bad Homburg? Was he, as Aaron Goldman suggests, trying to compensate for his own shortcomings in the years leading up to the war?

Both factors might have contributed to Vanisttart's extraordinary comportment. But Christabel Bielenberg gives us another idea: "The British did not go to war willingly, unless they had worked up a good old hate. . . . During the First World War, it had been my Uncle Northcliffe's business to do the hate rousing. . . . I could not hate because I knew too much."[129]

Here is another explanation for Vansittart's behavior. Clichés had the function to arouse hate. Clichés, in the form of demagoguery, served as a lethal weapon of war. But this weapon only worked with people who did not know all the facts. And it only worked because the recipients of the clichés put their faith in the cliché-monger, who had been a high-ranking official in a lawful and trusted government. Ironically, the opposite was true in Germany, where nobody believed the minister of

---

129 Bielenberg, *Past Is Myself*, 145. Her uncle was Lord Northcliffe, the newspaper publisher.

propaganda, who was *the* cliché-monger *par excellence*. Bielenberg wrote:

> I knew I would find it hard enough after the war to explain (to whoever wanted to listen) that I sincerely believed that Goebbels had never succeeded in making the Germans hate although he had used methods and arguments quite as ingenious as my uncle. In my opinion he had never aroused the "seething soul of the people" one way or the other. The Germans had not risen and torn the airmen to bits, who were killing them so indiscriminately night after night—I had never heard a cheer go up when an Allied bomber came crashing down in flames. But neither had they stirred themselves and cried to high heaven on the things being done in their name. After eleven years of Nazi rule, Germans it seemed to me, had become an ignorant and insensate mass, and I could only be grateful to the few, the few that I knew, who had shone out reassuringly like beacons, as constant to their principles in defeat as they had been when victory seemed just around the corner.[130]

Vansittart professed that, as in Sodom, the ten righteous men whose presence in Germany would have persuaded God to spare the country were all out. Bielenberg assures us that they were not. Here are the names of ten men whose righteousness was grounded in their Lutheran faith: Carl Goerdeler, Dietrich Bonhoeffer, Eugen Gerstenmaier, Hans-Bernd von Haeften, Adam von Trott zu Solz, Helmuth von Moltke, Bishop Wurm of Württemberg, Bishop Meiser of Bavaria, Colonel Hans Oster, Martin Niemöller; and there were thousands more.

"After the war it became clear that . . . the resistance movement was not as insignificant as Vansittart had assumed,"[131] writes Goldman. As Ritter says, it was by and large a movement of Christians, Protestant as well as Roman Catholic. Unfortunately, since the end of the war, it had become a generally accepted cliché that the Nazi years were marked by a monumental failure of the Lutheran Church, and there may be some justification or explanation for this view.

This assumption that the Lutheran Church failed is a cliché nonetheless, for it leaves out important relativizations. It ignores the

---

130 Bielenberg, *Past Is Myself*, 145–46.
131 Goldman, "Germans and Nazis," 186.

fact that as far back as 1933 some 6,000 pastors, one-third of Germany's entire Protestant clergy, had joined the anti-Nazi *Pfarrernotbund* (Pastors Emergency League).[132] Interestingly, this number corresponds roughly to the proportion of ministers actively opposed to the totalitarian authorities in East Germany after the war, according to Harald Krille, editor-in-chief of *Glaube und Heimat*, a weekly Protestant newspaper for central Germany.[133]

The cliché about the alleged "monumental failure" of the Lutheran Church in the Third Reich further ignores the thousands of clergymen critical of Hitler who were jailed, forbidden to preach, or drafted and often sent to the Russian front, from whence most did not return. And it completely overlooks the extent to which a Lutheran ethos motivated men like Goerdeler.

Goerdeler's internalized Lutheranism told him that Germans must rid themselves of this evil; it also told him that this should not be accomplished through insurrection, lest anarchy of the proportions of the Peasants' War or worse ensued. Competent leaders would have to stand ready to take over at once upon Hitler's arrest. That is why he drew up cabinet lists and a slate of names for every senior administrative post in Berlin and in the provinces. And this is why he formulated detailed policy plans for a government to be led by him. He had the makings of what Luther called a *Wundermann*, except that he lacked, in Luther's words, "smooth sailing on earth and so-called luck and success."

Instead, Goerdeler, who knew nothing of Luther's theology of the cross, lived a theology of the cross—all the way from betrayal by a woman whose family had received much kindness from him[134] to the cry of dereliction: Why hast thou forsaken us? But he *was* one of the ten righteous men of Sodom. Germany was spared. After forty-five years of

---

132 Cf. Ritter, *Goerdeler*, 114.

133 In a telephone interview in July 2006, Krille estimated "from personal observation" that 20 percent of the East German clergy actively supported the Communist government, 20 percent opposed it actively, and "the rest kept their heads down." Krille, a Thuringian and a committed Lutheran Christian, was born and raised under Communism.

134 The woman, Helene Schwärzel, recognized Goerdeler in a restaurant as he was on the run from the Gestapo. She denounced him and received a reward of one million marks before the OSS could rescue him. See R. Harris Smith, *OSS* (Berkeley: University of California Press, 1972), 227.

division, it is now reunified. In those forty-five years, Goerdeler continued to be a nonperson in the city of Leipzig, whose Communist rulers,
like so many left-wing historians in the West, would not give credit to a
righteous man who happened to be conservative.

The Communists are gone now, and today a square in front of
Leipzig's *Rathaus*, Goerdeler's former workplace, bears his name.

Chapter Five

Martin Luther Vindicated (II): Leipzig 1989

At no place has Christ's Gospel ever been stronger than where
it is the least liked. For when their hour came the tyrants went
under, and the Word remains on the agenda.[1]

This insight by Martin Luther has twice in this century been proven correct by events in Germany. First, this happened when Adolf Hitler's
tyranny came to an end in 1945 and then when the Communist dictatorship in East Germany collapsed in 1989. Under both regimes, the
Protestant church provided evidence ostensibly supporting both sides
of the argument over whether Luther had fostered quietism among his
faithful.

As a rule of thumb, Protestants in Hitler's Germany fell into three
groups of almost equal size: the pro-Nazi "German Christians," the anti-
Nazi confessional Christians, and an amorphous "neutral" faction in
the center. The most prevalent view of the Protestant church's role in the
Third Reich holds that the church ingloriously failed in its duty to stand
up to the demonic force of National Socialism. According to this view,
Luther is to blame. But as we have seen in the previous chapter, this does
not take into account the heroism and, in many cases, martyrdom of the

---

1 WA 19:401.6–9.

resistance. It neglects the internalized Lutheran Christianity that motivated its members. It ignores the fact that Western leaders consistently refused to take note of the resistance movement, much less consider its seriousness and strength. And it ignores the fact that the church leadership was divided along the lines described above; it ignores those bishops and pastors who spoke up precisely in the way Luther would have wanted them to.

In East Germany, the situation was only superficially comparable. On the one hand, not nearly as many Protestant clerics collaborated with the regime or supported its ideology; the pro-government "pastors' federation" (*Pfarrerbund*) never had more than two hundred members and was quickly dissolved. On the other hand, vanity made many church leaders cooperate with the authorities and even allow themselves to be used as informants by the Stasi, the East German secret police. More than one-and-a-half decades after Germany's reunification, armies of theologians, historians, and sociologists are still producing reams of paper on what has become a "preferred topic of research by scholars of contemporary history and sociology"—the relationship between church and state in the GDR.[2] They often reveal a disturbing intimacy between church bureaucracies and atheistic rulers.

There were many factors at work here. One was an ideological affinity with socialism. Another factor was, as in Nazi days, simply narcissism. As Harald Krille relates, "There were quite a few top churchmen who simply enjoyed playing 'insiders.' "[3] Then there was the evident need to assure the church's survival in an environment hostile to Christianity, which might have been the principal—though not sole—motivation behind the controversial *Kirche im Sozialismus* (church within socialism) approach by leading clerics of the League of Protestant Churches (*Kirchenbund*) in the GDR, which Peter L. Berger alluded to in the preface of this volume.

But rightly or wrongly, this policy of cooperation with the Communist state was based on Romans 13:1, which says that all governing

---

2 Horst Dähn et al., ed., *Staat und Kirchen in der DDR* (Frankfurt: Peter Lang, 2003), 7.

3 In a telephone interview with the author, July 2006.

authority is "instituted by God." Strangely, just as in Nazi Germany, it was not primarily confessional Lutherans who used this Pauline text to justify their collaboration with an anti-Christian system. According to sociologist Detlef Pollack, "the majority of the moderately placatory church leaders pushing the *Kirche im Sozialismus* line hailed from the ranks of the Union churches."[4] Among those leaders were Bishops Abrecht Schönherr, head of the eastern division of the territorial church of Berlin-Brandenburg; Eberhard Natho of the formerly Prussian "church province of Saxony" (not to be confused with the Lutheran Church of the former kingdom of Saxony); plus church lawyer Manfred Stolpe, second in command of the *Kirchenbund* and, after Germany's reunification, premier of the state of Brandenburg. None of these men is a confessional Lutheran—all have their theological roots in nine-teenth-century liberalism.

Moreover, writes Bruce W. Hall, using Romans 13 as an excuse, minority churches, such as Baptists, Methodists, and Seventh-day Adventists, were much more willing to make common cause with the Communists than the traditional territorial churches, be they Lutheran or Union (a mixed Lutheran and Reformed denomination imposed in the nineteenth century on formerly Prussian lands). Especially the German Adventists, who in the Third Reich "had given the National Socialists extraordinary backing," appealed to their members to join the Communist Party as far back as 1946, reports Hall.[5] He adds that when East Germany built the Berlin Wall in 1961, the Baptist leadership hailed this monstrous structure as an "anti-fascists bulwark" and "guarantor of peace and security."

In addition, fear, opportunism, and feeble faith prompted most East German Protestants to abandon the church and to deprive their children of Baptism and religious education so that, in the end, a mere 25 percent of the East German population belonged to one of the

---

4 Detlef Pollack, "Die politische und soziale Rolle der evangelischen Kirchen in der DDR aus sozialwissenschaftlicher Sicht," in *Staat und Kirchen in der DDR*, ed. Horst Dähn et al. (Frankfurt: Peter Lang, 2003), 77.

5 Bruce W. Hall, "Stand, Probleme und Erfahrungen eines amerikanischen Historikers bei der Erforschung der 'kleinen' Religionsgemeinschaften," in *Staat und Kirchen in der DDR*, ed. Horst Dähn et al. (Frankfurt: Peter Lang, 2003), 192–93.

Christian denominations. This meant that children were cut off from the source of Western civilization and its values. Thus it becomes increasingly obvious that the outrages committed by "neo-Nazi" skinheads against foreigners and the infirm today are rooted in this tragic development, as is the growth of extreme right-wing parties in the eastern German states.

Sixteen years after reunification, church membership has dropped even further in these territories because of a combination of factors. One is the introduction of the "church tax" collected by the government on behalf of the state-related denominations; another is the relentless migration of qualified workers and professionals to the western part of the country, where there are more jobs available. This has resulted in a drop of Protestants residing in the state of Saxony-Anhalt to a mere 15.9 percent of the population. (This is not to be confused with the Free State of Saxony, whose capital is Dresden, where the church is marginally better off.) Saxony-Anhalt used to be the Protestant heartland. It includes Lutherstadt Wittenberg, the city in which the Reformation began in 1517 and where Luther is buried under his former pulpit in the *Schloßkirche* (Castle Church).

Much has already been written about the *mésalliance* between the black frock and the red throne, so there is no need for me to elaborate on this sad aspect of Germany's most recent history. And where the decline of church membership is concerned, it will suffice to point to a historical-sociological factor, which has been "insufficiently explored so far," to quote Pollack, presumably because such research would fly in the face of political correctness. Pollack is referring to the "far-reaching social restructuring of the East German society since 1945." He goes on:

> Large parts of the educated bourgeoisie and the possessing classes [*Bildungsbürgertum sowie . . . Besitzbürgertum*] migrated west. The old elites in companies, schools and universities were driven out. Agriculture, the crafts and firms were collectivized. The result was an advancement of the lower classes into leadership positions, and a narrowing of the social-moral milieux of the elites. . . . The expulsion of the educated bourgeoisie and the collectivization of agriculture caused . . . a significant loss of Protestantism's social-structural backbone. The societal groups now setting the tone hailed

from the blue collar and (low-level) white-collar classes that had been critical of Christianity or hostile to it even before 1945.[6]

Citing the eminent Catholic sociologist Karl Gabriel, Pollack raises a fascinating point. This development must be seen in the context of a peculiarity of northern Germany's Christianization—it was largely imposed from above and therefore never took deep roots in the general population. "This way the Christian faith and popular culture never fully coalesced. . . . If Christian faith proved incapable of withstanding the pressures of sixty years of anti-church policies, then this must have been due in part to Christianity's failure of taking root among the people and being internalized by them."[7]

As the reader will realize, without this brief detour into the sociological, historical, and political circumstances of Lutherland's dramatic and wretched fall into unfaith, the significance of what follows cannot be fully appreciated nor will it be possible to draw lessons from this disaster to cope with future international conflicts. Handing the geographic heart of Germany's ancient civilization over to another godless tyranny after it had just been cleansed of Nazi rule was a staggering historical transgression on the part of the Western allies, which can only be explained with the unfathomable indifference to religious and cultural detail that has been plaguing U.S. foreign policy to this very day.

Having said this, however, one fascinating aspect pertaining to church history and Reformation theology is infinitely more relevant to this study. Whatever the sins of some church officials, they pale in the face of the faithfulness, civil courage, sacrifice, and wise comportment of individual parish pastors, deacons, and simple parishioners. Consciously or unconsciously, this minority acted in a truly Lutheran fashion by

---

6 Pollack, "Die politische und soziale Rolle der evangelischen Kirchen," 87. I have had personal experience with this in my childhood. When U.S. occupation forces turned over Leipzig to the Soviets in 1946, a new species of Communist teachers, called *Neulehrer,* turned up at my school. Of the eighty students in my class, only three of us admitted freely that we still attended church services. Every morning our *Neulehrer* told the class, "There are still three Christian swine [*Christenschweine*] in your midst. Beat them up after school until they come to their senses." This is how, aged 10 and undernourished, we learned to run fast, until we were smuggled into the U.S. zone of occupation.

7 Pollack, "Die politische und soziale Rolle der evangelischen Kirchen," 88.

opposing governmental injustice—not violently but with words, prayers, hymns, and candlelight. For what did Luther teach his followers? It is a Christian's duty to stand up courageously but with humility, for justice, truth, and personal convictions. And that happened in the GDR, which according to a local joke was neither German nor democratic nor a republic.

"The Free Word Has Broken the [Secular] Might" was the headline over one of the most stirring pieces of journalism written in the extraordinary days of East Germany's implosion. The article analyzed the church's role in the country's peaceful revolution. Its author was the late theologian Karl-Alfred Odin, who covered Protestantism for the venerable *Frankfurter Allgemeine Zeitung* of West Germany. Odin wrote: "Nobody directed the demonstrations in the G.D.R., nobody was detailed to keep order. Yet despite the justifiable fury against the Communist state apparatus . . . peace was always kept. How come? The answer lies in the prayers for peace and the candles. . . . With a candle in your hand you don't fight."[8]

These Christians, then, simply did not allow the two kingdoms to be "cooked and brewed into each other," to use Luther's imagery. "The Evangelical Church never intended [to act as a] political opposition," Odin continues. But he pointed out that, without overstepping their ecclesial confines, the Christian congregations nevertheless played a pivotal role. They provided pastoral care to opponents of the regime and to East Germans who had applied for exit visas and ever since were treated as outcasts by the Communist officialdom. Equally important, the congregations allowed their parish houses to be used by all kinds of *Gesprächskreise* (discussion groups) debating political, economic, and cultural questions they would not have been able to discuss elsewhere. Thus, writes Odin, shelters were established, and within these shelters developed a broad popular movement that showed through demonstrations that it was no longer prepared to tolerate the lack of freedom.

When this popular movement finally brought down the dictatorship, an unusual development occurred. Servants of the spiritual realm

---

8 Karl-Alfred Odin, "Das freie Wort hat die Macht gebrochen," *Frankfurter Allgemeine Zeitung* 298 (23 December 1989): "Bilder und Zeiten," (no page numbers).

suddenly found themselves in a position where they were often the only leaders qualified to prevent chaos and anarchy by assuming secular functions. Pastors became government ministers, members of parliament at all levels, county executives, and mayors. The Reverend Rainer Eppelmann, who under Communism had gone to jail for his refusal to serve in the military of a godless regime, suddenly found himself heading the East German Defense Ministry. In this position, it was Eppelmann's job to oversee the first stages of the dissolution of the country's once powerful National People's Army.

But did Luther not explicitly warn against brewing the two realms together? He did, but brewing the realms together is not exactly what happened in the final days of East Germany. Rather, the worldly realm lacked personalities who were, on the one hand, untarnished by any links to the previous government and, on the other hand, capable of stepping in to maintain the secular order. As we have seen in chapter 3, secular order corresponds to God's will; thus it turned out to be a blessing that in this exceptional case the spiritual realm possessed leaders it could lend to the state on a temporary basis. Most have since returned to their pulpits, though some have not. The latter have given up their ordination rights and are now serving as *leitourgoi gar Theou*, as God's agents, in the world rather than the spiritual kingdom. They are now ordinary citizens—like the rest of us.

LUTHER'S WORTHY HEIRS

In the late 1970s, I traveled as a reporter to East Germany, which I had not been allowed to visit for the preceding fifteen years and which I would not be permitted to enter for the subsequent decade. Initially, I received a visa to cover a fairly trivial subject—a luxury hotel for workers and peasants at the Baltic coast. But barely had I arrived in the GDR when I stumbled upon a much more exciting topic that was to occupy my mind for many years to come; it ultimately prompted me to study theology and write this book, which is based on my doctoral dissertation.

I discovered that there were many courageous people in East Germany who did precisely what Dietrich Bonhoeffer admonished Christians in our modern era to do. They "suffered with God in a godless world." Today, we know that in so doing they changed history. Luther had

worthy heirs in his own land, and they deserve mention, for they relativize an impression that has gained ground since the collapse of East
Germany and is threatening to ossify into a new cliché: the impression
that Luther's church has once again failed in an inhuman political system.

As I toured the part of Germany that had once been home to me,
I discovered the beginnings of the Christian protest movement that in
1989 would contribute heavily to the collapse of the Communist
tyranny in the GDR and the rest of the Soviet empire. Curiously, for all
the massive amount of scholarly research on East German church-and-
state issues done since reunification, those early ripples of what turned
into a deluge have hardly been explored. Intrepid Saxon pastors such as
Theo Lehmann of Chemnitz (then Karl-Marx-Stadt) and Christoph
Richter in Großhartmannsdorf, who were pivotal in this development,
are usually not mentioned in these treatises; yet they attracted thousands upon thousands of young people to their youth services, turning
these events into a hotbed of the "peaceful revolution" that would soon
envelop the entire country. One cannot help suspecting that the reason
for this omission might be scholarly snobbery at the centers of high
theology in reunified Germany because the main players in the Christian opposition, chiefly Lutherans, were of evangelical persuasion.
Moreover, I agree with Gerhard Lange's assessment: "Not always has the
great importance of oral history been given its due. . . . Much of what is
important for research has not been written down."[9]

During my reporting trips through East Germany in the 1970s, I
found an astonishing feature in the genesis of this protest movement.
Many of my interview partners told me that their movement had taken
off soon after Leipzig's thirteenth-century university church was blown
up on May 30, 1968, at the orders of Communist Party leader and chief
of state Walter Ulbricht. A native of Leipzig, Ulbricht hated his hometown's academic, Christian, and bourgeois traditions, which this grace-
ful sanctuary symbolized. To him, it was a blemish of the past on Karl-
Marx-Platz, Germany's largest square, which he intended to transform
into a "contemporary socialist parade ground." With the church, called

---

9 Gerhard Lange, "Die Anstrengungen der katholischen Kirche zur Aufarbeitung
   der Geschichte der katholischen Kirche in der DDR," in *Staat und Kirchen in der
   DDR*, ed. Horst Dähn et al. (Frankfurt: Peter Lang, 2003), 153.

Paulinerkirche, perished its organ, a masterpiece by local craftsman Johann Scheibe (1675–1748). It was Bach's favorite instrument in all of Leipzig. He had tested and certified it in 1717, six years before moving into the city for good.

Ulbricht's barbaric act, committed before the eyes of tens of thousands of weeping Leipzigers, had almost immediate consequences. Twenty days later, an international Bach festival took place in the Congress Hall next to Leipzig's famed zoo. Suddenly, in the presence of hundreds of musicians and music lovers from all over the world, an automatic mechanism unrolled a huge yellow banner showing the contours of the murdered church flanked by the dates of its consecration and its death (1240–1968) plus the inscription *Wir fordern Wiederaufbau* ("We demand reconstruction"). The authors of this act of defiance were five young physicists and physics students. They were captured and imprisoned. But many of their sympathizers throughout Leipzig and the GDR formed the nucleus of a protest movement that slowly snowballed into the avalanche that swept away Communism two decades later.

Not that the opposition consisted exclusively or even primarily of committed Christians. Most of the young people who began to flock to conservative pastors such as Lehmann, Richter, and others had never received any Christian instruction. In hundreds of interviews, they gave me the following reasons for their interest in the kind of Christianity that neither kowtows to the *Zeitgeist* nor "cooks and brews the two realms together":

- Young people were not looking for socialist rhetoric warmed over by clergymen. They had questions Marxism-Leninism simply could not answer. These questions were: Why are we here? Why is there suffering? Why do people get ill and die? What, if anything, happens after death?

- East Germans used to say that they lived and spoke on two tracks. There was the all-pervasive track of the Communist system with a rhetoric nobody believed. Then there was the private track, usually focused on West German television, which enabled people to cope with the unpleasant reality imposed on them by the regime. "Modern" anthropocentric churches reiterating the government's rhetoric did away with that latter level and thus became unattractive. On the other hand, a conventional church with its own language, rituals, and ethics that differed pleasantly from the regime's language, rituals, and ethics had a great appeal indeed.

• Young people often slipped into a church in search of an alternative to a system they clearly perceived as wrong. They liked to attend organ concerts and cantata services, which turned out to be valuable tools for mission because the music often triggered religious curiosity. In a break with German Protestant custom, pastors tended to keep their church doors open for strangers to wander about the sanctuary. More often than not, these were what, in East German clerical jargon, were called "nice heathens"—catechetical illiterates. Frequently, they thought the crucifix above the altar represented a gymnast. In Saxony, pastors or vicars spent much time in their churches on weekdays to be available to anyone who had questions.

In 1976, Manfred Stolpe, then the second in command of the Federation of Evangelical Churches (*Kirchenbund*) in the GDR and surely no champion of Lutheran orthodoxy, told me in an interview: "We are observing a curious development. Here in Berlin-Brandenburg our pastors are trying to be modern and liberal; they are trying to address the situation in the world we live in. And what happens? The churches are empty. We do not attract young people. In Saxony and Thuringia, on the other hand, where orthodox Lutheran sermons are preached, the Gospel is proclaimed, and traditional liturgies are sung, young people come *en masse*. Where do we go wrong?"[10] Where indeed? They went wrong in trying to accommodate the *Zeitgeist*, and in regions or parishes where this was attempted, the consequences proved disastrous for the church. In trying to square the goals of the church with those of the state, some

---

10 In view of the church leadership's precarious position in East Germany, this interview was conducted "on background"; his remarks were thus not for attribution at the time. Soon after reunification, Stolpe was accused of having been an "informal collaborator" of the Stasi (East German secret police), and he indeed admitted to having had contacts with this agency. Whatever the reasons might have been—his duties as the church's senior lawyer and second-ranking official clearly called for links to state authorities—Stolpe's remarks made to this West German journalist during an informal supper in his kitchen in East Berlin indicated a critical stance vis-à-vis the regime. For reasons of my own, I have never checked my "Stasi file," which doubtless would reveal the identity of East Germans who might have informed on me, but from what transpired during my GDR visits and their aftermath I have no reason to assume that Stolpe was one of them.

representatives of the ecclesiastical hierarchy fell into the same trap as the German Christians one generation before them.

It is tempting to create a new cliché at this point. The cliché would run thus: Whereas in the Nazi era the Union wing of German Protestantism[11] proved more immune to the National Socialist heresy, in the secular GDR Lutheranism proved more steadfast. But like every cliché, this one would also leave out relativizing factors. It must not be overlooked that the distortion of the doctrine of the two realms as propagated by the "German Christians" in the Nazi era was cheerfully perpetuated, albeit under a different political label and only up to a point, in Thuringia, a strictly Lutheran region. For a while, its bishop, Moritz Mitzenheim, kowtowed lamentably to the oppressive rule of Walter Ulbricht, the Communist Party leader handpicked by Joseph Stalin.[12] Conversely, prominent Union church leaders such as Bishop Hans-Jochim Fränkel of Görlitz or Pastors Eppelmann and Schorlemmer stood out because of their admirable degree of civil courage.

But it is true that, by and large, Lutheranism had learned from past mistakes and used the doctrine of the two realms correctly during the Soviet reign. "The Union churches had it easier with their doctrine," says Klaus Kaden, Leipzig's youth pastor at the time of the peaceful revolution and one of the originators of the prayers for peace. He continues: "To the Union churches Christ is king of all and that is that. It provided them with an easy way out of the dilemma a Socialist environment poses to a church. We Lutherans had to wrestle with the two realms over and over again, and that is precisely what gave us our strength."[13]

At this point, I must again quote Franz Lau:

---

11 The Union church is the official Protestant denomination in those German regions where in centuries past the rulers had decreed the merger of Lutheranism and Calvinism. The former kingdom of Prussia was one such region. Berlin and Brandenburg were Prussia's heartland.

12 However, according to Pollack, Mitzenheim changed course radically in 1953 by condemning the Communist state harshly when it threatened *Junge Gemeinde*, the feisty Protestant youth movement, and the *Evangelische Studentengemeinden* (Protestant Students groups). Moreover, the *Lutherische Bekenntnisgemeinschaft* (Community of Confessing Lutherans) in Thuringia was audaciously critical of the government and Mitzenheim's accommodating attitude. See Pollack, "Die politische und soziale Rolle der evangelischen Kirchen," 78.

13 Interview with the author, May 1990.

All those Christocratic theories are guided by a notion of Christ of which Scripture knows nothing. The term "kingship of Christ" is not biblical. The *vita Christiana* will always be lived in this world, as long as there are Christian house fathers and Christians who do not live in monastic colonies but pursue secular vocations. It may well be that the *vita Christiana* lived in the world today is much more difficult and filled with tension than in Luther's day. But that doesn't mean that we do not stand in two worlds of God.[14]

Lau was a professor of theology in Leipzig. His masterful work, *Luthers Lehre von den beiden Reichen*,[15] appeared at a critical time for Christians in the GDR who were at the height of the church struggle of 1952–1953. "No other book has influenced the postwar generation of Lutheran pastors in East Germany as much as this volume," says Jochen Ihmels, the former superintendent (regional bishop) of Rochlitz and a scion of an ancient dynasty of clerics in Saxony. In the early Hitler years, his grandfather, a bishop, had resigned in protest against the "German Christian" heresy. When I interviewed him in 1989, Ihmels was the chairman of the Confessing Church in Saxony. After the war, the anti-Nazi Confessing Church carried on as a brotherhood within the *Landeskirche*. Its primary function was to provide

---

14 Franz Lau, *Luthers Lehre von den beiden Reichen* (Berlin: Evangelische Verlags-anstalt, 1952), 95. It is true that under the episcopacy of Moritz Mitzenheim the hierarchical Thuringian church, which is strictly Lutheran, was also plagued by excessive collaboration with the Communist regime. But here the historical circumstances were different. In the National Socialist era, Thuringia was a hotbed of the "German Christian" heresy. After the war its policy of total subservience to the state was simply transferred to the Communist government. But at the time of the peaceful revolution in East Germany, the Thuringian church—and the *Kirchenbund*—were under the leadership of Werner Leich, an orthodox Lutheran who stood up to the Communist authorities. Although Erfurt, Heino Falcke's city, is the capital of Thuringia, it lies beyond the limits of the Thuringian Evangelical-Lutheran Church. Erfurt used to be Prussian. Thus its *Landeskirche* is a Union church. However, it is not my intention to denigrate the Union churches, most of whose pastors performed impressively in the face of the Communist challenge. I simply argue that the doctrine of the two realms served the Lutheran clergy, especially in Saxony, as a powerful weapon and shield against improper fraternization between the church and totalitarian authority. It protected the church to a considerable extent from the state's temptations.

15 *Luther's Doctrine of the Two Realms.*

the church at large with the theological ammunition for its dealings with the Communist state. This included a masterful comparison between the principal positions of Christianity and Marxism-Leninism culminating in the statement, "Marxism-Leninism is an anti-Christian doctrine of salvation"—a verity that would amaze many a Western theologian. Ihmels told me that Luther's doctrine of the two realms as interpreted by Lau had inspired him to stand by this statement: "A Christian is called to speak up and to be truthful; that's what I tried to do."

In clandestine leaflets that reminded the initiated of sixteenth-century Flacian pamphlets, the Confessing Church defined the role of a Christian in the GDR thus:

> A. [It is important] to resist the temptation to either accommodate comfortably [to the regime] or flee from responsibility. B. One can live as a Christian by [exercising] freedom and abstention. A Christian cannot accept every vocation or perform every [public] function. The more important one's position in society, the more difficult it becomes to persevere as a confessional Christian. C. One can live as a Christian by rejecting claims to absoluteness,[16] which violate the first commandment and [at the same time by] getting involved in behalf of one's fellow man. This is the yardstick by which one has to measure the extent to which cooperation in society is possible. D. One can live as a Christian by being prepared to struggle and suffer. The Christian does not seek confrontation, but neither does he dodge it if confrontation becomes unavoidable for the sake of truth. He relies on the weapons of the spirit and affirms [the weapons of] nonviolence as the means of struggle appropriate to the church. E. One can live as a Christian by obeying God's ten commandments and by having faith in his promises. This way a Christian in the GDR can radiate calm and confidence and prove himself as his Lord's witness.[17]

Indeed, the calm and confidence radiated by both Protestant and Roman Catholic Christians became their sharpest weapon in their confrontation with the atheistic doctrine of salvation that had

---

16 Meaning the Communist Party's claim to absoluteness.

17 Leaflet nr. D.483.2.78.1000, issued by the *Landesbruderrat der bekennenden evangelisch-lutherischen Kirche Sachsens* (Council of Brethren of the Confessing Evangelical-Lutheran Church of Saxony), February 1978.

been made the state religion of the GDR. In my research in the 1970s, I made an amazing discovery: Wherever confessional Christians lived and worked, they immediately became a powerful center of attraction to their environment. "You have to do nothing. People recognize you instinctively as a Christian, and so they come to you. You look different from all the others, you talk differently. You are not as uptight." This is what people told me in Pastor Theo Lehmann's *Schloßkirche* in Chemnitz, then Karl-Marx-Stadt, a church filled to capacity during every one of the pastor's four-hour youth services.

Colleagues and neighbors of Christians tended to seek them out to discover the source of their calm demeanor, signified in the German language by the wonderful vocable *Gelassenheit*, which is frequently associated with Lutheranism. Long before congregations began providing shelters in which the non-Christian opposition to the Communist dictatorship was able to evolve, simple Christians acted as the soft arms of the cross in its struggle with the harsh hammer and the compass—the symbols of East Germany's atheistic might. These arms included thousands of ecumenical *Hauskreise* or little prayer groups. They were often tiny, yet they functioned not unlike Communist cells in that they penetrated every aspect of life. Some of them were minute monastic communities of no more than two or three members living in an ordinary apartment; their mission was primarily just to be there.

The soft arms of the cross reached into factories, government offices, socialism's soulless high-rise apartment blocks, and even the National People's Army. Here are some examples:

- It was one of the many ironies of East Germany's forty-year history that the minority of children raised as Christians were discriminated against at school and taunted by party members; yet at the same time they were in reality highly respected by their classmates and teachers. Take the Holmer family of Gnadenthal near Berlin. Uwe Holmer is a Lutheran minister who, immediately after the collapse of East Germany, gave shelter to former party leader Erich Honecker and his wife, Margot, because nobody else would have them. When I interviewed the Holmers later, Sigrid Holmer told me:

  > It was a funny feeling having that couple under my roof. Here was Mrs. Honecker, who as minister of education tried every-

thing in her power to prevent children like mine from succeeding in Communist society. Yet I couldn't be angry with her because I knew how futile her efforts had been. I knew that one of my daughters was the only student in her class whom her teachers trusted even though she was an outsider, had never participated in the *Jugendweihe*, a Communist substitute for the confirmation ceremony, and had never belonged to the Young Pioneers. But what distinguished her from her contemporaries was the fact that, unlike most East Germans, she had not been taught to live on "two levels." She spoke as she thought, and she acted the way she spoke. And that's an attractive rarity in a dictatorship.

• Together, Roman Catholics and Protestants systematically visited new tenants in government housing developments. Seldom did they hear that the newcomers belonged to one or the other denomination. "Yet people were always glad when Christians came to see them," Christhart Wagner, a former youth pastor in Eisenach, told me. "Christians were the only ones willing to listen to people in those horrible tenements. During many of our visits we never got any further than the third floor because people had so much to tell us." This ministry was one important reason for the great trust the church enjoyed in the GDR, even among non-Christians. And it was precisely this trust that enabled the church to persuade them to act nonviolently. Without this nonviolence, the October revolution of 1989 would never have succeeded. Wagner commented, "Whether you declared yourself as a Christian in a bar or on a train, you inevitably encountered an enormous spiritual yearning among the people you met. For the Marxist-Leninist ideology touched nobody's heart."

• Andreas Gerschel, a deacon in Arnstadt, explained to me why he had entered the ministry: "During my military service I have always openly said that I was a Christian. As a result, officers came to me, a lowly private, to tell me their marital and career problems. They had to do this secretly because they were all Communist party functionaries. It was this experience that made me realize that I was called to be a minister."[18]

---

18 Interview with the author, summer 1990.

- The most successful missionary to the military of a godless government was a woman. Her name is Evilis Heisse, and she is a deacon's wife in the Erzgebirge Mountains, where the majority of the people have remained staunchly Lutheran through two atheistic dictatorships. Heisse set out to bring the Gospel to the soldiers garrisoned in her town. The National People's Army had no chaplains. So Mrs. Heisse kept an open house for the young men. Christian draftees spent every free hour there and often came with non-Christian comrades tired of drowning their inner emptiness in alcohol, which is a major problem in East Germany. Heisse reckons that the equivalent of an entire battalion has prayed, sung, eaten, and just relaxed in her small apartment. When their two years in the military were up, these men reentered civilian society as what Superintendent Richter in Leipzig called the "salt of the earth." Mrs. Heisse even distributed—illegally—the Bible to Soviet soldiers training nearby. How did she obtain hundreds of Russian-language Bibles? An underground network of Christian smugglers had brought them into East Germany.

Like Carl Goerdeler one generation before her, Evilis Heisse probably never asked herself: What would Luther do in my place? Like the members of Christian cells, like Christian visitors to socialist tenements and factories, she acted in an *internalized* Lutheran way that inevitably included a readiness to sacrifice. Mrs. Heisse's son and daughter wound up in prison for supporting their mother's activities. Indeed, many young East German Christians encountered almost two decades ago were not spared what Luther considered the quintessential Christian experience: Bearing witness (*to martyrion*) courageously in a hostile world also means bearing the cross. There was a teenager whose father had beaten him black and blue for practicing his faith. The father, a career officer, had lost his commission because of his son's activities. For the same reason, a high school principal locked up her daughter for several weeks. Another officer's son, who regularly attended Bible classes, was expelled from his school when he was about to graduate; his own father had instigated the expulsion.

A FIERY SELF-SACRIFICE *IN CASU CONFESSIONIS*

Doubtless, the most extreme form of martyrdom in East Germany was the fiery death of the Reverend Oskar Brüsewitz. On August 17, 1976, this village pastor, a former master cobbler, got out of his car in front of the *Michaeliskirche* in Zeitz. Dressed in his black clerical robe, he unfolded a banner reading, "The churches charge Communism with the suppression of our youth." Then he doused himself with gasoline and set himself on fire. He ran toward the church but collapsed after 20 yards. In an intensive care unit in Halle, he lived for another 100 hours. In his waking hours, the pastor hummed Lutheran hymns.

Brüsewitz's suicide was the single most powerful stimulus to the East German church hierarchy's moral courage in its dealings with the state. More than five hundred people, including eighty-two Protestant and Roman Catholic clergymen, attended Brüsewitz's funeral. His bishop denounced the Communist Party's attempt to question the pastor's sanity. With a clear reference to the Brüsewitz suicide, the synod[19] of the *Kirchenbund* insisted that the hierarchy muster the courage for taking an "unequivocal position." With direct reference to the pastor's self-sacrifice, the synod declared: "Frequently the impression prevails that the hierarchies [of the *Landeskirchen*] act according to tactical considerations. And it is no longer clear whether it is God who stands above every situation."

The Communist media portrayed Brüsewitz as a confused man. But he was clearly not. Christa and Esther Brüsewitz, his widow and one of his daughters, describe him instead as a gutsy man of God who often had his church bells toll for more than one hour to call lax Christians to prayer. He would thunder from his pulpit: "We are not looking forward to Socialism but to the kingdom of God." To the dismay of the Communist authorities, he placed a 20-foot neon cross on the top of his church spire so the truckers rumbling down the nearby highway from Leipzig to Gera would see it. When the GDR celebrated its twenty-fifth anniversary, Brüsewitz put up a huge sign reading: "2,000 years unvanquished Church of Jesus Christ." He was a cheerful man who trotted through the nine villages in his parish with his two daughters, all three of them blowing their trumpets. And he was a compassionate man who fed home-baked bread and homemade jam to the starving and begging Soviet soldiers roaming the Zeitz countryside.

---

19 Church parliament.

Would Luther have considered Brüsewitz's self-sacrifice as an acceptable form of protest *in casu confessionis*? This question probably eludes a definitive answer. In fact, could Luther ever have imagined circumstances under which the Christian faith would ever find itself in such dire jeopardy as it did four hundred years after his death—in his own land? Could it ever have occurred to Luther that the governing authority in Germany would do everything in its power to prevent the Christian education of children? Could it have occurred to him that a pastor would have to burn himself to death to remind ecclesial authority of its obligations in the face of this catastrophic turn of events?

One thing is certain. In his Lutheran way of thinking, Oskar Brüsewitz had determined that a *casus confessionis* existed. Religion, Christian education, and the family were in peril. This led Brüsewitz to the Lutheran conclusion that it was his duty to fight. But he did not fight in the style of Thomas Münzer by instigating an insurrection; he fought in a Lutheran fashion by taking the cross upon himself. "With this act brother Brüsewitz has moved the Church," Bishop Werner Leich of Thuringia later said to me. And when the Communist government fell in East Germany, many burghers of Zeitz approached Mrs. Brüsewitz, saying, "This we have your husband to thank for."[20]

We do not know to what extent Brüsewitz ever reflected intellectually on Lau's repristination of Luther's doctrine of the two realms. The fact is that he acted according to this doctrine, albeit in a highly idiosyncratic fashion. But many other theologians or theologically aware laypeople of the generation that was steeled by Ulbricht's church struggle in the immediate postwar period explicitly acknowledged Lau's influence—men such as Bishop Leich, Superintendent Ihmels, Superintendent Johannes Richter of Leipzig's *Thomaskirche*, Pastor Kaden, Theo Lehmann, and Moritzburg's Pastor Helmuth Wielepp, the quintessential Saxon Lutheran pietist who never doubted for one minute that prayer was more powerful than any ideology.

Decades before the prayers for peace in big-city churches managed to unhinge the Communist system, such prayers were commonplace in Wielepp's sanctuary. Every workday his church bells called the faithful to brief worship services. Now and then, young mothers sneaked their

---

20 This I have personally witnessed.

babies through side entrances to have the children baptized without their fathers' knowledge. Wielepp embodies all the virtues that have been attributed to Saxon clergymen for centuries. He is a powerful orator endowed with a glorious sense of humor, cheerful piety, and Lutheran truthfulness. He is a man who never minces words and consequently held his flock together. When Wielepp retired in the 1980s, 2,000 of the 2,800 burghers of Moritzburg were members of his congregation; Wielepp's services were always well attended.

The cross's gentle march toward victory over hammer and sickle began with men such as Wielepp long before the Communist Party designed that emblem and called it a part of the GDR. In 1946, when the last semi-free elections were held in the Soviet zone of occupation, the pastor was appointed poll supervisor in the small community of Weinböhla. When he discovered that the Soviet military administration had ordered the falsification of election results it considered unfavorable, Wielepp swiftly displayed the correct results on the bulletin board outside his church. Two days later the mayor announced the false figures, and Wielepp instructed his confirmands to cease greeting the mayor in the streets: "That man is a forger, he belongs in jail."

It is one of the curious verities of Christian life under Communism that such displays of civil courage by clergymen rarely had any serious consequences. Where a Christian confronts evil, it will ultimately retreat. Time and again this ancient insight was proven right in the forty-year history of East Germany. The Communists simply lacked the guts to challenge a pastor who, in addition to his parish work, drove a rickety truck with solid-rubber tires to all corners of Saxony to distribute pious tracts. They did not have the nerve to mess with a volatile cleric who, outraged by the inhumanity of the land reform that reduced independent farmers to agrarian proletarians, stormed into Moritzburg's town hall and informed the mayor, "You guys are worse than the Nazis."

But not only were parsons familiar with Lau's book on the two realms. One top church official who referred to Lau was Johannes Cieslak, a master stove-fitter who for years had been president of the Saxon synod. Cieslak had spent years in Hitler's concentration camps and then served in the dreaded penal battalion 999 in North Africa. He was taken prisoner by U.S. forces and sent to a camp for anti-Nazi POWs in

Massachusetts. There, two things happened to him. First, under the influence of U.S. military chaplains he returned to the Lutheran faith of his youth. Second, he observed Communist inmates at close quarters and realized that they were no better than the Nazis. So when Saxony came under Communist control, he decided not to settle in the U.S. zone of occupation, though he was given that opportunity. Instead, he returned to East Germany determined to resist tyranny in a nonviolent, Christian way—through the Word. He noted, "This is what I have learned from Luther—and Lau."

As the highest-ranking layman in the Saxon church, Cieslak kept reminding Communist officialdom "that it is not advisable to kick us Saxons around." Cieslak told me:

> When we found out that somebody was discriminated against because of his faith—for example, when a student received bad grades only because he was a Christian—we gave the party hacks such hell that they normally gave in. The problem was that most human rights violations were not reported to the church. But when the pastor knew about it, he or his superiors would take this up with public officials, and in most cases the matter was straightened out. Where we showed moral fortitude the Communists were scared of us.[21]

For Cieslak, the comportment of the individual Christian was the most powerful weapon in the cross's struggle with the hammer and the compass. "A Christian was able to do anything he wanted in the GDR," Cieslak stressed and added, "A Christian had to accept that he would be barred from certain functions." Cieslak's own children were not allowed to graduate from a regular high school—no practicing Christian could. Yet Cieslak's son Jürgen still managed to become a civil engineer, albeit in a roundabout way. He trained as an apprentice stove-fitter, attended night school, and obtained his high school diploma with such excellent grades that there was no way for the Technical University of Dresden to turn down his application.

Cieslak commented, "Christians are willing to accept disadvantages in order to live their faith." And that impressed some Socialists so much that, under the guidance of this stove-fitter, they themselves

---

21 Interview with the author, summer 1990.

became Christians and asked to be baptized. Cieslak stated:

> We knew that God was more powerful than the Party, and that gave us strength. Naturally we became scared when our doorbells rang in the middle of the night. But then we told ourselves: So what? We have a boss who is on our side. The secret police broke up our *Hauskreise* (prayer groups) claiming they had no right to assemble for Bible study outside church buildings. So we simply invited fellow parishioners to parties; they, too, were broken up when it became known that the Bible was read. In the end, the church formally rented the living rooms of congregants for Bible classes and thus deprived the *Stasi* of any pretext to interfere with us.

As president of the Saxon church parliament, Cieslak continually had to deal with Dr. Leverenz, who was the Communist Party's liaison to the churches in the district of Dresden. Cieslak said, "During these meetings it became obvious to me that the Marxists learned more about Christianity than we about Marxism." Cieslak received his greatest satisfaction when Dr. Leverenz asked him in private at one of the last meetings, "Please explain to me the Christian concept of sin." The old stovefitter has never found out if Leverenz converted, but he added, "I had the feeling that this man was on the right way."

The late Superintendent Richter of Leipzig's *Thomaskirche,* the church in front of whose altar Johann Sebastian Bach is buried, told me he thought that the forty years of Communism was one period in German history when the doctrine of the two realms was truly put to the test—and it proved itself. Richter commented, "The experience of living in this socialist society made me see the doctrine of the two realms in a totally new light." Using a German metaphor for which there is no English equivalent, Richter interprets the doctrine in the *Standbein-Spielbein* dialectic. As a rule, nobody stands firmly on the ground on both legs. Usually, the body rests on one leg, which the Germans call the *Standbein,* whereas the other leg is at ease. That leg is the *Spielbein.* According to Richter, a Christian in a totalitarian society will do well if his *Standbein* stands firmly on the ground of tradition and the reconciliation in Christ. When this is the case, the *Spielbein* can move in the world. This concept may sound harmless enough, but, as we have seen, it is a lethal combination for the totalitarian regime under which it is practiced. This is how Christians have undermined tyranny.

Was Gorbachev a Wundermann?

But the Christian endeavor to combat the Communist tyranny had help, as Bishop Leich also concluded: "I believe that God intervened in history to end this totalitarian regime and the division of our country. But God did not do this in a hocus-pocus kind of war. He made use of a set of circumstances such as our internalized distaste for violence, the faithfulness of the church, the economic and ecological disaster in Eastern Europe and the appearance of Mikhail Gorbachev."[22]

Does Gorbachev, then, meet the criteria for a *Wundermann*? Was he hewn from the same block as Cyrus, Alexander the Great, Vespasian, or Frederick the Wise? Many pastors interviewed for this study answered this question with an unqualified yes. Bishop Leich's response echoed Luther's exegesis of Psalm 101: "God even uses heathen as tools. It is possible that in Gorbachev's actions we discern God's hidden hand, whether Gorbi likes it or not."[23]

But a caveat is very much in order here. Once again, one needs to read Luther carefully and rethink his explanation of divine providence on the basis of the biblical statements. Luther would caution that, though we are assured of divine providence, without the benefit of the divine perspective we can only use our best judgment to discern what the divine plan is when analyzing world events (as well as events in our personal lives). Divine providence is a clear biblical teaching; therefore, we look for the hand of God in history. But this side of eternity we can never claim to know with certainty what the divine will or the divine plan is—whether an individual is indeed a *Wundermann* (specially sent by God), an obstacle, or even an opponent of God's plan (though it may not seem so to most observers).

For example, many would relegate Gorbachev to a secondary role and find the hand of God in Ronald Reagan's "big stick" diplomacy, the Strategic Defense Initiative ("Star Wars"), which forced the leaders of the Soviet Union to see that they could no longer compete with the United States militarily while their economy was collapsing. How many other events and persons, large or small, may have unwittingly, even

---

22 Interview with the author, summer 1990.

23 Interview with the author, summer 1990.

contrary to their wishes, carried out the divine plan by contributing to the disintegration of the Soviet Union?

In the final analysis, East Germany's peaceful revolution was an eminently Lutheran event, much in line with Lau's assessment of the doctrine of the two realms:

> Maybe it is the most important order of the day that the church perform its critical function vis-a-vis the world not in a lordly manner but in the form of service and obedience, in other words, with humility. In the final analysis, [the church] is not called to do this for the sake of the world but for God's sake, God who rules both realms but who is still one God whom we want to serve in the world.[24]

From a human point of view, that is precisely what happened on October 9, 1989, during and after what turned out to be the most crucial prayer services in the history of the East German resistance. Superintendent Richter preached in the *Thomaskirche* on Proverbs 25:15: "With patience a ruler will be persuaded, and a soft tongue will break a bone." Then his congregation, Christians and non-Christians alike, joined 70,000 other demonstrators and softly felled a forty-year tyranny. But more than that, they aroused the modern world from the utopian dream that the *eschaton*, that paradise, can be made a reality here and now by human efforts. With their actions, they finally settled the conflict between Luther and Münzer in Luther's favor. Before the eyes of hundreds of millions of television viewers around the world, the prejudiced misconception that Luther's doctrine of the two realms had turned the Germans into spineless sycophants and thus paved the way for Hitler was finally exposed as a banal cliché.

---

24 Lau, *Luthers Lehre von den beiden Reichen*, 96. See, for example, the excellent discussion on "God in History" in Heinrich Bornkamm, *Luther's World of Thought*, trans. Martin H. Bertram (St. Louis: Concordia, 1958), 195–217, especially the concluding statement: "For Luther Christ's cross was a pledge of God's wonderful, hidden rule in history; and in it he found, as every Christian finds, the help not indeed to understand history but to bear it and to be victorious over it."

Epilogue

Kairos and Betrayal

This study has been a plea for Martin Luther's acquittal from a charge that amounted to nothing less than the claim that he led Germany, Europe, and the entire world down the path to the worst cataclysm in the history of mankind. More than the reformer's good reputation is at stake here. What really matters is that after the collapse of the utopian era, we have rediscovered, albeit fleetingly, one of the finest treasures that has been handed down through the centuries. That treasure is Luther's doctrine of the two realms, a doctrine that enables the Christian to be guided by natural reason while operating in the secular realm without losing his citizenship in the spiritual realm. More than once in this century, parts of Luther's church have betrayed this liberating message, and other Christians have frequently defamed it. At least in part, the emptiness of Europe's Protestant churches every Sunday morning is the result of the ongoing betrayal of Luther's doctrine. This seems to indicate that the lessons of World War II and the East German experiences have still not been sufficiently learned.

"The devil never stops cooking and brewing these two kingdoms together," Luther said. "Secular leaders always want to be Christ's masters and teach him how he should run his Church and spiritual government. Similarly, the false priests and schismatic spirits always want to ... teach people how to organize the secular government. Thus the devil is very busy on both sides."[1] How right he was. Mindlessly, many Protestant ministers continue to "preach their churches empty," as the saying goes in Germany. They do so with secular and often contemptible messages. In West Berlin, for example, left-wing pastors instituted "requiem services for the departed bride" immediately after reunification, the "bride" being the GDR, whose Communist tyrants had their citizens shot like rabbits if they dared to cross into the free part of their homeland, including West Berlin.

The lament about Protestant preachers misusing the pulpit for ventures into the secular realm is by no means the exclusive province of conservative thinkers. As we have seen in the previous chapter, this malady is rooted in the theological crisis caused by nineteenth-century Protestant liberalism, which allowed secular creeds to infiltrate doctrine, thus blurring the distinction between the two realms. This is how anti-Semitic, Marxist, liberationist, feminist, and homosexual agendas managed to replace biblical and confessional truths in the kerygma of mainline Protestant churches in the Western world, sending them into a tailspin. This tendency to place man's desires, ideologies, biases, and saccharine political correctness above the Word of God has caused far too much damage during the Nazi era to be glossed over today by responsible intellectuals on the right or the left of the political divide. One prominent left-wing spokesman putting his finger on the church's wound is Michael Naumann, co-publisher of the renowned weekly *Die Zeit* and a former minister of culture. He scornfully accused preachers of "blathering from the pulpit often incomprehensible editorials on social and political issues. That's mostly stuff that I have read in every newspaper or even written myself."[2] Political scientist Klaus Motschmann accused the Protestant church of being "totally lost in the fog of the *Zeitgeist*."

The good news from Germany is that formerly "modernist" clerics, such as Wolfgang Huber, presiding bishop of the Evangelical Church in Germany at the time of this writing, have come to share this view. "*Sie sind nachgedunkelt* [They have darkened]," Germans like to say about

---

1 AE 13:194–95.

2 Uwe Siemon-Netto, "Young Pastors More Faithful," *United Press International* (15 January 2004).

such church leaders, meaning that they have become more confessional. Huber, once a stridently left-wing Heidelberg professor, has apologized for his former emphasis on secular concerns and now ceaselessly pushes for evangelism.

But much damage has been done already. Before his death in 1999, Johannes Gross, one of the wittiest essayists in postwar Germany and an orthodox Lutheran, pilloried the canine comportment of his nation's state-related Protestant church. He told me Protestant clerics behaved like dogs in front of whose noses a sausage is teasingly dangled and then cruelly whisked away. They yelp and snap at this piece of meat, salivating, but never quite manage to get it. In the present context, the bait happens to be the latest fad, or as Germans like to say, "the latest sow running down Main Street." Gross predicted that, consequently, only Roman Catholicism and evangelical Protestantism will survive in Germany. In other words, Lutheranism, which had shaped German culture for nearly half a millennium, would just wither away. A recent prognosis issued by the Evangelical Church in Germany (EKD) headquarters in Hanover seems to confirm Gross's dire forecast. It calculated that the membership of the Lutheran, Union, and Reformed *Landeskirchen* will drop from its current 26.5 million to 17 million by the year 2030. Protestantism has lost its status as the majority religion in Germany years ago. It has been overtaken by the Roman Catholic Church, which is also shrinking. And this is happening, ironically, at a time when pollsters note an increasing interest among Germans in matters of faith, when two-thirds of the population state that they consider religious education important and that they pray regularly.[3]

The elegant port city of Hamburg can serve as a paradigm for Protestantism's decline as a result of, or in tandem with, its secularist drift. Hamburg was once a bastion of sound Lutheranism. But in 1992, the Reverend Maria Jepsen was elected this city-state's—and world Lutheranism's—first woman bishop. Jepsen immediately embarked on promoting abortion rights and instituted the blessing of same-sex unions. Given that the cross is the heart and center of Lutheran theology, it was all the more astounding that this "bishop" proposed replacing the

---

3 Marcus Mockler, "So soll es wieder aufwärtsgehen," *ideaSpektrum* 27 (June 8, 2006): 16–19.

cross with the crèche as the symbol of Christianity. Her pronounce-
ments became so comical that before each of her sermons in the land-
mark *Michaeliskirche,* the congregation's staff would take bets on how
long it would take her to get to her favorite topic, homosexuality. The
loser had to pay a round of Dom Pérignon champagne. Within the first
ten years of Jepsen's episcopacy, the Lutheran Church in Hamburg lost
one-third of its membership. Still, the regional synod rewarded Jepsen
by re-electing her for yet another ten-year term. Today, a mere 26 percent of Hamburg's 1.6 million citizens describe themselves as religious,
which makes Hamburg the most secularized state in western Germany.
Only the formerly Communist East has more atheists or agnostics.[4]

I wrote at the beginning of this chapter that in 1989 we had rediscovered the liberating message of the doctrine of the two realms, but I
hasten to add with sadness that this rediscovery proved ephemeral. This
became clear when, soon after reunification, the then twenty-four territorial churches (their number has since shrunk to twenty-three as a
result of a merger) published a new hymnal. German hymnals include
the Augsburg Confession, though in the past the Union churches only
included its first twenty-one articles, while the Lutheran denominations
provided all twenty-eight articles.

However, in the new hymnals of most *Landeskirchen*—including
the territorial church of staunchly Lutheran Saxony—the Augsburg
Confession now ends with Article XXI. This means that even in a
Lutheran region worshipers no longer have easy access to a key element
in their church's theology—the doctrine of the two realms that is out-
lined with great clarity in Article XXVIII, titled "Church Authority" or,
alternatively, "Of Ecclesial Power."[5] This might seem a minor matter.
But in reality it is profoundly troubling because it shows the extent to
which Lutheran church bureaucrats have allowed themselves to be
browbeaten by Union theologians who dominate German Protestantism today. Union theologians do not generally subscribe to Luther's
dictum that the "two kingdoms must not be cooked and brewed
together." Many insist that there exists only one realm, the kingdom of

---

4 *ideaSpektrum* 18 (2003): 11.

5 This is not the case in Bavaria, a predominantly Catholic state whose minority
Lutheran *Landeskirche* includes strong confessional elements.

Christ, which is a dangerously flawed doctrine that even Reformed theologians in neighboring France, Calvin's homeland, are beginning to
question.

In Saxony, I found how insidious this infiltration of Union theology into that state's once staunchly Lutheran church has become. Bach's
Thomaskirche in Leipzig, once a mighty fortress of Lutheran orthodoxy,
imported a senior pastor from a western German Union church. Now
he uses the pulpit from which Luther once preached to rail against
United States policy. His colleague in the nearby *Nikolaikirche*, who had
been instrumental in East Germany's peaceful revolution, competes
with him in the art of political pulpiteering, thundering against the
attempts of the Berlin government to modernize the German economic
and social systems.

In 1989, many faithful Protestants in Germany, including this
writer, deluded themselves that they were witnessing a new dawn for
Lutheranism and its realistic doctrine, which would serve well as an
antidote against the mushiness of postmodern spirituality with its ever-
shifting values. Yet half a generation after the collapse of Communism,
we have discovered that just as in the case of great revivals or the sudden
and seemingly inexplicable growth of individual congregations, one of
Luther's most poignant observations applies to the larger picture as well:
There occur along the church's journey the occasional *Platzregen des
Heiligen Geistes*, "cloudbursts of the Holy Spirit." What happened in the
GDR was such a cloudburst on a grand scale. But then it was all over,
and one wonders if those called to preach the Gospel have even grasped
what had happened to them.

Some Protestant bishops, more than their Roman Catholic counterparts, actually seemed embarrassed about what had occurred in their
country. Instead of publicly giving thanks for what conservative Christians interpreted as a manifest intervention by God in history, liberal
church leaders such as Martin Kruse, then the presiding bishop of the
(Protestant) Evangelical Church in Germany, voiced their *Betroffenheit*,
a singularly tiresome German term meaning—loosely and imprecisely
translated—"perplexity combined with shame," almost implying that
what happened should not have happened.

Then on October 30, 1990, the unthinkable took place. Germany
was formally reunified. The whole world was stunned at this apparent

miracle that occurred without the loss of a single drop of blood. The whole Soviet empire unraveled in the wake of a breathtaking event in the very country that, little more than two generations earlier, had caused the second world war in a century and a holocaust that annihilated 6 million Jews, 500,000 Gypsies, and countless others. This reunification should have called for Germany's churches to ring their bells in joyous gratitude, as Luther himself would doubtless have urged every pastor in the land. But mostly Catholic bells tolled—plus Lutheran ones in Thuringia and a few other parts of the country. Generally, though, there was silence from Protestant spires as modernist ministers indulged their faithless perplexity.

The two German militaries—each the second largest in NATO and the Warsaw Pact, respectively—were bloodlessly integrated, an astounding feat by West German Lieutenant-General Jörg Schönbohm, a practicing Protestant who at the time of this writing is minister of the interior of the eastern state of Brandenburg. Bringing draftees from the largely dechristianized east into the armed forces of the united Germany presented a spectacular opportunity for military chaplains. For the first time, they had a chance to introduce these young men to the Gospel; in Communist days, the National People's Army employed no chaplains and did not allow any ministers of religion into its barracks. The Catholic Church jumped at this opportunity, but the Protestant denominations in the eastern territories wasted valuable years waffling over whether it was compatible with the evangelical faith for pastors to perform these duties in the employ of the government, a perfectly normal custom in Western countries such as France and the United States, where the separation between church and state is much more rigorously observed than in Germany.[6]

---

6 Although there is no absolute separation between church and state in Germany, chaplains in the *Bundeswehr* (armed forces), unlike their counterparts in France, Great Britain, or the United States, do not carry military rank nor do they wear military insignia. They are civilian ministers on loan to the Defense Ministry, which pays their salaries. With German forces now serving in peacekeeping missions in danger zones such as Afghanistan, the Baltics, Cambodia, and the Congo, chaplains accompany the troops everywhere. They have become popular as of late and are discovering that the military is a rewarding mission field where unchurched soldiers seek them out to talk about God.

Yet there is this pervasive thirst for transcendence in Germany as there is in other parts of the West. This should be the new Lutheran hour. At a time when both liberal Protestantism and considerable segments of evangelicalism are trapped on a roundabout because of their inability to keep the secular and the spiritual realms apart, there is a great need for a return to the sober voice of Luther. Peter L. Berger says that the doctrine of the two realms is one of the most valuable assets Lutheranism could offer to the contemporary United States, an assessment that would also apply to Germany.[7]

Even in the French Reformed Church, a renewed interest in Lutheran theology is gathering momentum, according to Jean-Luc Mouton, the former editor in chief of the newspaper *Réforme*. "Left-wing Calvinism is dead," he says. And it is dead only two or three decades after its most ardent proponents, led by theology professor Georges Casalis, went on pilgrimages to Communist-ruled countries. "Cambodia and Nicaragua have taught us that left-wing revolutions could not possibly be the Kingdom of God on earth. This has led some of the younger theologians in their mid-thirties to turn from Calvin to Luther."[8] In this process, they are turning their backs on Calvin's doctrine according to which there is only one kingdom, the kingdom of Christ. Calvin considered it essential for man to honor God by forging this one kingdom, which includes its social, political, and economic aspects. From the Lutheran point of view this implies "cooking and brewing the two kingdoms together." To Lutherans, the state of the world leaves little doubt that the devil is still its prince. Hence they view the doctrine of one realm as misguided.

Neo-Lutheranism's influence in contemporary France is not limited to the Reformed Church. Its two best-known proponents are Jean Daniel Causse and Elian Cuvillier, professors of systematic theology and New Testament, respectively, at the Protestant Institute (University) in Montpellier. Both also lecture regularly at Roman Catholic seminaries, where they familiarize future priests with the doctrine of the two realms as a serum against utopianism or *Schwärmerei*. In France, arguably the

---

7 Lecture at Concordia Seminary, St. Louis, Missouri, March 16, 2006.

8 Interview with the author, March 2001.

179

most secularized country in Western Europe, this argument is hitting home at a time of heated debate over *laïcité*, the doctrine on which that nation's rigid form of separation between church and state is based. Now even left-of-center politicians such as Régis Debray are calling for the reintroduction of religious instruction at public schools. In such a situation, a theology by which the two realms must serve each other but never interfere with one another could become very relevant indeed.

Meanwhile in Germany, where a huge collective hangover from two tyrannical regimes has seriously warped religious attitudes, it is quite likely that a new "Lutheran hour" could commence as suddenly as the nation's recent return to a healthy form of patriotism during the 2006 World Cup soccer tournament. Never before have that many black, red, and gold flags been waved cheerfully in a country that has eschewed any form of national emotion since World War II. Gradually, Germany seems to be shedding the insincere abstemiousness with regard to praiseworthy national legacies, which must ultimately include the teachings of the father of the Reformation.

It is obvious that the new thirst for transcendence cannot be satisfied by secularizing the church and thus excommunicating political adversaries de facto, which is what happens when one does not distinguish properly between the two realms. Let the conservatives, liberals, and independents—in the German context Christian and Social Democrats, Liberals, and Greens—lambast each other to their hearts' delight in the secular realm. But in the spiritual realm, that is, the church, all worldly discord must cease as long as the state does not interfere with the confession. Luther says that the two realms serve each other. They can only do this if secular conflicts are not carried into the church, for in the church everybody, regardless of his point of view on secular matters, stands under the Gospel.

Bonhoeffer considered the idea of a church made up solely of racially pure Germans a theological absurdity; the same applies to the ideologically correct church. The pastor proclaiming political dogmas from the pulpit leads his congregation out of the spiritual realm. He does not say anything new to those sharing his opinions, so they might as well sleep in on Sundays. Parishioners with opposing views are likely to avoid church "services" that are indistinguishable from partisan assemblies. Such a church will have no healing effect on the secular realm—quite the contrary. By adopting that realm's conflicts, it commits suicide. This is why sanctuaries are empty and the sects successful.

Ideology, utopianism, the *Zeitgeist*, and the cliché are phenomena of the secular realm, and they are related in their inability to relativize. Peter L. Berger points out that Luther has taught us an alternative to this dilemma:

> The Gospel liberates by relativizing all the realities in this world and all our projects in this world. The vocation of the church is to proclaim the Gospel, not to defend the American way of life, not to "build socialism," not even to "build a just society"—because, quite apart from the fact that we don't really know what this is, our notions of justice are fallible and finally marred by Sin. The "works-righteousness" in all these "different gospels" lies precisely in the insinuation that we shall be saved, "justified." But, as Paul tells us, "by works of the law shall no one be justified."[9]

The U.S. historian Mark A. Noll, who is not a Lutheran, sees a special role for Lutherans in an era marked by disillusionment, lack of orientation, and a desperate search for meaning. Noll believes that the time has come for Lutherans in the United States to stop being inconspicuous and start sharing their vast doctrinal and historical treasures with the rest of the country, an idea Peter L. Berger fully shares. Noll wants them first and foremost to remain "authentically Lutheran," but he also wants them to speak "Lutheranism with an American accent." And then "the resources that Lutherans offer to Americans, especially to other Protestants, would be of incalculable benefit.... Unlike most American Protestants, Lutherans have always insisted that history is important to faith."[10]

Noll thus supports the views of Johannes Richter, Leipzig's former superintendent, who, through forty years under Communism has discovered that a Christian's *Spielbein* is free to roam the world as long as the *Standbein* stands firmly on the ground of faith and tradition. As we have seen in the first chapter, Walter Künneth connects the *Zeitgeist* with modern society's hostility to history, with its "attempts to flee from history," with the utopian vision for a "history-free future for mankind,"

---

9 Erasmus Lecture given at St. Peter's Lutheran Church, New York, 1988.

10 Mark A. Noll, "The Lutheran Difference," *First Things* 20 (February 1992): 36–37.

and thus ultimately with its attempt to "flee from God." Noll's answer to this dilemma is this:

> Lutherans are in a position to teach a much sounder view of the past. . . . American evangelicals, who waste away with panting for the supernatural quick fix, and American liberals who want to fix things by themselves and right away, both need to learn from Lutherans that God's concern extends over decades and centuries as well as over days, weeks and months. Lutherans, who know something about the long view of history, should be insulated against the instability of innovation and the overconfidence of ignorance. Many of America's most energetic Christian leaders have cried with virtually the same words: "I have found something new. You must accept it or be lost." Against the lust for novelty, the Lutheran sense of history stands as a sober witness. . . . [T]hey are in a position to show that the accumulated testimony of the past is far more likely to plumb the depth of God's character and the vicissitudes of human nature than the idiosyncratic voice of the present.[11]

Being so deeply rooted in Lutheran Christian history was, of course, what motivated a man like Carl Goerdeler in his intrepid fight against evil. But this might also have been the reason why he was not understood in Washington DC. Noll concludes: "Americans have moved in a straight line from personal belief to social reform, from private experience to personal activity. For the colonial Puritans and nineteenth-century evangelicals this meant the mounting of crusades. It has assumed the necessity of moving directly from passion for God and the Bible to passion for the renovation of society."

This is what Bonhoeffer found so inadequate in U.S. theology—its reduction to a combination of religion and ethics. But something has changed since the immediate prewar years when Bonhoeffer was in New York challenging Reinhold Niebuhr on this issue. Now it is no longer just U.S. Protestantism but also the Evangelical (Protestant) Church in postwar Germany whom Bonhoeffer would have to call to task for constantly deviating from Luther because it pursues a way of thinking "which sets out from human problems and which asks for solutions on

---

11   Noll, "Lutheran Difference," 36–37.

this basis." Bonhoeffer commented: "Such thinking is unbliblical. The way of Jesus Christ, and therefore the way of all Christian thinking, leads not from the world to God but from God to the world. This means that the essence of the Gospel does not lie in the solution of human problems, and that the solution of human problems cannot be the essential task of the church."[12]

If Noll is right, we could be experiencing a Lutheran *kairos* almost half a millennium after Luther's reformation. Luther has an important message for the spiritually confused postmodern world: The created order is the *larvae Dei*, the mask behind which God hides. Man must be able to discern between that mask and God's words that are hidden in it. Man must not worship the mask but God. But he must not disdain the mask because "the kingdom, the realm, the governing authority, the teacher, the student, the father, the mother, the master, the mistress, the servant, the maid—all these are masks; they are persons whom according to God's will we must respect in awe and recognize as his creature. They must exist in this life. But it is not his will that they be ascribed divine essence."[13]

This, then, is the Christian reality in this world, a reality that the *Zeitgeist* is incapable of recognizing. Luther's church—in Europe as well as in many parts of the United States—stands at a crossroads. It can go on cooking the two realms into each other; it can persist in its foolish endeavor to prostitute itself to the spirit of time. But it must realize that in so doing it commits the anti-Lutheran and anti-Christian transgression of selling indulgences in the futile effort to stop its membership from dwindling. What are the indulgences of the twentieth century? They are ecclesiastical nods to wanton violations of God's order of creation. If that is the road the church will continue to travel, it will inevitably miss its *kairos*. Why? Because it beds with a spirit that is the antithesis of the Holy Spirit, the giver of life and creator of faith.

Will Protestantism eventually turn around after many deviations? Will it, after the rude awakening from two utopian dreams in half a century, shake off its latest postmodern follies and sever its links to the

---

12 Dietrich Bonhoeffer, *Ethics* (New York: Collier, 1955), 356.
13 WA 40/1:175.3–6.

Zeitgeist? To do that, it must rediscover its founder. Will it open its ears to Luther's voice, which has so often been misunderstood throughout history? Protestants would be well advised to do so. For Luther's voice, says Noll, "is a voice of unusual importance in Christian history." In Luther's voice, says Noll, "we hear uncommon resonances of the voice of God."[14]

14 Noll, "Lutheran Difference," 39.

SELECTED BIBLIOGRAPHY

Sociology

Arendt, Hannah. *On Revolution.* New York: Penguin, 1963.

Baur, Karl. *Zeitgeist und Geschichte.* Munich: Callwey, 1978. An in-depth study of the *Zeitgeist* phenomenon and its impact on society from the late Middle Ages to the present.

Berger, Peter L., and Thomas Luckmann. *The Social Construction of Reality.* Garden City: Anchor Press, 1967.

———. *The Heretical Imperative.* Garden City: Anchor Press/Doubleday, 1979.

———. *The Sacred Canopy.* Garden City: Doubleday, 1967.

Bossenbrook, William J. *The German Mind.* Detroit: Wayne State University Press, 1961.

Durkheim, Émile. *The Rules of Sociological Method.* Translated by Sarah Solovay and John H. Mueller. Edited by George E. G. Catlin. Chicago: Free Press, 1950.

Fest, Joachim. *Der zerstörte Traum.* Berlin: Siedler, 1991. A potent little book discussing the impact of utopianism on society and the end of the utopian systems with the collapse of the Soviet empire.

Gehlen, Arnold. *Man in the Age of Technology.* Translated by Patricia Lipscomb. New York: Columbia University Press, 1980.

Mannheim, Karl. *Ideologie und Utopie.* Frankfurt: Vittorio Klostermann, 1985.

———. "Das Konservative Denken." *Archiv für Sozialwissenschaft und Sozialpolitik* 57 (1927): 68–142; 470–95.

Noelle-Neumann, Elisabeth. *Die Schweigespirale—unsere soziale Haut.* Munich: Piper, 1980.

Schutz, Alfred. *Collected Papers.* Vol. 1. The Hague: M. Nijhoff, 1962.

Troeltsch, Ernst. *The Social Teaching of the Christian Churches.* Translated by Olive Wyon. New York: Macmillan, 1949.

Weber, Max. *Gesammelte Aufsätze zur Religionssoziologie.* Tübingen: Mohr, 1920.

———. *Die Protestantische Ethik II, Kritiken und Antikritiken.* Edited by Johannes Winkelmann. Tübingen: Gerd Mohn, 1987. On pp. 136ff., Felix Rachfahl, one of Weber's critics, discusses Lutheran resistance theories relevant to this study.

Zijderveld, Anton C. *On Clichés.* London: Routledge & Kegan Paul, 1979.

THEOLOGY

ON LUTHER, LUTHERANISM, MÜNZER

Bèze, Théodore de. *Du Droit des Magistrats.* Edited by Robert M. Kingdon. Geneva: Droz, 1970. In the introduction to this volume, Kingdon establishes the link between the Magdeburg Confession and Beza's treatise.

Barth, Karl. *Eine Schweizer Stimme.* Zurich: TVZ, 1945. In this work Barth links the names Hitler and Luther.

Berggrav, Eivind. *Man and State.* Translated by George Aus. Philadelphia: Muhlenberg, 1951.

Bonhoeffer, Dietrich. "Irrlehre in der Bekennenden Kirche." Pages 264–79 in vol. 2 of *Gesammelte Schriften,* edited by Eberhard Bethge. Munich: Chr. Kaiser, 1959. Here Bonhoeffer refers to Flacius and the *adiaphoron* problem.

Brauer, Siegfried, and Helmar Junghans. *Der Theologe Thomas Müntzer: Untersuchungen zu seiner Entwicklung und Lehre.* Berlin: Evangelische Verlagsanstalt, 1989.

———. *Martin Luther in marxistischer Sicht von 1945 bis zum Beginn der achtziger Jahre.* Berlin: Evangelische Verlagsanstalt, 1983.

Bubenheimer, Ulrich. *Thomas Müntzer: Herkunft und Bildung.* Leiden: Brill, 1989.

Ebeling, Gerhard. *Luther: Einführung in sein Denken.* Tübingen: J. C. B. Mohr (Paul Siebeck), 1965. Of particular relevance to this study is chapter 12, "Christperson und Weltperson," pp. 219–38, dealing with the doctrine of the two realms and Luther's thoughts of creation as God's mask (*larva Dei*).

Engels, Friedrich. *The German Revolutions.* Chicago: University of Chicago Press, 1963. Relevant because of references to Münzer and the Peasants' War.

Friedenthal, Richard. *Luther.* Munich: Piper, 1967.

Friedman, Jerome. "Protestants, Jews, and Jewish Sources." In *Piety, Politics, and Ethics,* edited by Carter Lindberg. Kirksville: Sixteenth Century Journal Publishers, 1984.

Gerlach, Wolfgang. *Als die Zeugen schwiegen: Bekennde Kirche und die Juden.* Berlin: Institut Kirche und Judentum, 1987.

Goertz, Hans-Jürgen. *Thomas Müntzer: Mystiker, Apokalyptiker, Revolutionar.* Munich: Beck, 1989.

Greiffenhagen, Martin, ed. *Das evangelische Pfarrhaus.* Stuttgart: Kreuz, 1984. A collection of articles by leading German theologians and other scholars on the enormous importance of the Protestant parsonage in the cultural and social devolopment of Germany.

Gritsch, Eric W. *Thomas Müntzer: A Tragedy of Errors.* Minneapolis: Fortress, 1989.

Hase, Hans-Christoph von. *Die Gestalt der Kirche Luthers: Der Casus Confessionis im Kampf des Matthias Flacius gegen das Interim von 1548.* Göttingen: Vandenhoeck & Ruprecht, 1940.

Hillerdal, Gunnar. *Gehorsam gegen Gott und Menschen.* Göttingen: Vandenhoeck & Ruprecht, 1955.

Holl, Karl. *Gesammelte Aufsätze zur Kirchengeschichte.* Vol. 1. Tübingen: J. C. B. Mohr, 1929. The chapter "Luther und die Schwärmer" deserves special attention in the context of this study.

Huegli, Albert. *Church and State under God.* St. Louis: Concordia, 1964.

Kegel, James D. "A Church Come of Age: American Lutheranism and National Socialism." Diss., Chicago: Lutheran School of Theology, 1988.

Klemperer, Klemens von. "Der deutsche Widerstand gegen den Nationalsozialismus im Lichte der konservativen Tradition." Pages 266–83 in *Demokratie und Diktatur: Geist und Gestalt politischer Herrschaft in Deutschland und Europa*, edited by Manfred Funke et al. Bonn: Bundeszentrale für Politische Bildung, 1987.

Künneth, Walter. *Das Widerstandsrecht als theologisch-ethisches Problem*. Munich: Claudius, 1954.

———. *Wider den Strom*. Wuppertal: R. Brockhaus, 1989. An important and prophetic little volume on the incompatibility of theology and the *Zeitgeist*.

Lau, Franz. *Luthers Lehre von den beiden Reichen*. Berlin: Evangelische Verlagsanstalt, 1952. This is arguably the most poignant study on Luther's doctrine of the two realms written in the aftermath of the Hitler tyranny. It served scores of East German theologians as a powerful guide on how to confront the new tyranny they were subjected to—this time the Communist one.

Lindberg, Carter. "Mask of God and Prince of Lies: Luther's Theology of the Demonic." Pages 87–103 in *Disguises of the Demonic*, edited by Alan M. Olson. New York: Association Press, 1975.

Luther, Martin. *Luther über Müntzer*. Witten: Luther-Verlag, 1973.

———. *D. Martin Luthers Werke. Kritische Gesamtausgabe*. 102 vols. Weimar: Hermann Böhlau, 1883–1999. These works are abbreviated as WA. Luther's letters are listed as WABr and his Table Talks as WATr.

———. *Luther's Works*. American Edition. General editors Jaroslav Pelikan and Helmut T. Lehmann. 55 vols. St. Louis: Concordia; and Philadelphia: Muhlenberg & Fortress, 1955–1986. These works are abbreviated as AE.

Mildenberger, Friedrich. *Theologie der lutherischen Bekenntnisschriften*. Stuttgart: W. Kohlhammer, 1983.

Motschmann, Jens. *So nicht, Herr Pfarrer!* Berlin: Ullstein, 1991.

Müntzer, Thomas. *The Collected Works of Thomas Müntzer*. Edited and translated by Peter Matheson. Edinburgh: T&T Clark, 1988.

Oberman, Heiko A. "The Nationalist Conscription of Martin Luther." In *Piety, Politics, and Ethics*, edited by Carter Lindberg. Kirksville: Sixteenth Century Journal Publishers, 1984.

Ritter, Gerhard. *Luther: Gestalt und Tat*. Frankfurt: Fischer, 1984.

Rupp, E. Gordon. *Martin Luther: Hitler's Cause or Cure?* London: Lutterworth, 1945.

———. *Patterns of Reformation*. Philadelphia: Fortress, 1969. This work is interesting for its discussion of the conflict between Luther and Münzer.

Scharffenorth, Gerta. *Den Glauben ins Leben ziehen*. Munich: Chr. Kaiser, 1982. Significant, within the context of this study, for its detailed discussion of Luther's doctrine of the two realms.

Scheible, Heinz, ed. *Das Widerstandsrecht als Problem der deutschen Protestanten 1523–1546*. Texte zur Kirchengeschichte 10. Gütersloh: Gerd Mohn, 1969.

Schmidt, Kurt Dietrich. *Kirchengeschichte*. Göttingen: Vandenhoeck & Ruprecht, 1960. The textbook on church history most frequently used at German schools of theology. Concise throughout, but especially strong on Reformation history. An important resource for the present study.

Spitz, Lewis W. "The Christian in Church and State." In *Martin Luther and the Modern Mind: Freedom, Conscience, Toleration, Rights*, edited by Manfred Hofmann. Toronto Studies in Theology 22. Lewiston: Edwin Mellon Press, 1985.

Tappert, Theodore G., ed. *The Book of Concord*. Philadelphia: Fortress, 1959.

Tödt, Heinz Eduard. "Die Bedeutung von Luthers Reiche- und Regimentenlehre für heutige Theologie und Ethik." Pages 53–126 in *Gottes Wirken in seiner Welt*, edited by Niels Hasselmann. Hamburg: Lutherisches Verlagshaus, 1980.

Treumann, Rudolf. *Die Monarchomachen*. Leipzig: Duncker & Humblot, 1895. A study of sixteenth-century revolutionary theories of state.

Troeltsch, Ernst. *Protestantism and Progress*. Translated by W. Montgomery. Boston: Beacon Press, 1966.

Waring, Luther Hess. *The Political Theories of Martin Luther*. New York: Putnam, 1910.

ARTICLES

Cooper, John W. "The Outlines of Political Theology in the Protestant Reformation." *Teaching Political Science* 10:1 (Fall 1982): 43–51.

Ford, Charles. "Luther, Bonhoeffer and Revolution." *Lutheran Forum* 25 (Advent 1991): 24–28.

Glenthøj, Jørgen. "Die Eideskrise in der Bekennenden Kirche 1938 und Dietrich Bonhoeffer." *Zeitschrift für Kirchengeschichte* 96 (1985): 378–94.

Graf, Friedrich Wilhelm. "Konservatives Kulturluthertum." *Zeitschrift für Theologie und Kirche* 85 (1988): 31–76.

Gritsch, Eric. "The Use and Abuse of Luther's Political Advice." *VII International Luther Congress* (Oslo, 1988).

Hinlicky, Paul R. "The Task of Lutheran Political Thought Today." *Word & World* 8:3 (1988): 271–81.

Klemperer, Klemens von. "Glaube, Religion, Kirche und der deutsche Widerstand gegen den Nationalsozialismus." *Vierteljahrehefte für Zeitgeschichte* 3 (1980): 294–309.

Lindberg, Carter. "Luther's Critique of the Ecumenical Assumption that Doctrine Divides but Service Unites." *Journal of Ecumenical Studies* 27:4 (Fall 1990): 679–96.

———. "Theology and Politics: Luther the Radical and Müntzer the Reactionary." *Encounter* 37:4 (1976): 356–71.

Noll, Mark A. "The Lutheran Difference." *First Things* 20 (February 1992): 31–40.

Olson, Oliver K. "Theology of Revolution: Magdeburg, 1550–1551." *Sixteenth Century Journal* 3:1 (1972): 57–79.

Schloemann, Martin. "Luthers Apfelbäumchen." In vol. 7 of *Wuppertaler Hochschulreden* (Wuppertal: Peter Hammer, 1976), 5–24.

Shoenberger, Cynthia Grant. "The Development of the Lutheran Theory of Resistance: 1523–1530." *Sixteenth Century Journal* 8:1 (1977): 62–76.

Strohm, Theodor. "Zum Ethos der Inneren Reformen des Freiherrn vom Stein." *Zeitschrift für Evangelische Ethik* 17:4 (July 1973): 193–212.

Stroup, John. "Political Theology and Secularization Theory in Germany, 1918–1939: Emanuel Hirsch as a Phenomenon of His Time." *Harvard Theological Review* 80:3 (1987): 321–68.

1SELECTED BIBLIOGRAPHY

Works Criticizing Luther

Dershowitz, Alan. *Chutzpah*. Boston: Little, Brown, 1991.

Mann, Thomas. "Deutschland und die Deutschen (1945)." In vol. 13 of *Gesammelte Werke*. Frankfurt: Fischer, 1974.

———. *Doktor Faustus*. Stockholm: Bermann-Fischer, 1947. In this allegorical novel, Mann develops the theme that Martin Luther paved the road to Hitler. For the genesis of this volume, cf. Gunilla Bergsten, *Thomas Mann's* Doktor Faustus (Uppsala: Svenska Bokförlaget, 1960).

———. *Die Entstehung des Doktor Faustus*. Frankfurt: Fischer, 1984.

———. "Warum ich nicht nach Deutschland zurückkehre." In vol. 12 of *Gesammelte Werke*. Frankfurt: Fischer, 1960.

———. "Die drei Gewaltigen (1949)." In vol. 10 of *Gesammelte Werke*. Frankfurt: Fischer, 1974.

McGovern, William Montgomery. *From Luther to Hitler*. Cambridge: Riverside Press, 1941.

Marius, Richard. *Luther*. Philadelphia: J. B. Lippincott, 1974.

Rose, Norman. *Vansittart, Study of a Diplomat*. London: Heinemann, 1978.

Shirer, William L. *The Rise and Fall of the Third Reich*. New York: Simon & Schuster, 1960.

Vansittart, Robert. *Black Record*. London: Hamish Hamilton, 1941.

———. *Lessons of My Life*. New York: Alfred Knopf, 1943.

Wiener, Peter F. *German with Tears*. London: Cresset, 1942. In this volume, Wiener describes Dean Inge as his "God-parent" (p. xi), calls Lutheranism an "anti-Christian religion" (p. 64), and avers, "I am convinced that we fight this war not against the Nazis or Adolf Hitler, but against the German mentality, their love for war and aggression. No less authority than Mr. Winston Churchill forsaw . . . that one day we would have to fight a war against a 'non-God religion.' . . . That 'non-God religion' is deep-seated in the hearts of the Germans" (p. 92).

———. *Martin Luther: Hitler's Spiritual Ancestor*. London: Hutchinson, 1945.

Articles

Doerne, Thomas. "Thomas Mann und das protestantische Christentum." *Die Sammlung* 11 (1946): 409ff.

Inge, William Ralph. "Nationalism and National Character." *Quarterly Review* (July 1941): 125–43. It is in this article that Inge accuses Luther of fostering two moralities.

Matheson, Peter Clarkson. "Luther and Hitler: A Controversy Reviewed." *Journal of Ecumenical Studies* 17:3 (Summer 1980): 445–53.

Christian Ethics

Bonhoeffer, Dietrich. *Ethics*. New York: Collier, 1955. Discusses the "crusading" tendency of Anglo-Saxon churches, a tendency from which Lutheranism "has almost entirely freed itself" (p. 356).

Pannenberg, Wolfhart. "The Basis of Ethics in the Thought of Ernst Troeltsch." In *Ethics*, translated by Keith Crim. Philadelphia: Westminster, 1981.

Thielicke, Helmut. *Theological Ethics.* Philadelphia: Fortress, 1966. Here Thielicke's discussion of *pecca fortiter*, anticipated eschatology and self-justification is of special interest to this study.

Rasmussen, Larry. *Reinhold Niebuhr: Theologian of Public Life.* Minneapolis: Fortress, 1991.

ARTICLE

Lindberg, Carter. "Reformation Initiatives for Social Welfare: Luther's Influence at Leisnig." *The Annual of the Society of Christian Ethics,* edited by D. M. Yeager (1987): 79–99.

LITERATURE ON ROMANS 13:1–7

Barth, Karl. *Der Römerbrief.* Stuttgart: EVZ, 1940.

Delling, Gerhard. *Römer 13, 1–7 innerhalb der Briefe des Neuen Testaments.* Berlin: Evangelische Verlagsanstalt, 1962.

Fischer, M. *Der Römerbrief.* Stuttgart: Kreuz, 1960.

Walker, Rolf. *Studie zu Römer 13, 1–7.* Theologische Existenz heute n. s. 132. Munich: Kaiser, 1966.

Wilckens, Ulrich. *Der Brief an die Römer.* Zurich: Benziger, 1978–1982.

SYSTEMATIC THEOLOGY

Braaten, Carl E. *Justification.* Minneapolis: Fortress, 1990.

———, and Robert W. Jenson. *Christian Dogmatics.* 2 vols. Philadelphia: Fortress, 1983.

Tillich, Paul. *The Protestant Era.* Translated by James Luther Adams. Chicago: University of Chicago Press, 1948.

———. *Systematic Theology.* 3 vols. Chicago: University of Chicago Press, 1951–1963.

Troeltsch, Ernst. *Writings on Theology and Religion.* Translated and edited by Robert Morgan and Michael Pye. Atlanta: John Knox, 1977.

ON LUTHERAN ROOTS OF THE EAST GERMAN REVOLUTION

Ebert, Andreas et al., ed. *Räumt die Steine hinweg.* Munich: Claudius, 1990. A collection of sermons and speeches by Protestant theologians on the occasion of the fall of the Berlin Wall.

Goeckel, Robert F. *The Lutheran Church and the East German State.* Ithaca: Cornell University Press, 1990. Here again the stereotype of Lutheran "quietism" is being promoted.

Sievers, Hans-Jürgen. *Stundenbuch einer deutschen Revolution: Die Leipziger Kirchen im Oktober 1989.* Göttingen: Vandenhoeck & Ruprecht, 1990.

Dähn, Horst et al., ed. *Staat und Kirchen in der DDR.* Frankfurt: Peter Lang, 2003.

ARTICLES

Fränkel, Hans-Joachim. "Die evangelische Kirche in der DDR." *Frankfurter Allgemeine Zeitung* 68 (6 April 1978): 9–10. One of the most important articles on the relations between church and state, written by the former Protestant bishop of Gorlitz, who of all church leaders in East Germany was the most uncompromising critic of the Communist regime.

Hempel, Johannes. "Was wird aus mir? Was wird aus der Kirche?" *Frankfurter Rundschau* 284 (7 December 1977): 14–5. The Lutheran bishop of Saxony on church and state in East Germany, with special reference to the doctrine of the two realms.

Henkys, Reinhard. "Leben mit Lenin und Luther." *Vorwärts* 41 (12 October 1978): 8. This article by the leading West German expert on the *Kirche im Sozialismus* concept addresses the tenuous relationship between church and state in East Germany.

Odin, Karl-Alfred. "Das freie Wort hat die Macht gebrochen." *Frankfurter Allgemeine Zeitung* 298 (23 December 1989): "Bilder und Zeiten," (no page numbers). A detailed description of how, thanks to the church's influence, the East German revolution took place peacefully.

HISTORICAL WORKS

ON CARL GOERDELER

Meyer-Krahmer, Marianne. *Carl Goerdeler und sein Weg in den Widerstand.* Freiburg: Herder, 1989.

Krause, Friedrich. *Goerdelers politisches Testament.* New York: Krause, 1945.

Ritter, Gerhard. *Carl Goerdeler und die deutsche Widerstandsbewegung.* Stuttgart: Deutsche Verlags-Anstalt, 1954.

Schramm, Wilhelm Ritter von, ed. *Beck und Goerdeler: Gemeinschafts-dokumente für den Frieden, 1941–1944.* Munich: Gotthold Muller, 1965.

Weizmann, Chaim. *Memoiren: Das Werden des Staates Israel.* Zurich: Phaidon, 1953.

Young, A. P. *The "X" Documents.* Edited by Sidney Aster. London: Deutsch, 1974. A crucial work for this study. Compendium of memoranda of British industrialist A. P. Young of his secret meetings with Goerdeler and Goerdeler's encounters with leading British figures.

OTHER WORKS ON GERMAN RESISTANCE AND EXILE POLITICS

Bethge, Eberhard. *Dietrich Bonhoeffer.* New York: Harper & Row, 1970.

Bielenberg, Christabel. *The Past Is Myself.* London: Corgi, 1970.

Glees, Anthony. *Exile Politics during the Second World War.* Oxford: Clarendon, 1982.

Hoffmann, Peter. *German Resistance to Hitler.* Cambridge: Harvard University Press, 1988. Cf. especially the bibliography, pp. 139–44.

Joffroy, Pierre. *A Spy for God: The Ordeal of Kurt Gerstein.* Glasgow: Collins, 1970. More than any other work, this story about a staunch Lutheran who infiltrated the SS shows the complexity of Christian resistance to tyranny and the almost insuperable barriers created by cliché thinking.

Kennedy, Paul. *The Rise of the Anglo-German Antagonism, 1860–1914.* London: Allen & Unwin, 1980.

Lützeler, Paul Michael, ed. *Hermann Broch: Briefe über Deutschland, 1945–1949.* Frankfurt: Suhrkamp, 1986. An exchange of letters between Volkmar von Zühlsdorff, who had returned to Germany from exile in the United States, and his friend, Hermann Broch, who remained in the United States. Among other things, von Zühlsdorff relates how the U.S. military government in Germany forbade the media from mentioning the German resistance against Hitler.

Schäfer, Jürgen. *Kurt Gerstein: Ein protestantisches Schicksal zwischen Bekennender Kirche und dem Vernichtungsapparat der SS*. Bochum: unpublished dissertation, 1987.

Smith, R. Harris. *OSS*. Berkeley: University of California Press, 1972.

On Religion in Nazi Germany

Poewe, Karla. *New Religions and the Nazis*. New York: Routledge, 2006.

Steigmann-Gall, Richard. *The Holy Reich: Nazi Conceptions of Christianity 1919–1945*. Cambridge: Cambridge University Press, 2003.

Articles

Hoffmann, Peter. "Ludwig Beck: Loyalty and Resistance." *Central European History* 14:4 (December 1981): 332–50.

————. "Peace through Coup d'État: The Foreign Contacts of the German Resistance 1933–1944." *Central European History* 19 (March 1986): 3–44.

Goldman, Aaron. "Germans and Nazis: The Controversy over 'Vansittartism' in Britain during the Second World War." *Journal of Contemporary History* 14:1 (January 1979): 155–91.

Roosevelt and Casablanca

Freidel, Frank. *Franklin D. Roosevelt: The Apprenticeship*. Boston: Little, Brown, 1952.

Kimball, Warren F., ed. *Churchill and Roosevelt: The Complete Correspondence*. Princeton: Princeton University Press, 1984.

Klingbeil, Kurt A. *F. D. R. and American Religious Leaders*. Diss., New York University, 1972.

Nisbet, Robert. *Roosevelt and Stalin: The Failed Courtship*. Washington DC: Regnery Gateway, 1988.

Article

Moltmann, Günter. "Die Genesis der Unconditional-Surrender-Forderung." *Wehrwissenschaftliche Rundschau* 6 (1956).

INDEX